Theology Out

of Place

A Theological Biography of

Walter J. Hollenweger

Lynne Price

SHEFFIELD ACADEMIC PRESS
A Continuum imprint
LONDON • NEW YORK

Published by
Sheffield Academic Press Ltd
The Tower Building, 11 York Road, London SE1 7NX
371 Lexington Avenue, New York, NY 10017-6550

www.SheffieldAcademicPress.com
www.continuumbooks.com

British Library Cataloguing-in-Publication Data
A catalogue record for this book is available from the British Library

Typeset by Sheffield Academic Press
Printed on acid-free paper in Great Britain by MPG Books Ltd, Bodmin, Cornwall

ISBN   0-8264-6027-5 (hardback)
       0-8264-6028-3 (paperback)

CONTENTS

ACKNOWLEDGMENTS

This book is primarily a theological biography of an individual scholar, Professor Walter J. Hollenweger. Through examination of his extensive interests, varied methods and wide-ranging reflection it is also an enquiry into the nature and function of Western academic theology in relation to Christian practice in the twentieth and twenty-first centuries.

During the five years of research and writing of this book Walter Hollenweger has given generously of his time for interviews, kept me informed of his ongoing projects and provided me with access to his personal archive material. With further generosity he has asked no questions of me and declined the offer of reading the manuscript before it was sent to JPTSup for consideration. I am most grateful to him for his practical cooperation and the authorial freedom given to me.

I am indebted to Werner Ustorf, Professor of Mission at the University of Birmingham, for reading the manuscript. His interest and perceptive comments have been invaluable. I have much appreciated Werner Ustorf's early assistance with some of my German translation and that of J. Michael Walpole in the later stages and proofreading of German text. I also wish to thank Dr Allan Anderson of the University of Birmingham for helpful discussions on Pentecostalism. All views and any errors remain, of course, my own.

Many others have assisted in a variety of ways: John Christopher Thomas, editor of the JPTSup Series, and colleagues at Sheffield Academic Press in bringing the work to publication; my family with their support and encouragement; Erica Hollenweger with her hospitality and conversation in Krattigen; the participants in the production of *Maria von Wedemeyer* at Berneuchener Haus, Kloster Kirchberg in 1997 by their friendship and sharing of views, and in particular the co-author and dramatic facilitator Estella Korthaus; all those involved with Walter Hollenweger's engagements in 1998 under the auspices of the Evangelisches Bildungswerk, Bayreuth/Bad Berneck; University of Birmingham research students of mission and Pentecostalism from many different countries and Christian traditions who have responded to papers I have presented and from whose writings I have gained much during the last 12 years.

This English Methodist has learnt a lot and enjoyed rich experiences during the creation of *Theology out of Place: Walter J. Hollenweger*.

Lynne Price, Birmingham, April 2002

INTRODUCTION

Our society today is frequently described in terms of what it is leaving behind; we are said to be postmodern, post-colonial, post-literary and post-Christian. There is a pervading uncertainty about what we are now and what sort of society will emerge in the future.

One response is nostalgia for past 'golden' eras such as Christendom, or more recently, the nineteenth century's unbridled optimism regarding technological progress combined with imperial wealth and power, but this is countermanded by a growing body of literature tarnishing the shining images. History is constantly being re-written as new information is discovered and disseminated; new voices add their interpretations of events—the governed, the enslaved, women, and minority cultures. Further, we inevitably view the past with our contemporary thought-forms and language, reflecting the different experiences of our time. As L.P. Hartley put it so memorably, 'The past is a foreign country; they do things differently there'.[1] Return is neither possible nor desirable.

Nevertheless, we are drawn to our particular histories because they have formed our present, are necessary to our own self-understanding, and contribute to formulating future action. So it becomes a matter of pressing importance that our eyes are opened to the more pluriform and nuanced picture of our identity which is emerging through the contributions of previously silenced or ignored groups. In worldwide terms, a static notion of cultural identity defined by the nation and deriving its authority from a supposedly unbroken tradition is, according to literary critic Edward Said, being challenged by new alignments made across borders: 'all cultures are involved with one another, none is single and pure, all are hybrid, heterogeneous, extraordinarily differentiated, and unmonolithic'.[2] At the same time, writers in various fields have pointed out that the so-called 'meta-narratives' of Christianity, philosophy, history and science proposing

1.   L.P. Hartley, *The Go-Between* (Harmondsworth: Penguin Books, 1970), p. 7.
2.   Edward W. Said, *Culture and Imperialism* (London: Vintage, 1994), pp. xxviii, xxix.

'large-scale theoretical interpretations purportedly of universal application' are increasingly rejected.[3] From one perspective relationships are
being discovered, from another they seem to be falling apart.

This is occurring when the continents are enjoying more electronic and
geographical communication than at any time previously and also growth in
awareness of their mutual interrelatedness, not least through ecological concerns and large-scale migration. There is more information widely available
on our world and its inhabitants than can be assimilated; faced with profuse
variety and competing interests, the twentieth century saw the birth of the
United Nations (1945) and the World Council of Churches (1948). Unity and
diversity, particularism and universalism, are the polarities on which we
hang the question marks at the beginning of the millennium.

In the Christian tradition Babel and Pentecost have sometimes been
juxtaposed to illustrate the divisive and uniting aspects of communication
between peoples. The irony is that the more channels of communication
and forums of discourse increase, the more the differences as well as what
is held in common are revealed. Christians should not be unnerved by this,
for it was clearly so in New Testament times. Yet, on the whole, we in the
West seem singularly uneasy with the present climate of change: the de-
cline and marginalization of the mainline churches along with the growth
of the house-church movement, Pentecostal and charismatic churches, are
set within other realities about which Christians are divided: relations with
people of other faiths, relations between blacks, whites and Asians, how to
address poverty and inequalities of opportunity, the place of women, non-
medical healing, sexuality—the list is endless.

Underlining the changes in the west is the worldwide situation of a
major shift of the distribution of Christians. Andrew Walls, Director of the
Centre for the Study of Christianity in the Non-Western World at the
University of Edinburgh, writes:

> Perhaps the most striking single feature of Christianity today is the fact that
> the Church now looks more like that great multitude whom none can
> number, drawn from all tribes and kindreds, people and tongues, than ever
> before in its history. Its diversity and history leads to a great variety of
> starting points for its theology and reflects varied bodies of experience. The
> study of Christian history and theology will increasingly need to operate
> from the position where most Christians are; and that will increasingly be
> the continents of Africa, Asia, Latin America and the Pacific.[4]

---

3.   David Harvey, *The Condition of Postmodernity: An Enquiry into the Origins of
Cultural Change* (Oxford: Basil Blackwell, 1990), p. 9.

4.   Andrew Walls, 'Christianity in the Non-Western World: A Study in the Serial

What it means to be a Western Christian in this minority situation at home and abroad has barely begun to be recognized. The traditional disciplines of Western academic theology—Biblical Studies, hermeneutics, systematics, and church history—already largely separate specialisms, seem ill-equipped to address the realities of our time. They rarely take as their starting point the ways in which Christian faith is experienced, acted upon and interpreted in concrete situations today. Not only is there an information gap between the Christian community and scholars, there is a gap between the fruits of scholarly research and reflection and how they can be utilized in Christian thought and action.

This book is concerned with contemporary theology in the context of our general cultural and specifically Christian condition. I begin to explore some ways in which the past, the present and the future can be approached both faithfully and critically through the work of an evangelist and academic theologian of missiology, Walter J. Hollenweger. His professional career has produced prolific writing on Pentecostalism, ecumenism and intercultural theology, three important and related subjects characterizing twentieth and twenty-first century Christianity. Alternately blowing holes through defences and building bridges across divides in his efforts to overcome boundaries between Christians and between Christians and non-Christians, Walter Hollenweger is difficult to locate in accepted categories of mission or theologizing. He is unconventional, sometimes contentious, never irrelevant. In the opinion of Werner Ustorf, Professor of Mission at the University of Birmingham, 'Hollenweger opts for a real theological encounter, the exposure of one's belief to the plurality of Christian experience, and to the explicitly non-religious, multi-religious and multicultural modernity of our time'.[5]

Nature of Christian Expansion', *Studies in World Christianity* 1.1 (1995), pp. 1-25 (24).

5.   'The Magpies Gotta Know: Hollenweger as an Ecumenical', in Jan A.B. Jongeneel *et al.* (eds.), *Pentecost, Mission and Ecumenism: Essays on Intercultural Theology* (Festschrift in Honour of Professor Walter J. Hollenweger; Frankfurt am Main: Peter Lang, 1992), pp. 27-32 (28).

Chapter 1

OUT OF PLACE: A BIOGRAPHY

Dear God, Sometimes I feel like a frog... Why must I be such an in-between
creature, neither fish nor bird, not quite at home in the water or the air?
From 'The Frog's Prayer' by Walter Hollenweger[1]

Walter Hollenweger was born out of place. The fact that his Swiss parents
were at that time in 1927 living temporarily in Antwerp, seems in retro-
spect to have signalled a note of dislocation which has echoed through his
varied career. It is precisely this characteristic of being out of step with
prevailing dominant trends of Christian thought and action on mission
which makes a study of his approach to evangelism and theology of
interest today; for against the brief outline of unsettling changes noted in
my Introduction, and despite the protestations of the 'frog', Hollenweger
seems strangely at home in a situation of reappraisal, fragmentation and
redistribution of power.

Knowledgeable and experienced in Pentecostalism, the World Council
of Churches, and British academic theology, he has engaged practically
and cognitively with tangible situations portraying the dominant contentious issues of the twentieth century—the re-examination and re-writing of
history, intercultural relations and communication, particularism and universalism—from the position of a committed Christian teacher and evangelist. The Bible and contemporary realities provide the reference points
for his thinking and this has resulted in insights, conclusions and questions
different from those reached by traditional Western academic theological
routes because, by and large, these do not directly approach the pressing
questions of today with sufficient regard to relating expertise from

1. 'Lieber Gott, manchmal komme ich vor wie ein Frosch... Warum muss ich ein
solches Zwischengeschöpf sein, weder Fisch noch Vogel, weder im Wasser noch auf
dem Trockenen wirklich zu Hause?' from 'Froschgebet', quoted by Richard Friedli in
his 'Hollenweger als Theologe', in Jongeneel *et al.* (eds.), *Pentecost, Mission and
Ecumenism*, pp. 15-26 (22-23).

separated specialisms, or with enough breadth of vision to embrace the contributions of non-Western Christians.

This chapter traces Walter Hollenweger's career, focusing on the events and experiences that have moulded his novel methodology. Attention is drawn particularly to the areas where he has found himself—or put himself—out of place with regard to general trends in church and missionary society policies or academic debate. It forms the basis for the ensuing consideration of topics of great Christian concern today—biblical hermeneutics, gospel and culture, ecumenism, mission and pneumatology—to which his refreshingly offbeat approach provides stimulus for further action and reflection.

Pentecostal Pastor

For two years Hollenweger resisted a call to ministry in the Swiss Pentecostal Church (*Pfingstmission*) that he attended as a teenager. His inclination to continue a potentially lucrative career in banking, and thus ensure the poverty that marked some of his childhood would not mar the future, was finally overcome through prayer. In committing himself to God he felt the power of the Spirit fall on him and was healed of a skin disease. This was the substance of his testimony to a Pentecostal gathering in Vienna in 1953, when he was assistant pastor at St Gallen.[2] Already at 26 he was a regular contributor to *Verheissung des Vaters*, the Swiss Pentecostal publication, writing on such subjects as freedom[3] and Christ as our example[4] or reporting on a holiday camp where many of the 60 8–14-year-olds 'heard the good news for the first time'.[5]

He recently recalled with some delight his modus operandi as a young pastor: he gathered new converts together for Bible study and subsequently trained and encouraged them to sing, speak or read in the church services. Then he would take them onto the street occasionally, complete

---

2.   *Jugendbote der freien Christengemeinden in Österreich* (Newsletter of the Free Christian Community in Austria), Heft 3, July 1953, p. 3. For a brief biography see Paul N. van der Laan, 'Walter Hollenweger: A Pluriform Life', and other chapters in Part I of Jongeneel et al. (eds.), *Pentecost, Mission and Ecumenism.*

3.   'Freiheit, die ich meine', *Verheissung des Vaters* 38.9 (September 1945), p. 16.

4.   'Christus unser Beispiel' (Phil. 2.5-11), *Verheissung des Vaters* 45.7 (July 1952), pp. 10-12.

5.   'Aus unserer Arbeit. Jugendlager-Berichte: Ferienlager "Les Pinsons, Bretaye"', November 1951, pp. 16-17, 24.

with a band and all wearing their best clothes, where they would sing until an audience gathered, before whom they were required to give their testimonies. At times people would argue or ask questions. 'You see,' said Hollenweger, laughing, 'that is not very much different from what I did afterwards at the university, only then I had more qualified knowledge! The same method—using the people with the little they knew, they had to put it into practice.' Sometimes an older member would be 'planted' in the crowd to affirm the preacher's message: 'Of course, I had prepared him beforehand. It looked all very spontaneous, but it wasn't!'[6] A love of teaching and a sense of drama have continued to be features of his life.

A year's study at the International Bible Training Institute in Leamington Spa from 1948–49 was Hollenweger's introduction to England; in 1952 he returned to attend the World Pentecostal Conference in London, where he acted as interpreter and led a Swiss choir and English brass band. Everything seemed set to continue along these lines: a young, energetic, committed pastor ministering to a rapidly growing congregation; a popular preacher, with a gift for languages of use in the international Pentecostal forum, happily married since 1951 to Erica Busslinger; a man who was fulfilling his vocation.

In 1958 Hollenweger resigned from the Swiss *Pfingstmission*. His suspension was anyway under consideration. According to Hollenweger there were two sets of factors culminating in this break: first, his continued study of the Bible raised questions which senior colleagues could not answer and were not interested in exploring;[7] and secondly, his popularity as a preacher and pastor, despite (or perhaps because of) the fact that his preaching did not follow the conventional Pentecostal lines of that time. He had, he says, more important things to preach about than whether jewellery should or should not be worn. 'I was silly, you know', he commented in a personal interview. 'I told them everything I learned; you see the blame is not all on their side. I was just silly but it would have come to a break anyhow, only later.' Today he relates with humour the

6. Interview, 8 August 1997.

7. Hollenweger writes a little about this in *Erfahrungen der Leibhaftigkeit: Interkulturelle Theologie I* (Munich: Chr. Kaiser Verlag, 1990), in the opening section 'Fragmente einer theologischen Autobiographie', pp. 11-13. Here he recalls asking a Reformed minister about notes in the Züricherbibel indicating, for example, that the story of Jesus and the adultress and the end of Mark's Gospel were later additions to the text. The reply he received was that liberal professors at the theology faculty at Zürich had smuggled them into the Bible! (p. 11) So he decided to find out about these things for himself.

fact that a Pentecostal congregation prayed publicly that he should fail his examinations and that fortunately God did not see fit to answer that particular request, but at the time he admits he was 'broken' by the split from 'his home' and grateful for the counselling sessions from a psychotherapist recommended by a fellow Pentecostal pastor. After hearing his story the counsellor advised Hollenweger not to try and re-establish contact with the authorities of the *Pfingstmission* and told him, 'Don't think that you have spoiled your vocation; perhaps this is the beginning of your vocation'.[8] In 1962 he was ordained as a minister of the Swiss Reformed Church, and though often a guest preacher and liturgist in many places since, he has never taken pastoral charge of a congregation since leaving the *Pfingstmission*.

In 1955 Hollenweger had begun theological studies at Zürich and Basel, which he continued until gaining his Doctor of Theology degree from Zürich University in 1966. As he put it himself in a Henry Martin Lecture delivered at Cambridge on 28 October 1997:

> I was raised in the experiential and oral spirituality of Pentecostalism. But I was trained in the most rigid methods of historical-critical exegesis. Among my teachers were Hans Conzelman, Eduard Schweizer, Gerhard Ebeling and Karl Barth. I knew Rudolph Bultmann and Ernst Käseman personally. I have great respect for the spirituality and integrity of these men.[9]

The outcome of this dual belonging has been that Hollenweger remains a Pentecostal in experience (speaking in tongues continues to be a part of his private prayer life, for example), but not in ideology. Unlike many people who undergo a difficult separation, Hollenweger has not made a wholesale rejection of what was formerly held dear but has instead held on to the riches of his Pentecostal heritage and experience while simultaneously adopting a critical approach to some of its rhetoric and theology. He is neither champion nor enemy of Pentecostalism, and is consequently variously appraised both by those inside and outside the movement; at times a support and at times the source of criticism, he is a non-aligned expert. This is not to say he is uninvolved, rather he is involved from different standpoints. The frog moves between the pond and the water lily leaf with agility.

8.   Interview, 29 October 1997.

9.   Manuscript of Lectures, p. 21; also in Walter J. Hollenweger, *Pentecostalism: Origins and Developments Worldwide* (Peabody, MA: Hendrickson, 1997), p. 322; German: *Charismatisch-pfingstliches Christentum* (Göttingen: Vandenhoeck & Ruprecht, 1997).

Pentecostal Scholar

When Hollenweger undertook his ground-breaking research on the Pentecostal movement, gathering primary material from worldwide sources in original languages and collating them in a massive ten-volume work for which he was awarded a doctorate, Pentecostalism was a marginal topic; few scholars had shown interest in the subject.[10] Hollenweger's foundational work, available and often still referred to by scholars today, was published in much-reduced form as *Enthusiastisches Christentum* in 1969 and in English as *The Pentecostals* in 1972 and became a standard reference.[11] His pioneering efforts to have Pentecostalism taken seriously as a subject of scholarly interest and concern by Western academia, and by Pentecostals themselves, have been more than justified in the ensuing years, when it has become generally apparent that this vibrant and diverse movement is internationally significant.[12] At the time, initial responses to the German edition reflected the novelty of the material to many readers inside and outside the movement, with some of the strongest criticism, from Pentecostals, directed against the author's use of historical-critical biblical exegesis.[13] In the Preface to the third edition of *The Pentecostals* in 1988, Hollenweger reflected on his original research in the light of further developments and considered that it had been vindicated in two

10. Nils Bloch-Hoell was a notable exception. *The Pentecostal Movement: Its Origins, Development and Distinctive Character* (London: Allen & Unwin, 1964); Norwegian: *Pinsebevegelsen. En undersøkelse av Pinsebevegelsens tilbivelse, utvikling og saerpreg med saerlig henblikk på bevegelsens utformning i Norge* (Oslo, Universitetsforlaget, 1956).

11. The full ten-volume work, *Handbuch der Pfingstbewegung*, 1965–67, is available at ATLA, Board of Microtexts, Divinity School, Yale University, New Haven. *Enthusiastisches Christentum: Die Pfingstbewegung in Geschichte und Gegenwart* (Zürich: Zwingli Verlag, 1969). First published in English as *The Pentecostals* (London: SCM Press, 1972, pbk 1976). North American: *The Pentecostal and Charismatic Movements* (Minneapolis: Augsburg, 1973); *The Pentecostals* (Peabody, MA: Hendrickson, 1988). Spanish: *El Pentecostalismo, Historia y Doctrinas* (Buenos Aires: La Aurora, 1975).

12. David Barrett's statistics are frequently referred to. See D. Barrett (ed.), *World Christian Encyclopedia* (Oxford: Oxford University Press, 1982) *idem*, 'Statistics, Global', in Stanley M. Burgess and Gary B. McGee (eds.), *Dictionary of Pentecostal and Charismatic Movements* (Grand Rapids: Zondervan, 9th reprint 1996 [1988]).

13. Hollenweger, *The Pentecostals*, p. 500. (All references are to the Hendrickson 1988 edn.)

important areas: 'Pentecostalism is in itself an ecumenical movement' and 'Pentecostalism's amazing capacity to incorporate oral and narrative structures from the American slave religion'.[14] Both motifs have been pursued by Hollenweger in subsequent works.[15] It is unusual to find a scholarly book on Pentecostalism today that does not cite Hollenweger's original work or his subsequent writings.[16] David Martin, in his recent book on Protestantism in Latin America, *Tongues of Fire*, refers to Hollenweger as 'the doyen of Pentecostal studies';[17] and Harvey Cox calls him 'the distinguished historian of Pentecostalism' in *Fire from Heaven: The Rise of Pentecostal Spirituality and the Reshaping of Religion in the Twenty-First Century*.[18] David Bundy, reviewing *Pentecostalism: Origins and Developments Worldwide* (1997) comments, 'In few instances since the Enlightenment has one scholar rested so gracefully at the summit of a discipline for half a century. His career is a remarkable achievement.'[19]

For decades Hollenweger has continued his interest in Pentecostalism and remained well-informed on the ever-increasing amount of research and writing on the subject, noting the shifts of interpretations, progress and

14. Hollenweger, *The Pentecostals*, p. xxviii.

15. See, e.g., 'Two Extraordinary Pentecostal Ecumenists: The Letters of Donald Gee and David du Plessis', *Ecumenical Review* 52.3 (2000), pp. 391-402; and Part I, 'The Black Oral Root', in *Pentecostalism: Origins*.

16. A few random examples of publications in English illustrating writers of various nationalities and denominations who refer to Hollenweger's writings on the subject: Rex Davis, *Locusts and Wild Honey: The Charismatic Renewal and the Ecumenical Movement* (Risk Book Series, 2; Geneva: WCC, 1978); Francis A. Sullivan, SJ, *Charisms and Charismatic Renewal: A Biblical and Theological Study* (Dublin: Gill & MacMillan, 1982); Charles Edwin Jones, *Black Holiness: A Guide to the Study of Black Participation in Wesleyan Perfectionist and Glossolalic Pentecostal Movements* (ATLA Bibliography Series, 18; Metuchen, NJ: American Theological Library Association and the Scarecrow Press, 1987); Allan Anderson, *Moya: the Holy Spirit in an African Context* (Pretoria: University of South Africa, 1991). See also a number of bibliographical references in Burgess and McGee (eds.), *Dictionary of Pentecostal*.

17. David Martin, *Tongues of Fire* (Oxford: Basil Blackwell, 1993 [1990]), p. 163.

18. Harvey Cox, *Fire from Heaven* (London: Cassell, 1996 [1994]), p. 148.

19. In *Encounter* 59.3 (1998), pp. 424-27 (425). See also Bundy's, 'Pentecostalism as a Global Phenomenon: A Review Essay of Walter Hollenweger's', *Pentecostalism: Origins and Developments Worldwide*', *Pneuma* 21.2 (1999), pp. 289-303, where he describes the book as a truly important one that 'brings research on Pentecostalism to a new level' and 'is in many ways an agenda for research' (303).

gaps,[20] and producing numerous journal articles, books, contributions to books, dictionary entries and conference papers on many aspects of the Pentecostal and charismatic movements. A bibliography extending to 1991 can be found in the Festschrift edited by Jan A.B. Jongeneel *et al.*, which was presented to Hollenweger at a ceremony at Utrecht University on Wednesday 9 September 1992. He had by this time retired from the post of Professor of Mission at the University of Birmingham and Selly Oak Colleges, and many of his colleagues and former research students (myself included) were present to hear his lecture on this occasion, entitled 'Pentecostalism and Academic Theology: From Confrontation to Cooperation', in which he made an impassioned statement:

> Nowadays we have institutes and specialists in every possible and impossible theological topic but not one single library, not a single institute, not one specialized doctoral supervisor in Europe for the hundreds and perhaps thousands of young Pentecostal scholars world-wide who are knocking at the doors of our academic establishments. That is a theological scandal without precedent.[21]

Pentecostalism: Origins and Developments Worldwide (1997), a major sequel to *The Pentecostals*, was written, he says, because 'Pentecostalism "has come to a crossroads" ' and as a consequence, in contrast to the early work, it is not historical, but theological. However, he asserts that it deals with theology in the form of histories rather than propositional statements.[22] With this approach Hollenweger once again ploughs his own furrow and eludes academic classification. The oft-quoted dedication in the original *Pentecostals*, 'To my friends and teachers in the Pentecostal Movement who taught me to love the Bible and to my teachers and friends in the Presbyterian Church who taught me to understand it', is extended in this latest book in a way which encapsulates Hollenweger's characteristic boundary-crossing:

> To my friends and scholars in the Pentecostal Movement who taught me to criticize and understand Pentecostalism's weaknesses and blind spots and to the friends and scholars in the universal church who showed me Pentecostalism's strengths and potentials. To the ex-Pentecostals who were

---

20. As, e.g., in Walter J. Hollenweger, 'After Twenty Years' Research on Pentecostalism' (Guest Editorial), *International Review of Mission* 75.297 (1986), pp. 3-12.

21. The lecture was subsequently published in *EPTA Bulletin*, the Journal of the European Pentecostal Theological Association, 11.1-2 (1992), pp. 42-49 (43-44).

22. *Pentecostalism: Origins*, pp. 1-2; quoting William Faupel.

> wounded and broken by Pentecostalism and who couldn't help but respond
> by fighting their former friends and to the new converts to Pentecostalism
> who found an inspiring spirituality and new life in Pentecostalism. All these
> are included in my prayers which accompany this book.

In conversation shortly before the publication of the English edition, Hollenweger told me that in putting Pentecostal theological questions on the map he was anticipating some negative reactions. Within the movement there were many people who were not aware of the work of the growing number of Pentecostal scholars and the existence of three academic journals, who would be challenged by the book.[23] And many academics would be 'flabbergasted' to learn that subjects like hermeneutics, soteriology, ecclesiology, liturgy, historiography and pneumatology were being discussed at an academic level within Pentecostalism.[24] Thus he warmly reviewed *The Globalisation of Pentecostalism* edited by Dempster, Klaus and Peterson and published in 1999, commenting that 'Pentecostalism has developed an important academic culture which is clearly shown in this book'.[25] In March 1999 the Society for Pentecostal Studies awarded Hollenweger their 'Lifetime Achievement Award'.[26]

Evangelist-Administrator at the World Council of Churches

Three years as Research Assistant for Church History and Social Ethics at the University of Zürich with Professor F. Blanke and Professor A. Rich, followed by one year as Study Director of the Evangelical Academy at Boldern from 1964–65, provided useful experience for Hollenweger's next appointment. As Executive Secretary of the Department on Studies in Evangelism at the World Council of Churches for the next three years, he arrived at an interesting time: only as recently as 1961 had the International Missionary Council become integrated with the WCC.[27] Thus there had been a shift from regarding mission as being the function of

23. There are now two more journals: *The Asian Journal of Pentecostal Studies* and *The Spirit & Church*. The three referred to are *EPTA Bulletin, Pneuma* and *Journal of Pentecostal Theology*.

24. Interview, 8 August 1997.

25. Review M.W. Dempster, Byron D. Klaus and Douglas Peterson (eds.), *The Globalisation of Pentecostalism* (Regnum, 1999), *Theology*, 103.813 (2000), p. 231.

26. At Evangel University, Springfield, MO.

27. Tom Stransky, 'International Missionary Council', in Nicholas Lossky *et al.* (eds.), *Dictionary of the Ecumenical Movement* (Geneva: WCC, 1991), pp. 526-29 (529).

the—mostly white, Western—missionary societies to seeing it as the function of the church. The first Commission for World Mission and Evangelism (CWME) Conference held in Mexico City in 1963 had defined the missionary task as belonging to the whole church together, in all six continents, and by nature to be both local and universal.[28] As part of the ongoing process a study called 'The Missionary Structure of the Congregation' was carried out, initially under the secretaryship of Hans Margull and passed to Walter Hollenweger. In his introduction to the report produced by the Western European Working Group, *The Church for Others*, Hollenweger described the work as 'excitingly theological and practical at the same time'.[29] Inspired by the thinking of Dietrich Bonhoeffer, this 1967 report considered mission from the perspective of the 'world setting the agenda' and 'the Church is the Church only when it exists for others'. Its influence permeated the controversial Section II Report 'Renewal in Mission' to the Fourth Assembly of the WCC at Uppsala in 1968, the writing of which Hollenweger was intimately involved with in his capacity as Secretary.[30]

That year Hollenweger became Secretary for Evangelism in the Division of World Mission and Evangelism and was given a wide brief to make explicit the WCC's concern for evangelism. The WCC publication *From Mexico City to Bangkok, Report of the Commission on World Mission and Evangelism 1963–1972* records that 'his work developed experimentally in four directions'. These were: developing links between Pentecostal churches in Europe and the Americas and the WCC; raising the question of 'meaningful communication' and experimenting with forms of worship, Bible study and narrative as well as producing a *Monthly Letter about Evangelism*;[31] working with local European churches, especially those in

28. World Council of Churches, *From Mexico City to Bangkok* (Report of the Commission on World Mission and Evangelism 1963–1972; Geneva: WCC, undated), p. 35.

29. 'The Church for Others: A Quest for Structures for Missionary Congregations' in World Council of Churches, *The Church for Others and The Church for the World* (Geneva: WCC, 1967), p. 4. The second part is the report by the North American Working Group.

30. The Introduction to the commentary on the report states: 'Of particular importance for the work of this Section is the report of the Study of the Missionary Structure of the Congregation entitled *The Church for Others* (WCC Publication)', *Drafts For Sections: Prepared for the Fourth Assembly of the World Council of Churches, Uppsala, Sweden 1968* (Geneva: WCC, 1967), p. 32.

31. Many of these letters were collected together and published in German as

Eastern Europe, and utilizing the medium of broadcasting; and fourthly, ecumenical work in Latin America focusing on enabling people to communicate the gospel in their own social and political context.[32] This stimulating and pioneering work took Hollenweger to many countries, particularly in Africa and Latin America, and brought him into contact with Christians from all strata of the churches.

Martin Conway, whose career intersected with Walter Hollenweger's at several points, recalled that in his farewell speech to the WCC Hollenweger began:

> 'On an occasion like this you either crack a few jokes and leave it at that, or else you risk saying the truth for once; I have decided to do the second'— and went on with a fierce critique of the self-satisfaction and in-turned bureaucracy that he had met among his colleagues.[33]

Conway also comments that Hollenweger has 'reflected relatively seldom in writing on the nature of the ecumenical movement'.[34] With regard to an analysis of structures and any attempt at a 'theology of ecumenism' this is probably true, but in other respects Hollenweger has paid the diverse realities of the world *oikoumene* enormous attention. When I asked Hollenweger recently about his time at the WCC, his response was that what he felt had been important was learning at first hand, rather than from books, that there were other types of Christianity, and that effective ecumenical relationships were founded not primarily on what people said, but on how they behaved towards one another.[35] These are the keys to appreciating the undoubtedly significant part he played in establishing dialogue between various groups of Christians, especially between those inside the WCC and those not (like almost all Pentecostals and all evangelicals) and between people of oral and literary cultures.[36]

Complementing his already regular contributions to the prestigious and popular German *Kirchentag*, personal exposure to the richness of Christian expressions of life and faith in the 'Third World' increased even

Walter J. Hollenweger (ed.), *Kirche, Benzin und Bohnensuppe: auf den Spuren dynamischer Gemeinden* (Zürich: TVZ, 1971).

32. World Council of Churches, *From Mexico City*, pp. 35-36.

33. Martin Conway, 'Helping the Ecumenical Movement to Move On: Hollenweger and the Rediscovery of the Value of Diversity', in Jongeneel *et al.* (eds.), *Pentecost, Mission and Ecumenism*, pp. 273-87 (273).

34. Conway, 'Helping the Ecumenical Movement', p. 274.

35. Interviews, 8 August 1997, 29 October 1997.

36. World Council of Churches, *From Mexico City*, p. 25.

further his commitment to innovative means of communication.[37] As a result of his extensive engagement with the four areas of experimentation noted above, Hollenweger developed his own particular style of communication through narratives, liturgies and dramas. These were not the normal staple diet of the WCC and not one they were to enjoy for long, for in 1971 he became Professor of Mission at Birmingham. However, during the following few years the fictional 'Mr. Chips' and 'Professor Unrat' took on the entertaining and provocative role of Hollenweger's chosen mouthpieces for comment on various aspects of the ecumenical movement.[38] It is in these articles, one of which was presented to the WCC Consultation on the charismatic movement at Bossey in 1980,[39] that much of Hollenweger's reflection can be found, admittedly not in conventional form. As I have noted elsewhere, his major criticisms of the WCC at that time were that it fell short of its own intention to be a world movement in its underrepresentation of 'Third World' Christians and operated within a Western conceptual framework which precluded easy communication with oral traditions.[40] It was, perhaps surprisingly, to be in the academic arena rather than in an ecumenical institutional one that Hollenweger was to further develop his own intensely practical route to improving this situation.

Professor of Mission

Professor J. Gordon Davies, Edward Cadbury Professor of Theology and Head of the Department of Theology at the University of Birmingham, had been a member of the Western European Working Group on the Missionary Structure of Congregation. There was at that time no chair of mission studies at an English university and Davies felt this should be

37. The *Kirchentag* is a bi-annual gathering for Bible study, worship and debate on political, social and economic and religious issues. Initiated by the Protestant Church, it currently attracts around 100,000 people from various denominations during the four-five days of events.

38. All the articles have been published together in German in *Glaube, Geist und Geister: Professor Unrat zwischen Bangkok und Birmingham* (Frankfurt: Otto Lembeck, 1975). Some have appeared in a variety of journals in English and we shall consider them later. In *Pentecostalism: Origins* Hollenweger points out that English publishers were not interested in this 'theological novel' (p. 379).

39. 'Saints in Birmingham', in Arnold Bittlinger (ed.), *The Church is Charismatic* (Geneva: WCC, 1981), pp. 87-99.

40. L. Price, entry 'Hollenweger, Walter J.', in Trevor A. Hart (ed.), *The Dictionary of Historical Theology* (Carlisle: Paternoster Press; Grand Rapids: Eerdmans, 2000).

rectified.[41] Agreement was reached with the Selly Oak Colleges to establish and fund a joint chair; both Gordon Davies and Paul Clifford of the Colleges went to Geneva to talk with Hollenweger and his colleagues. Hollenweger was given to understand that an English candidate would have been preferred, but 'only former missionaries' lacking adequate scholarly qualifications applied and after a full panel interview he was invited to become the first holder of the post.[42] The Pentecostal scholar, Reformed minister and ecumenical evangelist with international experience, together with his wife, was lured from Switzerland to Birmingham with the promise that he would be given the freedom to experiment with a new type of theology—intercultural theology—which was open to the universal dimensions of the Christian faith. This involved helping Westerners to realize that their way of theologizing was neither the only one, nor the normative one for all cultures, and introducing people from the non-Western world to critical understandings without, in his own words, transforming 'vital and spontaneous Christians into detached intellectuals'. In his farewell lecture in 1989 he was 'glad to say the promise had been kept'.[43]

Experimentation is necessarily a risky enterprise and circumstances proved particularly stimulating for different reasons in each of the two educational establishments. Just as Pentecostalism had been a marginal subject when Hollenweger embarked on his original research, missiology was a marginal discipline at the university. His inaugural lecture on a comparison of Marxist and Kimbanguist mission was to set the tone of things to come.[44] Something of the breadth of understanding Hollenweger held then of academic theology—and continued to hold—can be glimpsed in the information booklet *Theology at Birmingham*, which he wrote at the request of Gordon Davies on behalf of the department for prospective undergraduate students. The study of theology is described as an 'exciting experience' for those trying to understand the world and assess its problems in the light of the great religious traditions; the ecumenical and

---

41. See Daniel W. Hardy, 'God in the Ordinary: The Work of J.G. Davies (1919–1990)', *Theology* 98.792 (1996), pp. 427-40 (435).

42. Personal correspondence from Walter Hollenweger, 17 October 1996.

43. *The Future of Mission and the Mission of the Future* (Selly Oak Colleges Occasional Paper, 2; Birmingham: Selly Oak Colleges, 1989), p. 3.

44. *Marxist and Kimbanguist Mission—A Comparison* (Inaugural Lecture 23 November 1972; Birmingham: University of Birmingham, 1973).

international character of the department (and the city) is emphasized.[45]

Hollenweger concretized his understanding of narrative exegesis, evangelism and insights from intercultural theology in the writing and production of dramas with music, song and dance. Some, such as *Conflict in Corinth* and *A Bonhoeffer Requiem*, were performed by students in the department and much enjoyed, but few realized these 'revolutionized theological discourse'—an opinion given by George Mulrain from Trinidad and Emmanuel Lartey from Ghana.[46] 'If I wanted academic recognition I would have gone to Hamburg or to Berne and become a normal Swiss theologian', Hollenweger told me, 'but then I would have been missing my vocation. I think this [usual academic theology] is more of the same and doesn't bring anything. "Let the dead bury their dead".'[47]

At Selly Oak Colleges the situation was quite different. They knew what the professor was doing but were not entirely comfortable with it. Many of the individual colleges forming the federation had been established in the early twentieth century by various Protestant missionary societies and churches specifically to train missionaries for work overseas. Godfrey Phillips, a professor of Bangalore Theological College, had, on return to England in the 1930s retained his title when taking a key post at Selly Oak Colleges, so there was some history of an element of academic mission studies, though the emphasis was more on training than education in the broader sense and the Colleges had their own staff and programmes.

As noted in the previous section, a major rethinking of mission was taking place internationally in the 1960s and 1970s. Werner Ustorf observed in his speech welcoming Walter Hollenweger as an Honorary Fellow of the Selly Oak Colleges on 1 July 1996, seven years after his retirement, that Walter Hollenweger 'was so inspiring and good at this process of self-critical reflection' that after only two years, in 1973, the mission societies and colleges 'went ecumenical' and agreed to revive a tradition and set up a joint Department of Mission with its own dean, teaching staff and central programme. There are different possible interpretations of this move on the part of the Colleges; Ustorf suggests that 'the relationship between the Professorship and the Department was meant to be one of mutual

45. *Theology at Birmingham: BA Courses in Theology* (Birmingham: University of Birmingham, undated), pp. 1-3.
46. Emmanuel Y. Lartey and George M. Mulrain, 'Hollenweger as Professor of Mission', in Jongeneel *et al.* (eds.), *Pentecost, Mission and Ecumenism*, pp. 33-40 (36).
47. Interview, 8 August 1997.

sympathy and correction between two different models of mission'.[48] What is certainly true is that the new intercultural theological approach which Hollenweger experimented with and developed was not concerned with increasing the power and influence of Western missionary societies or the Western churches. He delighted in the variety of students and interdisciplinary studies, remarking in a substantial article on the subject for a German periodical that the Selly Oak Colleges were 'a logical impossibility and yet a concrete reality'.[49]

Concrete realities, however, are prone to practical problems. In a paper published in the *Selly Oak Journal* in 1986, Hollenweger wrote that 'the future of Mission Studies in Birmingham is by no means secure', and gave financial, social and missiological reasons why this was unfortunate. He recalled the original purpose of the Chair in Mission—'to secure for the subject of Mission Studies that academic standing which it had long been denied in Britain', and the promise that in his educational work he was 'allowed to start the process of reflection not exclusively with the Old Testament, the New Testament, the creeds, etc., but also with the troubles and questions of our time and my students, in short with what I called "Intercultural Theology" '.[50]

Hollenweger's lectures at the university to undergraduates and at the Selly Oak Colleges to students pursuing a variety of mission-related courses or research were rarely dull. During his last year in post I attended many of these and recall occasions when he climbed on top of and under furniture, strode expansively around the room, arms waving, or spoke with tears in his eyes. These demonstrative modes of communication served to highlight the points he was making and were not used for entertainment. Question and discussion times were often exciting, particularly at Selly Oak, where the audience was extremely mixed in all respects—nationality, experience, age, denomination, level of formal theological education, and

---

48. Text of Werner Ustorf's address. Werner Ustorf is the current Professor of Mission at the University of Birmingham and Walter Hollenweger's immediate successor. Martin Conway was at this time President of the Federation of Selly Oak Colleges; for his tribute on this occasion see 'Honorary Fellows 1996', *Selly Oak Colleges 'News and Views'* 20 (1996), p. 3, in which he says that Hollenweger's 'contribution to mission studies world-wide is second to none in this generation'.

49. Hollenweger, 'Theologiestudium anders', *Der Ueberblick* 9.1 (1973), pp. 51-52 (52).

50. Hollenweger, 'The Chair of Mission at the University of Birmingham', *The Selly Oak Journal* 4 (1986), pp. 13-17 (13).

place on the conservative–liberal continuum. An apparently simple but loaded question from the professor such as 'What is a Christian?' could occupy an hour of interactive discussion. People often left stirred, if not shaken, and this Hollenweger would regard as success. As he put it:

> Information must be precise and right but information you can get anywhere; inspiration you cannot get so easily. My first job is to stretch the students to consider things, to consider texts, to consider options which they have not considered before and to find it necessary and to find it interesting. That is the job of a teacher. There are of course people who say it is clear objective information we give, but that is boring, it is useless, and it is all over in communication theory and the natural sciences.[51]

One undergraduate student in the early 1970s who was inspired by Hollenweger's imaginative approach to theology and recently paid tribute to his teaching, is Michael Austin. Following five years as a Methodist minister in Honduras, where he was enriched by the people's method of life-to-text Bible study, he wrote the novel *Searching for Mother*. With the professional theatre company Palaver Productions he has subsequently written and produced for the British church and theatre.[52]

During his 18 years as Professor of Mission Hollenweger supervised the postgraduate research of 99 students of all ages, many denominations, from every continent, studying an amazing variety of subjects. Attendance at the monthly doctoral seminars held hospitably at the Hollenwegers' home made participants forcefully aware of the extent of the professor's expertise and breadth of interests. Graciously, he in turn acknowledges that he received 'an education in global theology, liturgy, economics and educational theories' from his research students.[53] In order to assist wider dissemination of the original studies produced, he and Professor Richard Friedli of Fribourg joined Professor Hans Margull of Hamburg to establish the series 'Studies in the Intercultural History of Christianity' published by Peter Lang of Frankfurt am Main, in which many of his students' dissertations were subsequently published.[54] Hollenweger continued to be

51. Interview, 29 October 1997.

52. Michael Austin, *Searching for Mother* (Palaver Publications, 1991). Palaver Productions theatre company aims to create high-quality theatre for the church and present work reflecting 'Christian' themes in the professional theatre; plays include *Temptations and Betrayals*, 1996. Austin lectured in Birmingham on 21 May 2000.

53. Hollenweger, *The Future of Mission*, p. 4.

54. See Hollenweger's article on the series which includes reviews of some of his research students' publications, 'Towards an Intercultural History of Christianity', in

an editor of the series until 1997. Many of his students have gone on to distinguished careers all over the world and maintain contact with him.

Another very practical outcome of his theological concerns was the key role he played in the establishment of the Centre for Black and White Christian Partnership at Selly Oak Colleges, an educational experiment formally established in 1978 to provide pastors from black independent churches with theological education and a recognized qualification. Hollenweger saw this as a step towards facilitating fruitful relationships between black and white Christians in Britain. Commenting some years later, he found it 'remarkable that the British mission societies, which are famous for their ecumenical and missiological pioneering work in the Third World, have almost totally missed the opportunity for a renewing intercultural dialogue in their own country'.[55] Together with Roswith Gerloff, whose initial research into African-Caribbean and African con-gregations in Britain provided information and contacts, a course was designed which was acceptable on academic grounds to the university and did not estrange the pastors from their own culture in which worship, prayer, song, dance and personal witness were vitally important. Professor Hollenweger's first task was to convince the university of the necessity and viability of the enterprise, in the knowledge that power politics were a real issue underlying the almost total absence of black competence in academia.[56] Subsequently he served as Consultant to the Director and Advisory Group of the Centre and provided the link with the Department of Theology, taught two courses on mission each year, and, with the tutor, Roswith Gerloff, set the examinations for that course.[57] The centre continues its work today.

Hollenweger is a prolific writer. During his time as Professor of Mission

International Review of Mission 76.304 (1987), pp. 526-56. At that time there were 40 volumes in the series, a third of the present number.

55. Walter J. Hollenweger, 'Interaction between Black and White in Theological Education', *Theology* 90.737 (1987), pp. 341-50 (342).

56. Walter J. Hollenweger, 'Black Competence', *Christian Action Journal* (Autumn 1982), p. 17.

57. Information taken from Roswith Gerloff, 'Theological Education in Black and White: The Centre for Black and White Christian Partnership (1978–1985)', in Jongeneel *et al.* (eds.), *Pentecost, Mission and Ecumenism*, pp. 41-59. See also *Pentecostalism: Origins*, Ch. 9. Bongani Mazibuko, who was co-ordinator of the centre for several years, has written on the history, content and evaluation of the centre in *Education in Mission—Mission in Education: A Critical Comparative Study of Selected Approaches* (Frankfurt am Main: Peter Lang, 1987).

he published a steady flow of articles on a wide variety of subjects in addition to Pentecostalism and the charismatic movement, which appeared principally in German and English publications, some in French and Spanish. His major three volumes on intercultural theology, in German only, appeared in 1979 (reprinted [×2] 1990), 1982 (reprinted [×2] 1992) and 1988.[58] 'Experiences of Life's Realities', 'Engagement with Myths' and 'Spirit and Matter' present Hollenweger's version of systematic theology. The first volume is a 'prologue to theology' establishing that all theology is culturally conditioned; the second is a Christology; and the third pneumatology. I put it to him that most academic theologians would not recognize these volumes as systematic theology. His reply was:

> It is not necessary for me that they recognize it. I think the time for systematic theology in the old sense is over anyhow… The first systematic theologian was Thomas Aquinas and he is a typical example of a contextual theologian because he had to introduce and work through Aristotle… Luther was very contextual, Cranmer was extremely contextual, Wesley was contextual. That is my tradition. The tradition is that they are contextual and fragmentary and selective, all of them.[59]

Applying systematic thought to systematic theology, he finds it inherently unsystematic. The subject matter treated in the three volumes ranges from Zwingli to Bonhoeffer, healing through prayer to business practice, Moses to Rumpelstiltskin, the church in first-century Corinth to Jesus in the Koran, confirming that Hollenweger's theologizing is indeed contextual, fragmentary and selective. And he would not have it any other way.

He revealed that most of his written work has been done in response to requests from other people with relatively few pieces self-initiated, and here the evangelist predominates over the academic—'I do not speak about the gospel unless I am asked'. His major contribution outside the area of Pentecostalism is, he feels, that he can communicate critical theological insights so that 'students and normal people and pastors can understand them'. This he sees as a much more important academic task than pursuing the route of a normative, classical theology which no longer

58. *Erfahrungen der Leibhaftigkeit, Umgang mit Mythen, Geist und Materie*, all published by Chr. Kaiser Verlag, of Munich. A proportion of the material in these volumes has been published in English as journal articles or contributions to books; I shall refer to them later. There is a one-volume abridged French version, *L'Expérience de l'Esprit: Jalons pour une théologie interculturelle* (Geneva: Labor et Fides, 1991).

59. Interview, 8 August 1997.

plays any significant role, even in Europe.[60] Indications of appreciation come from different quarters: an almost unbroken record of Bible studies, dramas or leading worship for 30 years at the *Kirchentag* speaks for itself. In 1995 Hollenweger was awarded the Sexau Community Prize for Theology. The witty and imaginative 'Laudatio' painted a picture of a united Europe and United Christian Council for Europe in the year 2030 supported, following the Third Vatican Council, by a Latin American Pope with Eugen Drewermann as a cardinal. From this perspective Walter Hollenweger would be viewed by a biographer as a 'Church Father of a Church of the Future'.[61]

The Dramas Continue

The major vehicle for this task of communication through narrative exegesis, which he experimented with first in 1980 and continues to employ with enthusiasm and vigour, is drama. In fact, it was the Swiss churches' commissioning of a drama to commemorate the 700th anniversary of Switzerland (1291–1991) which drew Hollenweger away prematurely from the Chair of Mission. *Friedensmahl* was staged nationwide with professional actors and local bands and choirs. Twenty-three of his innovative plays with music, song and dance have been published in German by Metanoia Verlag and produced all over Germany and Switzerland. Premières of the works have usually been performed by professional or semi-professional artists before large audiences; among the most notable were the *Bonhoeffer Requiem* at the 1987 *Kirchentag* in Berlin, *The Boy and the Moon* at Dortmund in 1991 and *Maria von Wedemeyer* at Leipzig in 1997 (co-authored with Estella Korthaus). Afterwards the plays have been taken up by many other non-professional and ad hoc groups, each bringing their own interpretation to the text. Sometimes Hollenweger is present at residential conferences where a play is rehearsed, performed and discussed by participants. None of the plays have been published in English, though manuscript copies of some are available and may be obtained from the publisher; *Jonah* was performed in Birmingham in 1986, to celebrate the 900th anniversary of St Lawrence's Church, Northfield, for example. It seems that while these enterprises do not have a

---

60. Interview, 8 August 1997.
61. Walter J. Hollenweger, *Wie erlebten die ersten Christen den Heiligen Geist? und Predigt über Joh. 20.29b* (Sexau: Evangelische Kirchengemeinde, 1995), pp. 1-27 (Laudatio 23-27).

wide appeal in England, demand continues in Germany and Switzerland.

Hollenweger is intending to write more plays and music in keeping with his teaching and evangelistic vocations. How he fits this in between guest lecturing and preaching, writing articles, facilitating weeks of Bible study, reviewing new publications, carrying out an editorial function with the *Journal of Pentecostal Theology*, attending some performances of his dramas when invited and giving time to researchers engaged with various aspects of his work, is something of a marvel but not a mystery: he works hard and he loves his work. A short book on hermeneutics entitled *Der Klapperstorch und die Theologie* ('The Stork and Theology') published in 2000 includes a Foreword by Hollenweger incorporating the criticisms of publishers who declined to produce it. The book is, according to Hollenweger, a highly critical assessment of theological education, which has not learnt how to tell the truth about the fruits of biblical scholarship without destroying the faith of the people.[62]

Comment

Walter Hollenweger is like a rolling stone which *does* gather moss. At each stage of his career he has taken what he has learnt and continued to work with it in subsequent settings. His initial nurturing in the Pentecostal Church, formal theological study, and the ensuing break, provided both the personal stability and the quest for change that characterize his attitude to his life and work. His insights into worldwide Pentecostalism in the 1960s—that it was in itself an ecumenical movement and that black narrative traditions were intrinsic to its growth and appreciation—were to prove highly relevant to the wider ecumenical movement in the form of the fledgling World Council of Churches, which perhaps was not quite ready for these reflections to be acted upon so concretely by the Secretary for Evangelism. Hollenweger's work there confirmed the realities of the diversity of the universal church. Rather than devote himself to levelling them he brought attention to the diversities as sources of mutual enrichment. Hence, as Professor of Mission, he developed his thinking on intercultural theology as an alternative to mission studies, which had traditionally been dominated by white Westerners and was no longer appropriate in the contemporary world where the distribution of Christianity had

62. Interview, 8 August 1997, and correspondence, 27 May 2000. Walter J. Hollenweger, *Der Klapperstorch und die Theologie: Die Krise von Theologie und Kirche als Chance* (Kindhausen: Metanoia Verlag, 2000).

changed and the colonial period ended. His study of the Bible, his recognition of the importance of narrative in the spread of Christianity, and his observations of the less dominantly cognitive exercise of faith in the 'Third World', all confirmed that evangelism was a dialogical and participatory activity. Not content with writing academically on the subject, Hollenweger acted on his convictions by devising the dramas based on these foundations for Europeans.

Hollenweger's first maxim, which all former students will be aware of, is 'the best criticism of the false is the praxis of the true'. He has not generally engaged in public debate with those who do not agree with him; he simply carries on doing what interests him and what he thinks fit. When critical comment is called for, he often uses the device of drawing on research and opinions from unexpected quarters to elucidate a view which is his own, as indicated in the dedication to his 1997 publication on Pentecostalism, obviating the need for head-on confrontation. There have, he acknowledges, been scuffles behind the scenes at the World Council of Churches, at the university and the Selly Oak Colleges, but he is not given to public abuse of individuals. Professor Beyerhaus of Tübingen, Hollenweger states in a recent book, wrongly thought he recognized himself in the fictional Professor Unrat.[63] To the recent influential writings of the late Lesslie Newbigin, a fellow ecumenist, former secretary of the International Missionary Council and colleague in the Mission Department at the Colleges from 1974–79,[64] Hollenweger has published no direct response, though their views on gospel and culture differ considerably. The gospel, Hollenweger frequently remarks, is like an onion, not a fruit with a hard core.

This refusal to enter the academic fray, combined with the wide variety of subjects that have captured his scholarly attention and his novel theological methodology, has meant that his work has not been within mainline discourse. He has always been out of place. It is appropriate that in a book on nineteenth- and twentieth-century Swiss theologians, Hollenweger

---

63. *Pentecostalism: Origins*, pp. 379-80 (n. 59). Professor Unrat is the character of the title of the 1904 novel by Heinrich Mann, 'Unrat' being the nickname given to Professor von Rath by his students. Mr Chips is used as the English equivalent, from the novel *Goodbye Mr. Chips* by James Hilton (London: Hoddert & Stoughton, 1984 [1934]).

64. See entry by Bernard Thorogood 'Lesslie Newbigin', in Lossky *et al.* (eds.), *Dictionary*, pp. 725-26.

should be included in the section 'Theology in Worldwide Horizons'.[65] Furthermore, for him practice and reflection are inextricably connected and consequently the outcomes may look messy and unsystematic to conventional theologians who are looking for answers to purely conceptual questions—answers that, from Hollenweger, are largely unforthcoming. But as with the subsequent vindication of his pioneering work on Pentecostalism, it may prove to be that in his idiosyncratic way he has not been offside but ahead of the field. By approaching in piecemeal fashion many of the 'bones of contention' [66] between Christians and between Christians and others, exemplified in real-life situations in different worldwide settings, he has identified ecumenism, Pentecostalism and intercultural relations as the dominant issues of the late twentieth and early twenty-first centuries.

65. Richard Friedli, 'Walter J. Hollenweger: Als Christ zusammen mit Gleichgültigen und Ungläubigen das Evangelium entdecken' ('Discovering the Gospel as a Christian in Cooperation with the indifferent and unbelievers: Hollenweger as Theologian'), in Stephen Leimgruber and Max Schoch (eds.), *Gegen die Gottvergessenheit: Schweizer Theologen im 19. und 20. Jahrhundert* (Freiburg: Herder, 1990). Reprinted, also in German, in Jongeneel *et al.* (eds.), *Pentecost, Mission and Ecumenism*, pp. 15-26.

66. Taken from the title of Hollenweger's book *Evangelism Today: Good News or Bone of Contention?* (Belfast: Christian Journals Limited, 1976).

Chapter 2

A DISPLACED, NOT MISPLACED, METHODOLOGY

David Tracy is one writer who has examined the way Western academic theology operates. In *The Analogical Imagination* he drew attention to the three 'publics' any theologian speaks in and to: society, the academy and the church. Many theologians, he said, resolve this intellectual and existential dilemma by choosing one of the three publics as their primary reference group and 'tend to leave the other two publics at the margins of their consciousness'.[1] Walter Hollenweger, as we have noted, has, notwithstanding the ambiguities of each constituency, operated professionally with reference to all three. Tracy puts the case for more openness in theology to take account of insights that come from outside the traditional 'classic' source material. Through his theological methodology Hollenweger has in many respects been doing just this for nearly 40 years.

David Ford, following the notion of Tracy's 'publics', confirms that most of the writers included in the two-volume collection *The Modern Theologians*, which he edited, concentrate on the academy and the church, while representatives of the new theologies in the second volume favour society.[2] He observes that the scope of modern Christian theology is diverse, in a manner 'often amounting to fragmentation'.[3] Most of the theologians who focus attention on the academy and the church, he notes, are Europeans dealing with systematic issues, while even with regard to the 'New Challenges in Theology' (Latin American Liberation, Black, Asian and Feminist theologies are listed under this heading) 'the main formal criterion [of selection] is that a theologian deals with a broad range of the classic Christian issues and offers a constructive response to them

1.   David Tracy, *The Analogical Imagination* (London: SCM Press, 1981), p. 51.
2.   David F. Ford (ed.), *The Modern Theologians: An Introduction to Christian Theology in the Twentieth Century, Volumes I and II* (Oxford: Basil Blackwell, 1989). Here Introduction to vol. I, p. 17.
3.   Ford, *The Modern Theologians*, II, p. vii.

and to modernity'.[4] Ford, in his Introduction, rightly emphasizes that 'the history of ideas is not enough' and that theology needs to recognize the contexts and interests in which it operates. Along with the Holocaust, post-colonial societies, technology and so on, specific to religion he includes here the Pentecostal movement, Christian and inter-religious ecumenism, the World Council of Churches, the Second Vatican Council, the spread of Islam and Christianity (especially in Africa), the new religious movements outside the main world religions, the multiplication of 'basic communities', and liturgical reforms. He then comments, 'Most of these feature in the theologies of these volumes, though *many are only implicit, or are ignored by theologians in ways that call for more explicit recognition*'.[5] Hollenweger has explicitly addressed each of the contexts and interests named by Ford. In his Introduction to *The Modern Theologians* Ford does not go on to explore the relationship between their common neglect and the Western academy's overriding preoccupation with the history of ideas and 'the classic Christian issues', but, like Tracy he is aware that conventional systematic approaches do not easily accommodate the realities of diverse world societies, a diverse church and a God who remains beyond the complete knowledge of the 'Queen of Sciences'.

Hollenweger, then, as he himself has observed, is not a typical Western academic theologian in relation to the three publics or the content of his material.[6] So how he approaches the 'God/World/Church' configuration will be of interest, not only, I suggest, to missiologists—who have debated the ordering of these factors at international level for a century from various perspectives—but also to theologians working in the traditional disciplines of biblical studies, hermeneutics, church history and systematics.[7] All are inevitably subject to the pressures of postmodernity outlined in the Introduction to this book; some have articulated concern about the trend to increased specialization that has contributed to the unhinging of disciplines.[8]

---

4.   Ford, *The Modern Theologians*, I, p. ix.
5.   Ford, *The Modern Theologians*, I, p. 15. Emphasis mine.
6.   Above, p. 18.
7.   On 'God/World/Church' see, e.g., the WCC discussions summarized in Lossky *et al.* (eds.), *Dictionary*, entries 'Ecumenical Conferences' and 'WCC Assemblies'; see Chapter 5 below.
8.   E.g., James Barr, in *The Bible in the Modern World* first published in 1973, already noted that 'many modern theologians appear to be able to work without giving much thought to the Bible's status' (London: SCM Press, 1990 [1973]), p. 9; Werner

Hollenweger's approach in effect straddles what is commonly thought of as a distinction between normative and applied theology—the former ostensibly aiming for what is conceptually true and the latter subsequently applying it to life situations. There are identifiable elements: learning from observation and experience; dialogue; revision of reflection and practice. It is a way of working in the fullest sense, not confined to the cognitive, and in this has much in common with Asian, Black, Feminist, Liberation, Process and Interfaith theologies which have developed in response to specific concerns which have come to prominence in the twentieth century (which is not to say they have no prior history) and for which the orthodox Western academic approach has been deemed inadequate.

In this chapter the objective is to demonstrate how Hollenweger's methodology and content are related and the way in which he balances the interests of all three publics. From the remarkable array of topics he has written on, four are selected to portray the depth of his reflection and flexibility of his writing genres. Context is a key consideration in his work, yet the international breadth of his attention obviates against parochialism and renders shared dialogue possible. On the Swiss Reformer and contemporary of Martin Luther, Huldrych Zwingli, we take five articles written for various publications, illustrating Hollenweger's engagement with a major figure from church history. A Mexican contribution to doing theology—'Flowers and Songs', by contrast, is a single article reflecting on an intercultural Bible study experience of lasting significance to Hollenweger himself. Pentecostal Boundaries offers a brief view of Hollenweger's work for and with the movement, indicating different approaches. Finally, 'Saints in Birmingham' introduces a dimension of his use of the narrative genre for theological communication and reflection.

Huldrych Zwingli: Reformer

Hollenweger's writings relating to Zwingli (1484–1531) are especially interesting because, although perhaps less well known, they indicate Hollenweger's propensity for drawing on both his contemporary context

---

Jeanrond criticized the preoccupation of theologians with the foundations of critical thinking rather than how the insights of biblical scholarship could be put to the use of Christians in their communities in an article 'Biblical Criticism and Theology: Towards a New Biblical Theology', in Werner G. Jeanrond and Jennifer L. Rike (eds.), *Radical Pluralism and Truth: David Tracy and the Hermeneutics of Religion* (New York: Crossroad, 1991), pp. 38-48 (42-43).

and his academic theological roots. Spanning more than two decades, the five pieces of work referred to here demonstrate quite clearly how Hollenweger keeps all three publics very much in mind in his theological reflection, even while each article is directed to a particular constituency.

The earliest, 'Zwingli Writes the Gospel into His World's Agenda', is a substantial article of 24 pages published in January 1969 by the *Mennonite Quarterly Review* 43.1.[9] The subtitle is 'The Story of the Swiss Reformer's Beginnings (1515–1522) Told in the Mood of Theological Reflection'. As a footnote makes clear, the terminology is taken from the 1967 WCC Report *The Church for Others*.[10] The story is told under four headings. The first 'The Context: Res Publica' relates Zwingli's vociferous response to the widespread sale of the services of Swiss soldiers to foreign interests and demonstrates that 'his worldly concern was his theological concern' in that the questions of war and peace and the responsibility of the Christian in society were constant topics of his theological writings.[11] The second section, 'The Key: Back to the Sources', examines how Zwingli dealt with his world's agenda and found that his study of the Bible provided the hermeneutic key for understanding, analyzing and changing his world. 'Did Christ teach us that?' was the question raised in relation to the use of Swiss mercenaries, and pressed further and more controversially on other issues than Erasmus, who asked the same question, was comfortable with.[12] The third section asks whether Zwingli discovered the gospel in the sense of the Reformation with or without Luther and concluded it was without: Zwingli discovered through Scripture that 'sin is too great to be overcome by education and the Gospel is an event which lies wholly in the initiative of God'.

> Luther was a monk. On his world's agenda was the question: How can I become just before God? Zwingli was a schoolmaster, a pastor and a humanist patriot. On his agenda was the question: How can God's will be done in society and church?[13]

---

9.   The article was published in Spanish in *Estudias Ecuménicas* 7 (1970), pp. 18-32; in German it is incorporated in vol. I of Hollenweger's *Intercultural Theology, Erfahrungen der Leibhaftigkeit*, pp. 299-328.

10.   *Mennonite Quarterly Review* (January 1969), pp. 70-94 (70). On *The Church for Others*, see Chapter 2, p. 13 and Chapter 6.

11.   Hollenweger, 'Zwingli Writes', p. 78.

12.   Hollenweger, 'Zwingli Writes', pp. 80-81.

13.   Hollenweger, 'Zwingli Writes', p. 92.

The conclusion, 'New Realities, Not Merely New Ideas' lists some of the changes Zwingli instituted, including the *Prophezei*, a team-ministry of cooperative Bible study open to the public.[14] The copious footnotes draw extensively on Zwingli's writings and on the work of Zwingli scholars, but Hollenweger's intention is not to prove (or disprove) the truth of Zwingli's conceptual theology; it is to show how the political, economic and social realities of Zwingli's context propelled him to renewed Bible study and subsequently to work for change in the society and church of his time.

Ten years after the publication of this article Hollenweger presented a paper to the Fourth International Conference of the Ecumenical Society of the Blessed Virgin Mary which was entitled 'Zwingli's Devotion to Mary'. His purpose, focusing on Zwingli, was to correct the widespread misconception that the Reformers maintained no special praise, devotion or liturgical place for Mary. As with the previous article, his first step was to set Zwingli in his context by describing his opposition to 'selling human flesh and slaying people for money', noting at this later date 'here we have a style of a theology of liberation 450 years before this term was invented. There is a ring of Helder Camara when Zwingli describes the foreign multi-national recruiters.'[15] Hollenweger asserted that Zwingli was falsely accused of vilifying Mary because his exposure of injustice was unpopular with the powerful but could not be dismissed on Christian grounds, so another way had to be found to discredit him. Zwingli's sermon on the Virgin Mary showed that he was not out of line with some contemporary Catholic understanding and, moreover, he ensured that the Marian feasts were kept in Zürich. That Zwingli was the most socially and politically aware of the Reformers is reflected, according to Hollenweger, in his reform of the liturgy and his devotion to Mary.

A third article was written in 1984 for *Leben und Glauben* and asks the Swiss Churches 'What remains of Zwingli's reformation?'[16] Here

14. Hollenweger, 'Zwingli Writes', pp. 93-94.

15. Walter J. Hollenweger, 'Zwingli's Devotion to Mary', *One in Christ* 16.1-2 (1980), pp. 59-68 (62). Helder Camara was a Brazilian Roman Catholic Archbishop who championed the poor and non-violent social change.

16. Walter J. Hollenweger, 'Was ist von Zwingli's Reformation geblieben?', *Leben und Glauben* 59.44 (2 November 1984), pp. 6-7. Other articles published the same year are 'Huldrych Zwingli, réformateur de l'église et de la société', *Mensuel* 7 (March 1984), pp. 16-18, and 'Huldrych Zwingli: Ein Leben zwischen Krieg und Frieden' ('Huldrych Zwingli: A Life between War and Peace), *Kirchenbote für den Kanton Zürich* 70.1a (1 January 1984), pp. 6-8 (reprinted in *Der Sämann*, 100.1, January 1984, p. 8). The latter was also the title of a radio feature on Radio DRS, Zürich 1.1.1984,

Hollenweger challenges his co-nationals with the suggestion that signs can be seen more clearly in the ecumenical arena: parallels are drawn between Zwingli's criticisms of the church institution and religious elites and Leonardo Boff's criticisms in *Kirche: Charisma und Macht* (*Church: Charism and Power*, 1981); the Church of England has been more influenced by Zwingli than is commonly known in respect of its Communion liturgy, devotion to Mary, Bible translation and attitude to war as evidenced by its official position on the use of atomic weapons. The article closes provocatively: how long will it be before the Swiss Churches discover the modern reformer of church and society in Zwingli or will he, like other Swiss—Barth, Corbusier, Jung and Piaget—be better understood abroad than in Switzerland?

Reviewing W. Peter Stephens's 1986 book, the *Theology of Huldrych Zwingli* for *Zwingliana* in 1988, Hollenweger is afraid that the book will be taken as 'pure history' and Zwingli's relevance for today overlooked. Among the Reformers, for example, Zwingli is the one who gives the greatest freedom for dialogue with non-Christians—a matter of pressing contemporary concern. Stephens, he suggested, did not want to spoil his high-quality book with application to contemporary realities; this was in keeping with current academic theology's self-understanding—but not in keeping with Zwingli's![17]

Writing again for an academic audience with his contribution to the Festschrift for Zwingli scholar Gottfried W. Locher in 1992, Hollenweger's article 'Zwingli's Influence in England' opens with his acknowledgment of Locher's influence on his own study of the subject.[18] He examines the

with the addition 'erzählt von seiner Frau' ('told by his wife'). *Zwingli zwischen Krieg und Frieden, erzählt von seiner Frau* (Kaiser Traktate, 76; Munich: Chr. Kaiser Verlag, 1983 and 1984 (2); (repr. Kindhausen: Metanoia Verlag, 1992). 'Huldrych Zwinglis ökumenische Bedeutung' ('Huldrych Zwingli's Ecumenical Significance') was the title of lectures given in Leipzig and Berne the same year.

17. In *Zwingliana* 17.6 (1988), pp. 550-51 (551). '…was ist die Relevanz solcher theologischen Aussagen für uns heutige? Mir scheint, dass von allen Reformatoren Zwingli derjenige ist, der uns im Gespräch mit den Nichtchristen die grösste Freiheit gibt…' 'Stephens wollte sein gediegenes Buch nicht mit Aktualisierungen belasten und verunzieren. Das ist sicher im Sinne unseres heutigen Verständnisses von Wissenschaft und Theologie—gewiss aber nicht im Sinne Zwinglis.'

18. Hollenweger, 'Zwinglis Einfluss in England', in Heiko A. Oberman *et al.* (eds.), *Reformiertes Erbe* (Festschrift für Gottfried W. Locher zu seinem 80. Geburtstag; Zürich: TVZ, 1992), pp. 171-86. Also in the 1969 article, 'Zwingli Writes', Hollenweger had acknowledged Locher's assistance: 'G. Locher, in a long

England–Zürich exchanges of letters, writings and people in the sixteenth century, including the polemic against Zwingli's sacramental understanding, before pointing out liturgical similarities between Zwingli and Cranmer, as reflected in *The Book of Common Prayer*. These were: (1) the rejection of the transubstantiation of the elements of bread and wine into the body and blood of Christ and its replacing by the changing of the members of the community into the body of Christ; (2) the insertion of the call to healing, 'Come unto me all ye who labour and are heavy laden…' from Zwingli's *De canon missae epichiresis* (1523); and (3) the active participation of the community through an antiphonal chorus.[19] The important insight Zwingli and Cranmer shared, according to Hollenweger, was that in regard to the organization of the people into the body of Christ, what evaded theological definition could nevertheless be celebrated in common.[20] This insight offered the possibility that, in the wake of an ecumenical and intercultural writing of history, the Lord's Supper would no longer be celebrated as a banquet of accredited and correct believers, but as a meal whose unfinished character was also recognized in theology and liturgy; as such, other convictions, rites and models of activity must no longer be condemned or their proponents excluded from the meal of peace.[21] The article, as Hollenweger pointed out at the beginning, takes Locher's research and carries it further.

In his writings, Hollenweger addresses Zwingli as a contextual theologian, man of social awareness and action, church Reformer, liturgical

conversation, allowed me to draw from his knowledge of Zwingli's development' (p. 75 n. 31).

19. Hollenweger, 'Zwinglis Einfluss', p. 182: '1. Die Ablehnung der Transsubstantiation der Elemente Brot und Wein in Leib und Blut Christi und ihre Ersetzung durch die Wandlung der Gemeindeglieder in den Leib Christi. 2. Die Einfügung des Heilandsrufes, "Kommet her zu mir alle, die ihr mühselig und beladen seid…" aus Zwinglis "De canone missae epichiresis" (1523)… 3. Die aktive Beteiligung der Gemeinde durch einen Wechsel-Sprechchor.'

20. Hollenweger, 'Zwinglis Einfluss', p. 185. 'Dieser Leib wird konstituiert durch die Ausrichtung auf das, was sich der theologischen Definition entzieht, das wir aber trotzdem gemeinsam feiern können…'

21. Hollenweger, 'Zwinglis Einfluss', p. 186: 'Vielleicht werden wir im Gefolge einer ökumenischen und interkulturellen Geschichtsschreibung und Theologie dazu kommen, das Abendmahl nicht mehr als das Bankett der akkreditierten und richtig Glaubenden zu feiern, sondern als das Mahl derer, die sich ihrer Stückwerk-Existenz auch in Theologie und Liturgie bewusst sind und darum solche, die andere Überzeugungen, Riten und Handlungsmuster vertreten, nicht mehr verurteilen und von unserem Friedensmahl ausschliessen müssen.'

revisionist and ecumenical inspiration—not as matters of unique but limited interest to the academy, but as having practical importance for contemporary Christians. Zwingli's method of theologizing, through Hollenweger's analysis, proves to be strikingly appropriate today—and one with which Hollenweger himself is in accord. Attention to context (historical, social, economic, geographic, religious factors) effectively redresses an unhelpful bias towards the concerns of biblical scholarship, hermeneutics, church history or systematics. While these dimensions are also given proper attention, they do not become ends in themselves, but contributions to the ongoing processes of practice and reflection in concrete situations. Attention to context raises legitimate questions for each of these disciplines. Zwingli knew it in the sixteenth century, and Hollenweger knows it half a millennium later.

'Flowers and Songs': A Mexican Contribution to Doing Theology

This article arose from his work in the middle period of his career at the World Council of Churches and was first published in 1970, originally in Spanish and subsequently in German, French, English, Italian and Dutch in a variety of publications. That it remains central to his thinking is evident from a revised and annotated version appearing in his 1997 major book, *Pentecostalism: Origins and Developments Worldwide*.[22]

'Flowers and Songs' opens with a question: 'Is a theological dialogue possible between the Third World and the theological systems of Europe and America?' It arose from Hollenweger's experience and observation at the WCC that the 'rules of the theological debate' were those of Westerners and contributions from Third World theologians who thought differently were absent. In these circumstances it was not surprising that so few Third World Churches were members of the WCC. In his capacity as Secretary of the Division on World Mission and Evangelism Hollenweger was involved in experiments designed to look for non-Western categories for thinking theologically and for presenting theology. The search could only be conducted through dialogue: Mexicans should be enabled to speak for themselves as people of significance free from the inhibiting domination of Western intellectual concepts and racial prejudices.

---

22. Ch. 7, pp. 81-98. This is the version referred to here. In English it can also be found in Walter Hollenweger, *Pentecost between Black and White: Five Case Studies on Pentecost and Politics* (Belfast: Christian Journals Limited, 1974), pp. 33-54, and *International Review of Mission* 60.238 (1971), pp. 232-44.

Hollenweger's next section deals briefly with elements of the philosophy and educational system of ancient Mexican (Nahuatl) civilization. Drawing on the work of scholars in the field, he identifies the key role of the *tlamantini*, the one who 'knows things', the one 'who makes others develop a face'. The educational medium was not the textbook but poetry: 'Flowers and Songs' alludes to the way in which description was used rather than definition in this non-systematic philosophy, reflecting the Nahuas' scepticism about whether human beings could possess truth. 'With the arrival of the Spaniards, the songs died away, the flowers were trampled underfoot, the quetzal-feathers torn out' wrote Hollenweger, before giving more conventional data to illustrate the dire consequences of political and religious imperialism for this ancient civilization whose outstanding competence in mathematics, astronomy and architecture have more recently been recognized.[23] He continues, 'It is not unfair to say that Mexico's present widespread illiteracy and economic dependence were created by Europeans, and have been maintained by Americans'. However, remnants of the Nahuatl tradition have survived, he suggests, and can assist Mexicans to 'develop a face'. Examples can be found in the stories of two Pentecostal groups (later both united in the *Iglesia Cristiana Independiente Pentecostés*) which had developed their own church organization and social initiatives (a bank and farming cooperative respectively) theologically and economically independently of foreign missions. The pastors were all Mexicans and, unlike ministers of mainline churches, earned their living in the same way as other members of the church so that they were not estranged either from colleagues at work, or the Christian community.

The foregoing is a prelude to Hollenweger's summary of the WCC-initiated seminars held in five cities, which were organized through local people and embraced participants from all sections of society—intellectuals and those with little or no formal education, people of Spanish and Indian descent, Catholics, Protestants and Pentecostals.[24] The 'Flowers and Songs' method involved theological discussion based on fictional or biblical stories and utilized films and pictures. For example, a silent film of

23. Hollenweger notes there were a few Christians who defended the rights and dignity of the indigenous population against the prevailing political and religious colonialism but who were not heeded. In particular he refers to the Dominican, Fray Bartolomé de las Casas under the heading 'A Heretic Defends the Indians'.

24. A full report of the six seminars in Spanish only, in *Concepto Latinamericano III*, ' "Flores y Cantos": Un Concepto Mexicano'; *Concept* Special Issue 32 (Geneva: WCC, October 1970).

the passion and resurrection with Christ portrayed as a clown and Gerardo Murillo's story 'Guardian Angel' were used and stimulated discussion on Christology and pneumatology. Bible studies included the four Gospel accounts of Peter's confession, and the story of Philip and the Ethiopian eunuch, giving rise to fascinating insights and observations from the participants on contemporary confessions of faith and interpretation of Scripture. The role of the academic theologian was to introduce Western historical-critical understandings of biblical material as a contribution to the ecumenical and intercultural discussions. Hollenweger closes the 1997 version with a sober, but not despondent, outlook on Catholic–Pentecostal dialogue.[25]

The project itself, and Hollenweger's personal involvement, demonstrate change in action following reflection, while the article reflects on the necessity for dialogical engagement—not only that which took place between people during the seminars, but also with the historical and contemporary Mexican context of the participants through reference to scholarly research. The diversity of material included in the article is a hallmark of much of Hollenweger's writing. The Bible and the realities of life are the two major reference points; church history has a place, but a qualified one, for Hollenweger not only championed the 'losers' rather than the 'victors' of fifteenth- and sixteenth-century religious colonialism, but also highlighted 'alternative' church movements in contemporary history. Systematic questions also arise through the seminar discussions, for example on Christology and pneumatology, but no attempt is made by Hollenweger to systematize answers. The hermeneutical process is in the hands of members of the ecumenical Christian community—ongoing and unfinished. Through this different distribution of academic priorities employed in a concrete situation, ecumenism, Pentecostalism and intercultural theology become explicitly articulated and take their place as major concerns of the present and immediate future of Christianity and theology.

25. The Ecumenical Press Service issued a release on 16 April 1970 headed 'WCC Evangelism Secretary heads Bible Study in Mexico' describing the first seminar held in Monterrey. It noted that Hollenweger's method of Bible study 'in a post- and pre-literary culture was based on a mutual dialogical interpretation of the biblical text in which all are teachers and pupils at the same time'. Local press coverage described the seminar as 'excellent', 'an active, practical, renovating school of Christianity' and the local radio station devoted an hour to modern methods of interpreting the Bible with Baptist, Reformed, Catholic and Jewish participants.

The particular and concise demonstration of Hollenweger's method which this article offers shows how the opportunity is created for pressing practical and cognitive Christian issues to emerge and, moreover, enables them to be held together: the articulation of beliefs arises from the lived experience of Christians in dialogue with the Bible and with their past and present contexts. The article can, perhaps, be viewed as paradigmatic of Hollenweger's agenda and modus operandi. Reflecting on a WCC initiative, it is poised chronologically between his original research on worldwide Pentecostalism (and his key insights that it was itself an ecumenical movement heavily dependent on oral, narrative media) and his future development of intercultural theology as the way forward for mission studies.

Pentecostal Boundaries

The original, massive research on the Pentecostal movement worldwide which Hollenweger carried out in the 1960s did not lead him to engage extensively with specific scholarly studies which he advocated should be carried out on the histories, practices and beliefs of the movement in specific geographical environments.[26] Rather, he chose to engage in a communicative, interpretative and critical role as theological intermediary between the Pentecostal movement and mainline churches, which together with the preponderance and continued growth of the movement in parts of Asia and Africa, has heightened the necessity for mediation between oral and literary cultures, and also among Pentecostals themselves. In this process he has drawn on the ever-increasing body of research carried out internationally.[27] Thus Hollenweger's concern is global and ecumenical, while his approach, which relies heavily on recounting narratives set in their historical, religious, political and social contexts and reflecting on them, takes account of the particular. Ingo Lembke, reviewing the Festschrift for *Jahrbuch Mission 1993*, comments that:

> the phenomenon which is Hollenweger astonishes because he builds
> intercultural bridges at a time when contextualization, reconfessionalization

26. Hollenweger, *The Pentecostals*, pp. 497-98.

27. The bibliography in *Pentecostalism: Origins* confirms his extensive study of scholarly research published in English, German, Spanish, French, Italian and other languages. He has also reviewed a large number of books over the years for a variety of academic publications, including the *International Review of Mission, Expository Times, Reformatio, Ecumenical Review, Theology, Evangelische Kommentare, Scottish Journal of Theology* and *Zwingliana.*

and fundamentalism are rampant. At the same time he is proof that it is possible to formulate one's own point of view without building up new frontiers, but on the contrary to overcome frontiers...[28]

Hollenweger's own viewpoint is clearly stated in the Preface to his 1974 publication *Pentecost between Black and White*, where he says, 'The body of Christ can only come to its full maturity when all the gifts of all its members reach full interplay with each other'.[29] This book, as the publishers point out, 'is not only informative and descriptive but is a penetrating analysis of Pentecostalism written in a popular vein'. The depth of knowledge and summaries of other scholars' thinking are embodied in a remarkably accessible style. With regard to the Kimbanguists in the Congo, black Pentecostals in the United States, Indian Pentecostals in Mexico, Catholic Pentecostals, and the Jesus People, on whom he presents case studies in this book, Hollenweger's purpose is to show that 'in these movements there is a hitherto unexplored potential for real partnership between black and white, poor and rich, illiterates and intellectuals'.[30] The case study groups, Hollenweger suggested, function as catalysts of religious and social transition in society and are distinguished by the oral and narrative media which they employ. From this those in the West may learn something about models of thinking and communication which they lack or are underdeveloped.

This viewpoint—the necessity for the full interplay of Christian gifts—is pursued relentlessly in numerous directions, for Hollenweger is adamant that the Pentecostal movement in all its forms should also be the subject of scholarly, critical analysis. Apart from his two major volumes on Pentecostalism, which are accessible to both intellectuals and non-specialists, I draw attention to two articles for the academy: his paper for a conference on Pentecostal and Charismatic Research in Europe held at Utrecht

28. Ingo Lembke, Review of Janqeneel *et al*, *Pentecost, Mission and Ecumenism*, in *Jahrbuch Mission* 25, 1993 (ed. Verband Evangelischer Missionskonferenzen; Hamburg: Missionshilfe Verlag, 1993), pp. 200-201: 'das Phänomen der Person Hollenwegers darin erstaunt, dass er interkulturelle Beziehungen herstellt und inter-konfessionelle Brücken baut gerade in einer Zeit zunehmender Kontextualisierung, Rekonfessionalisierung und wachsenden Fundamentalismus. Gleichzeitig ist er ein Beweis dafür, dass es möglich ist, einen eigenen Standpunkt zu formulieren, ohne damit Grenzen zu ziehen, sondern im Gegenteil—Grenzen in erster Linie zu überwinden...'

29. Hollenweger, *Pentecost between Black and White*, p. 10.

30. Hollenweger, *Pentecost between Black and White*, quotations from the back cover. The book has 118 pages of unreferenced text and 20 pages of bibliography.

University in 1989 names the priorities as historiography, missiology, hermeneutics and pneumatology.[31] An article for the *Journal of Pentecostal Theology* in 1992, 'The Critical Tradition of Pentecostalism', rejoices in the increasing number of Pentecostal scholars and bemoans the lack of attention paid to them by its church leaders and members.[32]

Welcoming the *Dictionary of Pentecostal and Charismatic Movements* published in 1988, Hollenweger in his review nevertheless criticizes its focus on North American and European Pentecostalism to the exclusion of non-Western material which would have provided 'A picture of a genuine third-world movement with all its theological contradictions, social pains, and political compromises...'[33] The importance of a fully international dialogue among Pentecostals is again underlined in his contribution to the 1994 book *Charismatic Christianity as a Global Culture*, 'The Pentecostal Elites and the Pentecostal Poor: A Missed Dialogue?'[34] Here, taking account of the increase in the number of affluent Pentecostals since the beginnings of the modern Pentecostal movement when it was predominantly a religion of the poor, Hollenweger challenges them to 'dig into their past in order to find the language and tools to dialogue with Pentecostals who are poor today'. The exclusion of the poor from dialogue, he asserts, has to do with the 'disrespect' shown to oral and narrative patterns of thought.[35]

Hollenweger thus embraces a number of roles as a specialist in Pentecostalism—mediator, exponent, critic, participant and observer, addressing all three publics and using a variety of literary vehicles.

Saints in Birmingham

A factor which makes Hollenweger's theologizing particularly challenging is that he takes his own content and methodology seriously and acts upon them. Not satisfied with the conceptual articulation that bridge-building is

31. Walter J. Hollenweger, 'Priorities in Pentecostal Research: Historiography, Missiology, Hermeneutics and Pneumatology', in Jan A.B. Jongeneel (ed.), *Experiences of the Spirit* (Frankfurt am Main: Peter Lang, 1991), pp. 7-22.

32. Walter J. Hollenweger, 'The Critical Tradition of Pentecostalism', *Journal of Pentecostal Theology* 1 (1992), pp. 7-17 (7).

33. Review of Burgess and McGee (eds.), *Dictionary of Pentecostal* in *International Bulletin of Missionary Research* 13.4 (1989), pp. 181-82 (182).

34. Walter J. Hollenweger, 'The Pentecostal Elites and the Pentecostal Poor: A Missed Dialogue?', in Karla Poewe (ed.), *Charismatic Christianity as a Global Culture* (Columbia: University of South Carolina Press, 1994), pp. 200-214.

35. Hollenweger, 'The Pentecostal Elites', p. 200.

necessary between Christians from different historical and geographical contexts and from oral and literary cultures, he unashamedly embodies his insights through his style of communication where he feels it is appropriate. One such occasion was the World Council of Churches Consultation on the Significance of the Charismatic Renewal for the Churches held at Bossey, Geneva, Switzerland, 8–13 March 1980. Hollenweger had previously revised and abridged the WCC consultative group paper produced at the Schwanberg (Federal Republic of Germany) meeting in 1978, entitled 'Towards a Church Renewed and United in the Spirit'. This paper dealt with the hopes and expectations of the charismatic renewal and with ecclesiological, cosmological and sacramental approaches to the Spirit, before addressing some practical considerations regarding gifts of the Spirit and discernment.[36] In his Introduction to *The Church is Charismatic: The World Council of Churches and the Charismatic Renewal*, Hollenweger wrote that the 1978 paper was a compromise document which did not adequately reflect some of the most important experiences of the meeting, such as one woman who did not take part in the discussions but prayed, fasted and had a number of visions. At Bossey, therefore, Hollenweger's paper entitled 'Saints in Birmingham' was a narrative, not an academic treatise.[37] It tells the story of the fictional Mr Chips arriving in Birmingham city centre at the moment of an actual historical event—the bombing of a public house when the Protestant–Catholic, Loyalist–Nationalist conflicts in Ireland extended to mainland Britain; an incident in which many people were killed and injured. Mr Chips was taken to an 'evening of spirituality' at the home of a friend, and through descriptions of the participants, their words, songs and music, Hollenweger addresses issues of prayer, reconciliation, healing and doubt. The paper ends with an imaginary service of reconciliation organized by the local Council of Churches and presided over by the leader of a black church.

---

36. The material in this section is taken from Bittlinger (ed.), *The Church is Charismatic*; see in particular pp. 21-28. The next step in the discussion process was a letter sent by Dr Philip Potter, General Secretary of the WCC, to member churches, national councils and regional conferences inviting them to identify issues which the Bossey Consultation should address. Speaking to the consultation, Dr Potter noted that the response had been 'copious'. He added, 'Walter Hollenweger as usual—he's a Pentecostal man but he's always good at giving orders—wrote me a letter instructing me that I must read all those replies and this was a unique event in the ecumenical movement' (p. 74).

37. In Bittlinger, *The Church is Charismatic*, pp. 87-99.

Ingrid Reimer, in her article 'A Critical Participant Looks Back to the Bossey Consultation', commented:

> I recall the Swiss professor from Birmingham. All he did was tell a story. And just as we were saying to ourselves: 'ah, yes, now he'll begin his real address', his contribution was already over. That really vexed me. I had, of course, already heard of Professor Hollenweger's narrative style of presentation, known as 'intercultural theology'. But it took me some time to realize just how this narrative form makes it possible to do justice to the intricacy of a theme.[38]

Hollenweger uses 'Saints in Birmingham' with just this purpose in *Pentecostalism: Origins*.[39]

Comment

The role of intermediary is a difficult one, for there is a constant danger of misunderstanding from all quarters. That Hollenweger is aware of this is evident from his published prayers, nine of which are included in *Pentecostalism: Origins*, and most of the same ones in a 2000 book illustrated with reproductions of batik by Solomon Raj. The mosquito asks why it must sting people and if there will be mosquitos in the kingdom of God, the caterpillar looks forward to 'an eternal Sunday morning' when it will be a butterfly, the turtle in its protective shell cannot get through to other people, the singing bird wants to sing 'for those who listen and for those who don't listen'. Most specifically, the dirt-eating earthworm, pecked at by magpies, asks why he has to be an earthworm. He is told by God that he is important, for without him there is 'no life, no plants, no vegetables, no animals, no people, no university, no government, no science and art

38. Bittlinger (ed.), *The Church is Charismatic*, p. 216. Hollenweger also wrote about the Bossey meeting for *Reform* 7 (March 1981), p. 7, under the title 'The Embrace of Africa with the West', describing some of the participants, exchanges and proceedings, paying tribute to the way in which Philip Potter personalized his theological analysis, and referring to his own 'Mr. Chips' contribution. He commented, 'Without giving up the critical function of academic research, theology became visible. The pain and the joy of theological confrontation and reconciliation could be felt and experienced...the Bossey consultation produced a bridge between Western and Third World spirituality.'

39. *Pentecostalism: Origins*, ch. 2: 'The following story tries to cover all aspects of Charismatic/Pentecostal spirituality in order to give an introduction to this type of religion' (6). In *Umgang mit Mythen* (II, *Intercultural Theology*), 'Saints in Birmingham' is offered as an example of a 'true myth', pp. 166-78.

and no magpies in all their academic glory'. The prayer ends, 'But, dear God, I wonder whether you couldn't tell that to the magpies too'.[40]

If Hollenweger's objective were to assess the conceptual orthodoxy of particular manifestations of Christianity then a conventional dogmatic approach might be appropriate—appropriate but not fruitful, for this would continue the debate only within the confines of Western academia and with little reference to the other 'publics' of churches and societies, and in the process perpetuate the misconception that Western understanding of Christian faith and life is normative for all Christians. This position is in itself untenable—it does not match the reality of contemporary worldwide, post-colonial Christianity and takes insufficient account of the variety of beliefs, ways of worship, ethical values and social and political responses among even mainline traditions themselves during their varied histories. Facing the realities demands a different methodology, a dialogical one, through which questions can emerge and in which propositional discussion is only one element of the theological process.

This chapter has introduced the special blend of method, content and communication which are the hallmark of Hollenweger's theology, placing it in the forum of theology as a worldwide enterprise and not simply as a Western academic prerogative. The implications of this displaced methodology, responsive to the particular and universal dimensions of Christianity, endorsing oral and literary approaches to God, world and church, taking the concrete realities of life as the context of reflection, will be explored further. First, we examine Hollenweger's approach to hermeneutics, for in his appropriation of the Bible and biblical scholarship we discover the driving force of his thinking and practice.

---

40. *Pentecostalism: Origins*, pp. 180, 80, 199-200, 286-87, 40 respectively; *Züritüütschi Gibätt: Gebete–Prières–Prayers* (Meilen: Ch. Walter Verlag, 2000). I have been present on several occasions when Hollenweger has used the Prayer of the Earthworm: at his farewell lecture at the Selly Oak Colleges some of the audience were a little surprised; at the close of a session preparing an anointing service at Berneuchener House with people participating in *Maria von Wedemeyer* in 1997 and at the close of his sermon at a public service of anointing at a church in Bayreuth in 1998 the impact was very strong on many people. The sense of personal resonance, relief and uplift was both visible on their faces and articulated after the events.

Chapter 3

NARRATIVE EXEGESIS: LOVING AND UNDERSTANDING THE BIBLE

Hollenweger as theologian was propelled into responding to realities in a way, and on a scale, required of few academics in the course of their careers. The transitions from Pentecostal pastor to academic study of the Bible, from research on the worldwide Pentecostal movement to the international ecumenical movement, from mission studies to intercultural theology, are significant. What makes Hollenweger particularly interesting is that, through the transitions, he retained and utilized elements of each milieu, developing an original approach to theological praxis and reflection. As he pointed out in *Erfahrungen der Leibhaftigkeit*, 'Both theologies, the oral and the written, exist within me…' He grew up with oral theology— singing, praying, street meetings and debates, and then learnt written theology at university. 'Since then I have repeatedly travelled the way between the two cultural forms.'[1] He attended, as we have seen, to all three publics of the academy, the churches and society and thereby developed a way of working in which method, content and mode of communication were each important. Against this background we can begin to discern his use of narrative exegesis in relation to the Bible.

The Inheritance of Western Critical Scholarship

He who holds the Bible to be a foundation book of Christian faith—and I am of this opinion—has to wrestle with the fact that already in the Bible the search for the truth and the articulation of faith appears as an ongoing process.[2]

1. Hollenweger, Preface of *Erfahrungen der Leibhaftigkeit*, 'Fragmente einer theologischen Autobiographie', pp. 28-29: 'Die beiden Theologien, die mündliche und die schriftliche, leben in mir selber… Mit der mündlichen Theologie bin ich aufgewachsen. Ich habe sie gesungen, gebetet, in Strassenversammlungen und öffentlichen Streitgesprächen geübt. Die schriftliche Theologie habe ich an der Universität gelernt… Seitdem bin ich die Wege zwischen den beiden kulturellen Ausformungen der Theologie mehrmals gegangen.'

Hollenweger uses the term 'narrative exegesis' to describe much of the work he has engaged in. His method differs from that of biblical scholars and systematic theologians currently engaged with the subject of biblical interpretation. The term does not appear as an entry in *A Dictionary of Biblical Interpretation*. According to the editors, R.J. Coggins and J.L. Houlden, the volume was published in 1990 in response to 'a certain lack of confidence' about the meaning of the Bible in order to provide a reference source for the burgeoning of terms, methods and techniques in 'this territory which may appear something of a maze'.[3]

Many theologians are still struggling to come to terms with the implications of the critical insights offered by biblical scholarship. Maurice Wiles has summarised key insights succinctly:

> The rootedness of the texts in the particular social-cultural understandings of their times; the variety of theological standpoints represented by the various scriptural authors; the differing degrees of historical accuracy characteristic of different scriptural writings.[4]

Narrative theology (as distinct from the study of the Bible as literature), stimulated in particular by the work of Hans Frei, has been one attempt to cope with the perceived threat to the authority of the Bible.[5] Wiles has observed that theology and the church still expect the Bible to establish doctrine and provide firm guidance for its practical life. In his article 'Scriptural Authority and Theological Construction: The Limitations of Narrative Interpretation' he criticizes writers like Charles Wood, Ronald Thiemann and George Lindbeck for the inadequacy of their attempts to

---

2.   Walter J. Hollenweger, *Conflict in Corinth & Memoirs of an Old Man: Two Stories that Illuminate the Way the Bible Came To Be Written* (New York: Paulist Press, 1982 [German original 1978]), p. 75.

3.   R.J. Coggins and J.L. Houlden (eds.), *A Dictionary of Biblical Interpretation* (London: SCM Press, 1990), Preface, p. v.

4.   Maurice Wiles, 'Scriptural Authority and Theological Construction: The Limitations of Narrative Interpretation', in Garrett Green (ed.), *Scriptural Authority and Narrative Interpretation* (Philadelphia: Fortress Press, 1987), pp. 42-58 (43-44).

5.   Authors in G. Green, *Scriptural Authority and Narrative Interpretation* are students, colleagues and friends of Hans Frei, whose publications *The Eclipse of Biblical Narrative* (1974) and *The Identity of Jesus Christ* (1975) drew attention to the fact that with two centuries of preoccupation with hermeneutics, the issue of the Bible as a narrative description of reality had been overlooked. Continued interest in Frei's work is reflected in the publication of George Hunsinger and William C. Placher (eds.), *Theology and Narrative: Selected Essays Hans W. Frei* (Oxford: Oxford University Press, 1993).

find through narrative interpretation ways to defend against the implications, while not denying the validity, of biblical scholarship. Given the
key critical insights, he is of the opinion that it is not possible to perpetuate
the idea of one biblical narrative and one interpretation of it.[6]

Gerard Loughlin suggests the doctrine of the Trinity is:

> the means by which the Church positions itself within the stories it writes
> and tells and by which it is written and told. It is by its doctrine of God that
> the Church is able to perform its stories, stories which are...the continuing
> event of God.[7]

A doctrine (unquestioned) is put forward as the solution to the problem
of the diverse socio-cultural context in which the books of the Bible were
written, the different theological standpoints of the authors and the
different degrees of historicity of the texts. Hollenweger, on the contrary,
has commented that, 'The springtime of exegesis was also the autumn of
systematic theology'.[8]

George Stroup, in *The Promise of Narrative Theology*, had offered a
systematic approach using narrative theology to look at Christian identity
and the meaning of revelation. He was writing in response to the dilemma
of theologically trained ('liberal') pastors in the face of the popular tendency in conservative churches to offer a distinct Christian identity by
clinging to an inerrant Bible.[9] Hollenweger, reviewing this book, focused
not on identity or revelation, nor on narrative theology, but on the
dilemma Stroup identified: the division of the church into producers and
consumers of theology. He suggested 'a new form of narrative Bible
exegesis which is informed by critical scholarship' by which the origins,
transformation and re-adaptation of the biblical stories are made accessible
to the whole people of God. Critical storytelling reveals, he asserted, 'the
breath-taking modernity of many of the biblical narratives because most of
them are about how Israel and the early church wrestled and dealt with
conflicts in their own ranks'.[10]

Hollenweger, then, is not engaged with developing a systematic theology

6.   Wiles, 'Scriptural Authority', pp. 47-51.
7.   Gerard Loughlin, *Telling God's Story: Bible, Church and Narrative Theology*
(Cambridge: Cambridge University Press, 1996), p. 197.
8.   Hollenweger, *Conflict*, p. 65.
9.   George Stroup, *The Promise of Narrative Theology* (London: SCM Press,
1981), Preface and ch. 1.
10.   Walter J. Hollenweger, 'What Happens to Scripture in Church and School?',
Journal of Beliefs and Values 4.2 (1983), pp. 14-19 (18, 19).

on the basis of a unitary biblical narrative. What Hollenweger definitely is concerned with is an informed utilization of the Bible by all Christians today; the fruits of biblical scholarship are to be valued and, as such, should not be a matter of private discussion within the academy. The academy seems to be concerned about the increasing complexities of the theoretical debates rather than with the dissemination of scholarly findings and the critical assimilation of interpretations arising from the churches and society. Hollenweger is not concerned to provide or prove authoritative statements on hermeneutics (understood as a theory of interpretation); he is concerned that the whole church—and interested others—participate in the ongoing process of the search for truth and articulation of faith. 'Narrative exegesis (as I practise it) cannot produce a new hermeneutics but it can at least open our eyes to the catastrophe which we have brought on ourselves.'[11] The catastrophe referred to in 1981 was the lack of will in the academy to place exegesis where it belonged—'in the universal community of all Christians' with the result that, in Walter Wink's phrase, historical-critical research had become bankrupt.[12]

It does not seem that the situation has changed much. Hollenweger returns to the subject in a 1995 article:

> Academic theology is bankrupt, not because what it produces is worthless, but because it cannot bring its products to where they are more necessary than daily bread, namely into the church and society... For example, it has been known for a hundred years that Noah and Methuselah were not historical persons. In spite of this, how Noah could have sorted all the animals into his ark so that they didn't eat each other, and why Methusulah became so old, are still discussed in our communities.[13]

11. Walter J. Hollenweger, 'The Other Exegesis', *Horizons in Biblical Theology* 3 (1981), pp. 155-79 (156). This article is also included in *Umgang mit Mythen*, pp. 134-58.

12. Hollenweger, 'The Other Exegesis', p. 165.

13. Walter J. Hollenweger, 'Theologie Tanzen: Warum wir eine "narrative Exegese" brauchen', *Evangelische Kommentare* 7 (1995), pp. 403-404 (403). 'Die wissenschaftliche Theologie ist bankrott, nicht weil das, was sie produziert, wertlos ist, sondern weil sie ihre Produkte nicht dorthin bringen kann, wo sie nötiger sind als das tägliche Brot, nämlich in Kirche und Gesellschaft... Es ist zum Beispiel seit hundert Jahren bekannt, dass Noah und Methusalem keine historischen Personen sind. Trotzdem wird in unseren Gemeinden immer noch diskutiert, wie wohl Noah alle die Tiere in seine Arche einsortierte, dass sie sich nicht auffrassen und warum Methusalem so alt wurde.' See also the articles 'Minjung-Theologie in der Schweiz?', in Samuel Jakob and Hans Strub (eds.), *Kirche Leiten im Übergang-Konturen Werden Sichtbar*

David Clines, in his 1997 publication, also notes that:

> the development of biblical criticism has left the church almost entirely
> untouched... Why is the church being kept in ignorance of what is known
> in the Academy about the Bible. How can church leaders possibly think it
> profits the Christian community to be kept out of the picture, even about
> elementary facts about the Bible?[14]

Clines traces the shifts of academic focus this century from the biblical
authors to the text and, currently, from the text to the readers. He proposes
a model for biblical interpretation focusing on the users of the Bible,
which takes account of the indeterminacy of meaning of the Bible and the
authority of interpretative communities.[15]

Hollenweger would concur with Clines at several points: identification
of the information gap has been a constant theme in Hollenweger's writing; 'Flowers and Songs' was one example (mentioned in Chapter 2) of
his taking readers' interpretations seriously; the existence of a variety of
possible interpretations of biblical material and the plurality of interpretative communities is even more evident in the worldwide context of
Hollenweger's research than in Clines's Western focus. As he stated in a
1995 article:

> If the New Testament presents us with a number of different christologies,
> liturgies, theologies, ethics, how much more do we have to say farewell
> nowadays to a streamlined universal theology, when Christianity has taken
> root in many more cultures and languages.[16]

In this article he referred to the work of Juan Luis Segundo and James
Cone, for example, as representatives of communities of interpretation
whose voices were now heard alongside the dominant white Western ones.
Fourteen years earlier he had commented:

(Festschrift für Ernst Meili; Zürich: Theologischer Verlag, 1993), pp. 284-90; and 'Das
einzige wirklich interessante Thema ist "Gott"', *Der Evangelische Erzieher* 46.3
(1994), pp. 219-28, especially section 3, 'Die Aufgabe der Wissenschaftlichen
Theologie', pp. 225-27.

14. David J.A. Clines, *The Bible and the Modern World* (Biblical Seminar, 51;
Sheffield: Sheffield Academic Press, 1997), pp. 88-89.

15. Clines, *Bible*, ch. 1 'The Bible and the Academy'; ch. 4 'The Bible and the
Church'; here pp. 91-92.

16. Walter J. Hollenweger, 'Theology and the Future of the Church', in Peter
Byrne and Leslie Houlden (eds.), *Companion Encyclopedia of Theology* (London:
Routledge, 1995), pp. 1017-1035 (1025).

The Christians in the suburbs of California, many times described and
ridiculed by Harvey Cox, hear in the gospel something different from the
peasants of Solentiname. But who hears the truth?... I believe that the
biblical interpretations of the peasants of Solentiname is the truth of the
peasants of Solentiname.[17]

In more general terms he has stated that one person does not have a
global perspective: 'The synthesis of all viewpoints is—theologically
speaking—the prerogative of God.'[18]

However, there are differences in the response of the two theologians to
the situation. Clines describes himself as a 'hireling of the state' (as a Professor of Biblical Studies) and 'not a servant of the church'; he advises the
church about its use of the Bible in his spare time.[19] Hollenweger alter-
nated or combined both state and church obligations. Clines, while pointing out that there is a whole variety of interpretations in the history of the
church which could be usefully drawn on by Christians today, is essentially concerned with how the academy could utilize information on user
interpretations to assist its critical task. Hollenweger is concerned with
how non-academics and academics can together engage in the ongoing
theological process. For him this is not a matter of simplifying or popu-
larizing cognitive data and debates to dispense authoritative wisdom but
an expression of a much deeper and broader understanding of the purpose
of Bible study.

Hollenweger, it seems to me, actually demonstrates confidence in
scholarship's critical insights into the authorship, creation, forms, contexts
and ambiguities of material in the Bible. Whereas for some there is a
'certain loss of confidence' about the meaning of the Bible as a result of
academic research, for Hollenweger historical-critical knowledge is not
only a very positive contribution to understanding the diversity of present-
day Christianity and plurality of interpretations, but also reveals a model
of ongoing struggle to articulate faith in the context of life's realities.

17. Hollenweger, 'The Other Exegesis', p. 162. The reference is to Ernesto
Cardinal, *Love in Practice. The Gospel in Solentiname* (New York: Orbis Books,
1974), in which he describes the commune he co-founded in Nicaragua which attracted
large numbers of peasants. Segundo's *A Theology for Artisans of a New Humanity* (5
vols; New York: Maryknoll, 1974) (see Hollenweger's review in *Ecumenical Renewal*
27.3 [1975], pp. 291-93) and Cone's *God of the Oppressed* (New York: Seabury,
1975). Hollenweger, 'Theology and the Future', pp. 1026-27.

18. Hollenweger, *Erfahrungen der Leibhaftigkeit*, p. 69. 'Die Synthese aller
Gesichtspunkte ist—theologisch gesagt—das Vorrecht Gottes.'

19. Clines, *Bible*, p. 87.

A good example of this insight can be found in his paper, 'What is the Word of God?', presented to a conference of Protestant Religious Education teachers at Mariazell in 1987.[20] Beginning with the story of Jacob wrestling with the person at Penuel in Gen. 32.22-32, he points out that the Yahwist interpretation is that God is merciful to Jacob. Verse 32, however, reflecting a postexilic context, is concerned to explain and reinforce a dietary law: 'Therefore to this day the Israelites do not eat the sinew of the hip which is upon the hollow of the thigh, because he ['the man'] touched the hollow of Jacob's thigh on the sinew of the hip.' This, said Hollenweger, would not be preached as a sermon today, and is not the word of God for Christians today. Without v. 32, there is an old story, older than the Yahwist, which the author found and transformed. The oldest layer is a pre-Israelite, pre-Canaanite, local legend, of a man (later rendered as Jacob) who fought with a river demon (Isch) in order to cross the ford. The oldest layer with its belief in demons is not the word of God for us today either, says Hollenweger, unless we believe in the ghost stories told in the Swiss Alps.[21] Hosea refers to the story, writing that 'He [Jacob] wrestled with the angel and won' (12.4-5). Hollenweger points out that Hosea also knew the tradition but used the story as a negative example to address his context: for Hosea the word of God here is how people should not conduct themselves with God. There are therefore already four possible interpretations in the Bible. A fifth is provided by biblical scholar Claus Westermann, whose commentary on Genesis Hollenweger had drawn on, which is that, when the sun came up, Jacob knew God was with him and with that knowledge went to meet his brother. 'This statement', said Hollenweger, 'is naturally right, but is it sufficient? With it Westermann underestimates his own profession of interpretation, for to come to this conclusion one does not have to be an Old Testament biblical scholar. Why the whole academic apparatus?'[22]

---

20. 'Was ist das Wort Gottes?', *Schulfach Religion* 6.1-2 (1987): (Dokumentation der Fortbildungstagung für Evangelische Religionslehrer in Mariazell vom 22-27 März 1987), pp. 25-36.

21. An example of Hollenweger's dry sense of humour, bearing in mind his defence of myth and his home in the Swiss Alps!

22. Hollenweger, 'Was ist das Wort', p. 32: 'Diese Aussage is natürlich richtig, aber genügt sie?... Westermann unterschätzt dabei seinen eigenen Beitrag zur Auslegung, denn um zu diesem Schluss zu kommen, muss man nicht alttestamentlicher Bibelwissenschafter sein.' C. Westermann, Genesis (BK1, 1-3, 3 Bde); Neukirchen, 1974-1982.

Hollenweger's answer to the question 'what is the word of God' is that 'The whole, the whole process of interpretation is the word of God'.[23] But he does not stop there: the process illuminated by scholarship must be made known to the community: 'Only together, in the community, in the annoying, yet realistic many-voicedness of the Bible, is the word of God to be found.'[24]

Other writers have, of course, stated that the proper place for biblical interpretation is the Christian community. Karl Barth opened his *Church Dogmatics* with the statement 'theology is a function of the church'. More recently Hauerwas and Loughlin, for example, have reaffirmed this.[25] But Hollenweger does not view the church as a closed system; the contexts in which it functions are also annoying and many-voiced. In the light of critical scholarship the Bible is 'foundational' as a model of how people in various historical, social and political contexts described and interpreted their experiences of faith and life—a model which can guide contemporary Christians in the same task.

Furthermore, form criticism in particular, and especially in relation to the New Testament, had revealed the oral origins of much biblical material. Long before the Bible reached its book form, Judaism and Christianity knew their histories as oral religion.[26] Narrative exegesis belonging to the oral culture was, in other words, intrinsic to the Bible. The academy had lost touch with these roots: the Gospel of Mark, Hollenweger pointed out, would not pass examination as a piece of theological research: it is anecdotal, uses words without defining them, does not explain its hermeneutical method, does not acknowledge sources and is without a conclusion. The Gospel is an example of oral theology:

> it operates through the medium of the story, not the statement. It does not use definitions, but descriptions... Mark has recorded the community memory of his church and put it into a theological framework without destroying the traditional oral elements.[27]

23. Hollenweger, 'Was ist das Wort', p. 32.

24. Hollenweger, 'Was ist das Wort', p. 34: 'Nur zusammen, in der Gemeinde, in der ärgerlich aber doch realistischen Vielstimmigkeit der Bibel ist das Wort Gottes anzutreffen.'

25. Stanley Hauerwas, 'The Church as God's New Language', in Green (ed.), *Scriptural Authority and Narrative Interpretation*, pp. 179-98; Loughlin, *Telling God's Story*.

26. Hollenweger, *Erfahrungen der Leibhaftigkeit*, pp. 69-74.

27. Hollenweger, *The Future of Mission*, pp. 8, 9.

The central importance of finding an appropriate way to use the inheritance of Western critical scholarship has, if anything, increased over time for Hollenweger. The sources we have drawn on so far have been from a diversity of articles, extracts from his books and workshops spanning almost 20 years. It is significant that, in the year 2000, he returned to articulate the necessity of addressing the situation in one short volume written in a style accessible to all. *Der Klapperstorch und die Theologie: Die Krise von Theologie und Kirche als Chance* ('The Stork and Theology: The Crisis of Theology and Church as Opportunity') carries on its cover a cartoon drawing of a stork flying to deliver a large bound book in place of the familiar baby. The crisis as Hollenweger sees it, is that scholarly knowledge about the Bible is not communicated: questions and ambiguities are not shared by academics or clerics with others. 'One day children will realize that babies are not brought by the stork. One day our indistinct (which is to say "untrue" and insincere) speech will be uncovered. The situation will explode.'[28]

Sharing the Inheritance

Hollenweger's response has been practical and experimental, a multi-faceted attempt to address each of the three publics in a way that overcame the restrictive barriers between the previously delineated areas of interest and expertise of those publics. This demanded a genre through which reciprocity was possible, namely, narrative. As he expressed it in the article for the academy in 1981, 'The form of the story permits the use of different languages in one and the same piece of writing and thus finds a literary form in which the contrast of styles corresponds to the struggle of different cultures and classes'.[29]

Hollenweger employs narrative as the medium for sharing the inheritance of critical scholarship with non-specialists. It is a genre which, he pointed out, enables the different exegetical options to be made visible. Narrative exegesis has the advantage of presenting different points of view simultaneously.[30] Much of his work has developed in this direction, that is,

---

28. Hollenweger, *Der Klapperstorch*, p. 46. 'Eines Tages realisieren die Kinder, dass die Babies nict vom Storch gebracht werden. Eines Tages wird unser undeutliches (sprich: "unwares" und unaufrichtiges) Reden aufgedeckt. Die situation wird explodieren.'

29. Hollenweger, 'The Other Exegesis', p. 164.

30. Hollenweger, *Conflict*, p. 66.

in very practical experiments to share scholarly biblical information in forms useful to church members and society. He has acknowledged that narrative exegesis lacks precision, but pointed out that linear argument presenting one point of view also has disadvantages: the argument may be rejected and nothing of value taken from the exegesis, or if one link in the line of argument is weak, the whole argument collapses. Lack of precision is a price Hollenweger has been willing to pay for the communication of biblical exegesis to audiences of mixed cultural and educational backgrounds.[31] As he put it to the academy, far from being given up, critical scholarship should be applied to the whole field between 'sender' and 'receiver', and thus provide 'one way of escaping from our religious and academic ghetto and not only claiming but demonstrating theology's place in the world in which we live'.[32]

Hollenweger drew encouragement from some current (1970s) innovative practical European Bible studies and said of them:

> By demonstrating a method of grassroot-theology these works are not merely practical guides for passing on already known theological insights but *applied methodology for a theological interaction between different languages and different worlds.*[33]

Secondly, these studies provided experience of telling and hearing stories. Thirdly, particularly in the work of Hans-Ruedi Weber, political and economic contexts could be taken into account, along with visual arts and the contribution of imagination and fantasy to Bible study.

From its inception the WCC had held consultations on the authority and interpretation of the Bible. Series of discussions had produced statements and reports at regular intervals: Wadham (1949), Montreal (1963), Bristol

---

31. Hollenweger, *Conflict*, pp. 66-68.

32. Hollenweger, 'Intercultural Theology', in J.G. Davies (ed.) *Research Bulletin 1978* (Institute for the Study of Worship and Religious Architecture; Birmingham: University of Birmingham, 1978), pp. 90-104 (102). This paper is published in German as ch. 1 of Hollenweger's *Erfahrungen der Leibhaftigkeit.*

33. Hollenweger, 'The Other Exegesis', pp. 169-71 (169); Hollenweger's emphasis. Others mentioned are Anton Steiner and Volker Weymann, Willi Erl and Fritz Gaiser, Ingo Neumann. Later, in *Pentecostalism: Origins* (111), he also commends Theophil Vogt's *Bibelarbeit. Grundlegung und Praxismodelle einer biblisch orientierten Erwachsenenbildung* (Stuttgart: W. Kohlhammer, 1985). Vogt shares Hollenweger's concern about the growing specialization of the academic theologian and the growing theological illiteracy of the people of God and regrets that the fruits of Bible studies using the oral medium are ignored by the academy.

(1967), Louvain (1971), Locuum (1977).[34] These studies not only reflect various current trends in Western biblical scholarship, but also reflect the different perspective offered by the international arena. Hans-Ruedi Weber, reviewing the reports in a 1981 book, noted particularly insights such as the cultural and confessional conditioning affecting the way Christians understand and live the Bible (Montreal), and the interpretative process visible in the Bible as a response to situations as well as events and revelations, which indicated the need to take contemporary historical situations into account in the ongoing task of interpretation (Louvain).[35] It is against this background of ongoing study, discussion and questioning that Hollenweger (who worked at the WCC from 1965–71) set himself the practical task of enabling engagement with the Bible as a text and engagement with the Bible as an ongoing process of interpretation in diverse and changing contexts.

Hollenweger's experiments in narrative exegesis of the Bible have taken various forms. The basic form is that of story and is illustrated by *Conflict in Corinth & Memoirs of an Old Man*, first published in German in 1978 and in English in 1982. The first narrative is based on 1 Corinthians 12–14 and the second on Ezekiel 37;[36] together they only cover 60 pages of large print (without the Commentary and Notes). We will look at *Conflict in Corinth*, the subject and approach to which Hollenweger had previously tested in many geographical locations, including the *Kirchentag* and a Catholic seminary in Trinidad, and with different groups of people.[37]

34. These can be found in Ellen Flesseman-van Leer (ed.), *The Bible: Its Authority and Interpretation in the Ecumenical Movement* (Geneva: WCC, 1980).

35. Hans-Ruedi Weber, *Experiments in Bible Study* (Geneva: WCC, 1981), pp. 45-55.

36. Hollenweger, *Conflict. Memoirs of an Old Man*, which is based on Ezekiel, is related by a man who, as a child, was taken to Babylon and looks back on the experience of the Exile and return to Jerusalem. His reflections cover three generations of the family, differences of opinion about preservation or renewal of the religious tradition in Exile, differences of opinion on priorities in Jerusalem (the building of houses or Temple). This story ends with a postscript written by the narrator's Babylonian wife after his death: 'Is this the new life that Ezekiel spoke of? Or is Yahweh, as your father once said, only to be experienced beyond our experience?' Hollenweger states in the Notes that the story addresses the theological problem, 'How does one deal with a promise which has not been fulfilled?' (p. 74).

37. Hollenweger, 'Intercultural Theology' (1978), p. 102. In this paper Hollenweger analyses the sociological profile of the church in Corinth before presenting the narrative and a critical appraisal of narrative exegesis. It concludes with an application

The story is told by a secretary-slave employed by the bank in Corinth invited to a citizen's meeting of Christians where part of Paul's letter to them is read for the first time. He observes the affluent, the dockworkers and slaves from other parts of the Roman Empire, literate and illiterate, those familiar with the Hebrew Scriptures and the synagogue and those not, sharing bread and wine, and responding to Paul's letter in different ways—discourse, vision, singing, speaking in tongues. 'Red Chloe', an ex-courtesan and now, as a Christian, champion of the underpaid and underfed dockworkers, leads the more spontaneous contributions to the gatherings and is also the one who draws attention to the dubious authenticity of the section of the scroll relating to women not speaking in public (1 Cor. 14.33b-36). The narrator tries to make sense of what he is told about Jesus being dead, but present, yet coming; he is attracted to the citizens' meetings, but is aware of the social and political risks of being identified with the 'socialist' Christians. The story ends with him wondering what to do: 'Is there any good reason for becoming a Christian?'

Background research to *Conflict in Corinth* was drawn particularly from two recent essays by Gerd Theissen and Dieter Luhrmann on the sociology and social structures of the early Christian communities. The Notes also list the scholarly literature discussed in these essays.[38]

Referring to the Corinthian text in his first volume of *Intercultural Theology*, Hollenweger suggests that his emphasis on the conflict between oral and literary cultural groups in Corinth is an original one, not found in the familiar commentaries. The situation in this early Christian community was an 'intercultural adventure', responded to by Paul, not by dividing the groups, but by the writing of a theological myth, the body of Christ, in which the parts have different functions but all serve the same body. For Paul, the body of Christ was not mystical but a social reality, and, adds Hollenweger, as sociologically dysfunctional and politically subversive

to intercultural theology. In German this article is in *Erfahrungen der Leibhaftigkeit* (34-51). Texts from the *Kirchentag* studies, *Konflikt in Korinth/Memoiren eines alten Mannes*, were published by Chr. Kaiser Verlag of Munich in 1978 with a fifth edition in 1987. These two exegeses have also been published in French, Italian and Indonesian, singly, together, or with other exegeses.

38. Hollenweger, *Conflict*, p. 69. Gerd Theissen, 'Soziale Schichtung in der korinthischen Gemeinde: Ein Beitrag zur Soziologie des hellenistischen Urchristentums', *Zeitschrift für neutestamentliche Wissenschaft* 65 (1974), pp. 232-72; Dieter Luhrmann, 'Wo man nicht mehr Sklave oder Freier ist: Ueberlegungen zur Struktur frühchristlicher Gemeinden', in *Wort und Dienst* (Jahrbuch der Kirchl. Hochschule Bethel, NF 13, 1975, pp. 53-58).

today as it was in the context of the Roman Empire.[39]

Conflict in Corinth thus provides, in a very accessible yet scholarly way, a case study of pneumatological, ecumenical and intercultural processes and debates.

Hollenweger made his debut at the *Kirchentag* in Hanover in 1967, invited initially in his WCC capacity as someone who could give a Bible study in English. Soon his sessions were drawing large audiences, which Hollenweger attributes to his different approach. 'People do not want to be preached at. They want to learn something and then they want to get really into the thing and make an experience and not just be before the preacher.'[40] He was invited yet again to give sessions at the 1999 *Kirchentag* in Stuttgart, and has contributed at all but one in the intervening years.

Not only did he experiment with a creative narrative approach to biblical texts; music and movement became part of the proceedings. The studies presented at the 1981 *Kirchentag* in Hamburg were published

39. Hollenweger, *Erfarhrungen der Leibhaftigkeit*, pp. 73-74. 'der Konflikt zwischen den zwei Kulturen, sich nicht in den geläufigen Kommentaren findet... Was nun aber interessant ist in Korinth, ist die Art, wie dieser Konflikt von Paulus angegangen wird. Die Gemeinde spaltete sich nicht nach Kulturen auf, hier die Mündlichen, dort die Schriftlichen, hier die Analphabeten, dort die Bürgerlichen. Man gründete keine Volkshochschule für die Sklaven. Das ist das faszinierende inter-kulturelle Abenteuer in Korinth... Paulus beschreibt die interkulturelle Gemeinde von Korinth im theologischen Mythos vom Leibe Christi, in dem die Glieder verschiedene Funktionen haben, aber dem gleichen Leibe dienen. Dies war im Kontext des römischen Reiches so fremd wie heute, soziologisch dysfunktional und politisch subversiv. Darum ist das Modell auch verschwunden... Der Leib Christi war eben für Paulus kein Corpus mysticum, keine mystische, sondern eine soziale Wirklichkeit.'

40. Interview, 11 June 1998. Interest in Hollenweger's sessions was also generated by a service which he led. According to his own account, a Dutch Catholic priest had been invited to preach at the eucharistic service, but was forbidden to do so, creating a dilemma for the organizers. Hollenweger decided 'to be obedient' and offered to explain to the people. He told the congregation of thousands that the priest had come to express his ecumenical fellowship and describe the ecumenical revival that was happening in many parts of the world but was not allowed to do so, so he would be silent. Hollenweger placed him in the centre of the platform beside a Brother from Taizé (Protestant), who explained what they would have done had they been allowed. The congregation began to call 'we want to hear the Catholic'. Hollenweger continued his account, 'Of course I had orchestrated that a little bit. I said "WAIT" we are not allowed to.' At a press conference afterwards Hollenweger refused to say which bishop had forbidden the priest's speaking. Initially German newspapers did not report the service, but did so after coverage by the Dutch press.

(German only) and provide an illustration: *Besuch Bei Lukas* contains four narrative exegeses on Exodus 14, Lk. 2.1-14, 2 Cor. 6.4-11 and Lk. 19.1-10.[41] The fourth study, 'Camels and Capitalists' is a story set in the year 90, and opens with, 'After the marriage of my son Aquila with the prophetess Maria, a dispute took place in the Christian community at Sinope'.[42] The reality of both rich and poor within the community had to be addressed. Hollenweger peoples the story with an interesting selection of characters, some biblical and others not, like the cheeky Swiss business man who was not a Christian and the historically anachronistic Marcion. At a meeting an old woman, Johanna, drew attention to a saying of Jesus—it is easier for a camel to pass through the eye of a needle than for a rich man to enter the kingdom of God—and the story of Dives and Lazarus. The owner of a shipping line, Marcion, pointed out that he gave money to poor Christians and also provided employment; if he sold everything and gave the proceeds away, many would lose their livelihoods. Luke, the assistant bishop, reminded the meeting of Jesus' encounter with 'the stinking rich financier, Zaccheus'. The bishop commented that Jesus did not criticize Zaccheus because he was a colonialist and a capitalist. The narrator observes that both Johanna and Marcion were trying to defend their positions in society as well as in the kingdom of God, though he learnt from Marcion later that he gave away a great part of his fortune. 'Was that not one of the reasons why there were muttered voices condemning him as a heretic?'[43]

The first exegesis, described by a journalist present at the *Kirchentag* event, involved the audience forming the Red Sea, the Israelites passing through and the Egyptians being engulfed. Miriam, from the podium, danced to the beat of a kettledrum and 'shortly the whole company in the hall was on its feet dancing'.[44]

41. Walter J. Hollenweger, *Besuch Bei Lukas* (Munich: Chr. Kaiser Verlag, 1986 [1981]). Other *Kirchentag* Bible studies published by Kaiser are *Erfahrungen in Ephesus* 1985 (1979) and *Das Fest der Verloren* 1984 (1983).

42. Hollenweger, *Besuch*, p. 43. 'Nach der Hochzeit meines Sohnes Aquila mit der Prophetin Maria entstand in der Christengemeinde Sinope ein Streit.'

43. Hollenweger, *Besuch*, p. 48. 'Mir war klar, dass sowohl Johanna wie auch Marcion ihre gesellschaftliche Position als die dem Reiche Gottes gemässe zu verteidigen suchten. Von Marcion allerdings erfuhr ich später, dass er einen grossen Teil seines Vermögens verschenkte. Ob das nicht mit ein Grund ist, warum sich Stimmen regten, die ihn als Irrlehrer verurteilten?'

44. Hollenweger, *Besuch*, pp. 59-61. The article by Robert Leicht, 'Der Tanz mit dem grossen Weib Mirjam' is reproduced in *Besuch bei Lukas* from the *Süddeutsche*

The book contains a commentary, a bibliography of exegetical and general literature and detailed notes; there is a suggestion that the studies could be produced in local communities as an active rather than passive form of working with the content and history of the Bible.

Hollenweger has developed the dramatic and artistic elements in his work, refining and modifying his original Bible studies. *Conflict in Corinth* has been expanded into a drama with music, song and dance, and in fact, he has recently again partly re-written it for a particular event—an international conference of the Old Catholic Church. He has changed the characters to people from all over Europe and all those attending the conference will take part in some way, including a bishop, who will afterwards celebrate the Eucharist according to the Old Catholic liturgy.[45]

Kamele und Kapitalisten was subsequently published by Metanoia Verlag as a one-act Bible play with music, dance, drama and song, as were many others, including *Gomer—Das Gesicht des Unsichtbaren* (*Gomer— the Face of the Invisible*), which takes up the subject of 'wrestling Jacob' referred to above. Hosea's widow and children leave Samaria after its conquest by Assyria and travel to Bethel where they continue their discussion on the various versions of the story, punctuated by the comments of a chorus: was Jacob wrong to try and manipulate God? What is God really like? Was Jacob, is Israel, being punished by God? Can the past cast any light on the present situation? Writing about the drama, *Gomer*, in *Umgang Mit Mythen* ('Encounter with Myth') Hollenweger describes how he learnt from the biblical authors how they dealt with myth, using Hosea's reference to the Jacob story to demonstrate that the original myth was historicized, socialized and relativized in a different context.[46]

From the 'Flowers and Songs' Mexican Bible studies and discussion, Hollenweger developed the drama *The Adventure of Faith* (German, *Das Wagnis des Glaubens*).[47] Act 1 portrays an early church meeting where Philip's baptism of the Ethiopian is debated; Act 2 considers Peter's fraternising with Cornelius; Act 3 Ananias's dealings with Saul/Paul. All centre around a question still relevant: 'Are there not events and texts which have today to be interpreted in terms of Jesus, in opposition to both

Zeitung 20/21.6.198, pp. 59-60. 'Binnen kurzem ist die ganze Hallenbelegschaft tanzend auf den Beinen.'

45. Interview, 11 June 1998.
46. Hollenweger, *Umgang mit Mythen*, pp. 112-21 (114).
47. Hollenweger, *Pentecostalism: Origins*, p. 97 n. 82.

Christian and non-Christian tradition?' This drama was produced in Bir-mingham in 1997.[48]

A publicity leaflet from Metanoia dated September 1995 lists 22 plays by Hollenweger, many with original music written by Hans-Jürgen Hufeisen, with whom he has collaborated since 1981.[49] Hollenweger continues to write new biblical dramas, including two co-authored with Estella Korthaus: *Maria von Wedemeyer*, which will be discussed later, and one on apocalyptics, *Neuer Himmel—neue Erde,* performed in 1999 for the first time and for which he also wrote the music.[50]

The dramas added the dimension of participation which Hollenweger has made a vital part of biblical interpretation. The audiences are not passive receptors of information, they are involved in the exegetical process. This, Hollenweger discovered through experience, was an effective learning method, an observation considerably reinforced by his teaching role at Birmingham. It was especially at the Centre for Black and White Christian Partnership, which he helped to establish, at the Selly Oak Colleges that Hollenweger was alerted to the necessity for a creative teaching method. Many of the black British pastors who attended the courses were unfamiliar with the conceptual monolinguistics and mono-culture of academic theologizing.[51] They were accustomed to more con-crete, experiential expressions of faith and life in which dreams, visions, dance, song, fasting and healing were of great significance, and so a medium had to be found that bridged the literary and oral approaches. Also, Hollenweger soon realized, one which kept his students awake!

---

48. Hollenweger, *Pentecostalism: Origins*, p. 97. See Chapter 5 below.

49. Those listed are *Mirjam, Mutter Jesu; Gomer—das Gesicht des Unsichtbaren* (both previously published by Exodus Verlag, 1987); *Michal: Die Frauen meines Mannes*; *Der Kommissar auf biblischer Spurensuche*; *Ruth, die Ausländerin*; *Kamele und Kapitalisten*; *Der Handelsreisende Gottes*; *Vorsicht Baustelle. Betreten auf eigene Gefahr!*; *Johannestexte*; *Im Schatten Seines Friedens*; *Kommet her zu mir alle, die ihr mühlselig und beladen seid & Die zehn Aussätzigen*; *Hiob—oder Gottes Wette; Ostertanz der Frauen & Veni Creator Spiritus (eine Pfingstliturgie)*; *Fontana, die Frau am Brunnen und der siebte Mann & Herr, bleibe bei uns, denn es will Abend werden*; *Hiob im Kreuzfeuer der Religionen*; *Jona, ein Kind unserer Zeit*; *Das Wagnis des Glaubens*; *Requiem für Bonhoeffer: Den Toten aller Völker*; *Jörg Ratgeb.* Others have since been published including *Hommage an Maria von Wedemeyer*, and *Neuer Himmel—neue Erde*, both co-authored with Estella F. Korthaus.

50. Interview, 8 August 1997, and correspondence 5 April 1999, 25 January 2001.

51. See Chapter 2 above, pp. 37-39. From the literature referred to there, *Pentecostalism: Origins*, ch. 8, is particularly relevant here.

Most of the course participants were engaged in full-time employment—indeed some were pastors in addition to other occupations—and often travelled considerable distances to attend the college. Looking back, he recognizes the influence of this learning/teaching experience on the development of his narrative exegetical method to engage people's physical, spiritual and affective participation as well as the purely cognitive.[52]

Comment

This selective, but not unrepresentative, glimpse of Hollenweger's response to the Bible and critical scholarship illustrates the novel path he has followed. Attention to the public of the church is clear—it should have access to biblical scholarship and participate in the interpretative process. His attention to the public of society is demonstrated in the insistence that the interpretative process can only take place in its various geographical, historical, social, political and economic contexts.

For the public of the academy Hollenweger's contribution is not easy to assess: he does not conform to the conventional rules of engagement. While drawing consistently on the work of biblical scholars—always fully referenced in notes and bibliographies—he does not debate the issues with which they are immediately concerned. Rather, he moves with the weight of the findings and utlilizes them with confidence in the realms of the other publics of church and society. The key question for him is not 'what is the Truth?' but, as he put it in a 1993 article, 'How do we produce a body-of-Christ-theology, a theology which is not only understood by the people but a theology in whose production the people of God participate and which they can recognise as their own?'[53]

Chris Peck, writing in 1995 on the growth of participatory methods of Bible study in England, noted the growing consensus that the developments—experienced through a variety of activities including role play,

---

52. 'Some [dramas] I have also developed in Birmingham for the black students and then adapted them to the *Kirchentag*. You see it works both ways. Because I have these black students and they went to sleep when I taught them so I had to do something. They said to me, "what we have not played, danced and sung we have not understood". So I said, "how does one dance, sing and play university theology?" They said, "We know how to dance, sing and play but the content must come from you". So I produced the content and they produced the choreography and the drama and the music and they were very gifted so I learned it from them.' The *Bonhoeffer Requiem* was the outcome of this process. Interview, 11 June 1998.

53. Hollenweger, 'Theology and the Future', p. 1024.

group identification, drama, painting, fantasy and storytelling—deserved serious attention.[54] Like Hollenweger (whose week-long dramatizations of biblical books he mentions in passing), Peck draws attention to the divorce of Bible study from the life of the Christian community. Through participatory studies, he suggests, 'what is presented as an attempt to engage in objective, rational, universal analysis from within the boundaries of academic institutions becomes exposed as being culturally and historically conditioned' when examined from other perspectives. On the basis of his own considerable experience, Peck calls for boundary-crossing for mutual correction between the academy and participatory groups: the former could help construct participatory Bible studies and facilitate dialogue between text, context and experience; participants in the latter could offer their insights and challenge asssumptions that have divorced the academy from the day-to-day experience of the community it serves.[55]

Hollenweger has been, and continues to be, one such boundary-crosser. Moving into the practical usage of scholarship rather than staying within conceptual discourse endorsed the value of academic enterprise. Further, and more importantly, the insight that the Bible was foundational for Christians today with regard to what it had to teach of the discernible processes forming its content (as much as through the content per se) effectively opens new vistas of possibilities for exegesis. Just as people of faith in biblical times struggled to make sense of God, life and the world in the circumstances, languages and thought-forms of their respective contexts, people today are engaged in the same process: the difference is that today they have the model of biblical authors to guide them.

The adaptation and reinterpretation of material by the biblical authors for their own communities in the light of contemporary circumstances is the key to appreciating Hollenweger's narrative exegetical method. The medium for communicating critical insights is also, in a way, the message, for when participants actively engage with the material they see the relevance for their own contexts and become interpreters.

Howard Cooper, writing as a rabbi and analytic psychotherapist, has made very interesting observations that dovetail neatly with Hollenweger's understanding of biblical narrative and practice of narrative exegesis.

---

54. Chris Peck, 'Back to the Future: Participatory Bible Study and Biblical Theology', *Theology* 98.785 (1995), pp. 350-57.

55. Peck, 'Back to the Future', pp. 350-57 (352, 357). Reference to Hollenweger 351. Peck also traces the development of participatory Bible studies to the 1970s and refers to Hans-Ruedi Weber's *Experiments in Bible Study*.

Drawing on Robert Alter's *The Art of Biblical Narrative* and Gabriel Josipovici's *The Book of God*, Cooper observes that the ancient Hebrew writers' use of narrative to convey a people's historical development necessitates that 'the meaning of events is not fixed'. He continues:

> One could even suggest that the Hebrew scriptures aim to produce an indeterminacy of meaning... What is distinctive about biblical literature is that conflicting points of view co-exist within it. Events are laid alongside each other, without comment (just like in life), and we are never allowed to know whether the pattern we see emerging at one point is the true pattern... It is this stance of 'calling into question' assumptions, certainties, the stories we tell ourselves—and living with the questions—which describes too the task of the therapist.[56]

If 'calling into question' and 'living with the questions' describes the approach of biblical authors and the task of the therapist, it also describes that of the academy: scholarship has a critical function. Hollenweger democratizes the task: he says the entire Christian community should be involved in the process. For this to happen, we could say, the academy needs to put its knowledge and insights to therapeutic, rather than didactic use.

We have drawn attention to Hollenweger's emphasis on the oral origin of much biblical material and noted his treatment of the pre-Israelite myth of Jacob and the river demon. It is no surprise, therefore, that he has a positive view of myth which has taken him against the tide of prevailing opinion. The Introduction to his book *Umgang mit Mythen*, published in German only in 1982, explains why he engaged so fully with the topic. He was asked by his colleague at Birmingham, John Hick, to write for the book *The Myth of God Incarnate* (1977). The initial outline seemed to Hollenweger to be continuing the de-mythologizing trend which had been prevalent since Rudolph Bultmann's sensational essay. Yet it had also been proved that most christological statements in the New Testament were served by Greek and Jewish mythological categories. The 'astonishing' conclusion had been drawn that therefore they could not possibly be true. Looking for something new to bring into the debate, he sought in his contribution to show how important mythical language is for theology and, also, underlined the meaning of mythical connections for English society as well, through examples such as the degree congregation at the

---

56. Howard Cooper, 'Living with the Questions: Psychotherapy and the Myth of Self-Fulfilment', in Sidney Brichto and Richard Harries (eds.), *Two Cheers for Secularism* (Northamptonshire: Pilkington Press, 1998), pp. 93-106 (102-103). Alter, New York: Basic Books, 1981; Josipovici, New Haven: Yale University Press, 1988.

university.[57] He was 'excommunicated' from the participating team.[58]

Umgang mit Mythen was Hollenweger's response: an exploration of myth as a category for reinterpreting the gospel. In it he describes a variety of 'sacred' myths (e.g. Christmas, the Eucharist) and 'secular' myths (eg William Tell, the Marxist class struggle) identifying criteria for a 'true myth'. I have referred above to the example of *Gomer* included in *Umgang mit Mythen*; an example from the New Testament is in the Letter to the Colossians (1.15-20). Analysing the text, Hollenweger demonstrates how the author corrects the prevailing myth known to the Christian community at Colossus—that of a cosmic force that holds the world together. The author adds interpolations, corrections and subsequent interpretations and Hollenweger finds in the biblical author's handling of the cosmic myth a model for specifying the criteria of a true myth: it is related to actual human history (the author relates mission and the church as a social entity to the myth); the cosmic myth is related to a historical event (the life of Jesus of Nazareth); and thirdly, the author's 'true myth' expresses an 'overspill of hope' which is not contained in history.[59] From the biblical guidelines, Hollenweger moves us to the arena of mission and intercultural theology, highlighting the centrality of the biblical myths, their plasticity of interpretation in concrete situations, and their offer of hope for a lived reality beyond present difficulties. Biblical myths such as the Eucharist and Easter have meaning and power for those outside the churches:

57. Hollenweger, *Umgang mit Mythen*, p. 9: ' "Umgang mit Mythen" wurde ein Thema für mich, als ich eingeladen wurde, einen Beitrag zu dem von meinem Kollegen John Hick herausgegebenen Buch "The Myth Of God Incarnate" zu schreiben. In den ersten Entwürfen, die mir meine Kollegen zustandten, wurde frisch-fröhlich drauflos entmythologisiert, als wären seit Rudolph Bultmanns aufsehenerregendem Aufsatz nicht vierzig Jahre ins Land gegangen, als hätte die wissenschaftliche Mythenforschung seit Bultmann nicht einen differenzierten Umgang mit Mythen nahegelegt. Es wurde nachgewiesen, dass die meisten christologischen Aussagen des Neues Testaments sich griechischer und jüdischer mythischer Kategorien bedienten (was kaum ein informierter Bibelleser bestreitet). Daraus wurde die erstaunliche Folgerung gezogen, dass sie demzufolge unmöglich wahr sein können. Ich wunderte mich über den Versuch, diesen unterdessen etwas staubig gewordenen Ladenhüter aufzupolieren und neu in den Verkehr zu bringen. Ich versuchte in meinem Beitrag für das geplante Buch zu zeigen, wie wichtig die mythische Sprache für die Theologie ist. Ich unterstrich die Bedeutung des Mythenzusammenhangs gerade für die englische Gesellschaft.'

58. Hollenweger, *Umgang mit Mythen*, p. 10: 'Ich wurde sang- und klanglos aus dem Mitarbeiter-Team exkommuniziert'.

59. Hollenweger, *Umgang mit Mythen*, pp. 158-63: 'Der Mythos der Kolosser.'

Hollenweger refers to the writings of Marxists Roger Garaudy and Milan Machoveč to substantiate this.[60]

David Bosch described *Umgang mit Mythen* as 'a book on Hermeneutics, Systematic Theology, Practical Theology, Ethics and even Economic Theory' as well as on missiology.[61] Interestingly, it has also been described as a book for non-academics: Werner Simpfendörfer wrote:

> Hollenweger's new volume of intercultural theology illustrates once again his gift for narrating difficult theological matters in stories and experiences in a way which brings them alive. By this way of doing theology he shows us what a paradigm shift among professional theologians might look like. Though questions may be left unanswered here and fresh problems arise, this, far from being frustrating, has a stimulating effect because this narrative style of a frontier commuter claims and mobilizes the theological capacities of lay men and women whose destiny and experience it is, day by day, to have to cross frontiers and to build bridges.[62]

Focusing on process rather than content accommodates much more readily the dialogical and contextually sensitive theological methodologies which have developed in the last half of this century: Black, Asian, process, interfaith, feminist and liberation. No longer oddities hovering on the fringe of 'proper' theology, they can be viewed as within the mainstream of biblical exegetical tradition. Hollenweger, from his international and ecumenical perspective combined with his critical knowledge of the Bible, was aware earlier than many Western theologians of the legitimacy of these enterprises and read widely from the works of non-Western theologians.[63]

---

60. Hollenweger, *Umgang mit Mythen*, pp. 100-102, Garaudy; pp. 138-39, Machoveč (in English 'The Other Exegesis', 158-59); *Erfahrungen der Leibhaftigkeit*, pp. 285-86, Machoveč. Machoveč's book *A Marxist Looks at Jesus* (London: Darton Longman & Todd, 1976) was described by Cyril Rodd as 'one of the most important recent studies of the life of Jesus', in the entry 'Sociology and Social Anthropology', in Coggins and Houlden (eds.), *Dictionary*, p. 638.

61. Review in *Missionalia* 10.3 (1982), pp. 128-29.

62. Review in *Ecumenical Review* 35 (1983), pp. 103-105 (105). At the time of writing, Simpfendörfer was General Secretary of the European Association of Lay Training Centres.

63. His intimate knowledge of the writings of Segundo and Cone have been noted above. These are but two examples of the extensive reference Hollenweger makes in almost all his works to Black, African, Asian and Latin American authors. Feminist writers are not so well represented. His considerable editorial and reviewing work over the years has contributed to his wide reading, as well, of course, as his professorial teaching and examining roles. He contributed the entry 'Black Christian Interpretation' to Coggins and Houlden (eds.), *Dictionary*, pp. 90-92.

Today, theologians such as Kwok Pui-Lan, a feminist and biblical scholar, to take a random example, are able to draw on a growing body of Asian literature to discern how the society's myths, stories and legends are being used in the exegetical task.[64] Kwok Pui-Lan sees this imaginative and dialogical approach as 'challenging the historical-critical method, presumed by many to be objective and neutral'.[65] Hollenweger, as we have seen, would defend critical scholarship, but not its claim to objectivity and neutrality—that claim can no longer be sustained in theology any more than in the physical sciences. He would also defend an imaginative and dialogical approach to exegesis. For him, the Bible remains foundational— not as a source of proof texts to support particular dogmatic positions, but in a much more complex way a truly universal collection of inspired writings whose meanings become clear only as succeeding and diverse communities engage with them in the midst of present realities and share their insights with each other. In answer to the question 'Who interprets Scripture correctly?' his reply is: 'no one person interprets Scripture correctly on his own. It is only in conflict, debate, and agreement with the whole people of God, and also with non-Christian readers that we can get a glimpse of what Scripture means.'[66]

I recall the work of an author I introduced this chapter with. Loughlin closes his book on 'Bible, Church and Narrative Theology' with an Epilogue entitled 'Eating the Word'. He suggests that the image in the book of Revelation of John being given the book to eat, 'which is both Christ's risen body in the bread of the Eucharist and the divine logos in the word of Scripture' is a figure for narrativist theology. [67] The Eucharist, he says, is itself 'a narrative that enfolds the participants within the biblical story'.[68] This image does not fit Hollenweger's approach. His narrative exegetical method bursts out of dogmatic and institutional bounds. Not only does he exhibit confidence in biblical critical scholarship, he also exhibits confidence in the inherent strength of the Bible itself, in all its diversity. It does not need such protective control and regulation. He is conservative with regard to the centrality of the Bible, but radical with regard to its interpreters and interpretations.

64. Kwok Pui-Lan, *Discovering the Bible in the Non-Biblical World* (Maryknoll, NY: Orbis Books, 1995).

65. Kwok, *Discovering the Bible*, p. 13.

66. See ch. 23, 'Hermeneutics: Who Interpets Scripture Correctly?', in *Pentecostalism: Origins.* Here, p. 325.

67. Loughlin, *Telling God's Story*, pp. 244-45.

68. Loughlin, *Telling God's Story*, p. 223.

Chapter 4

INTERCULTURAL THEOLOGY: ESCAPING THE GHETTO

The Western Theological Academy and Intercultural Theology

Intercultural theology, wrote Hollenweger in 1978, is 'that academic discipline which operates in a given culture without absolutising this culture'. Theology, if it is not to be sectarian or culturally imperialistic, must attempt to be open to the universal and sacramental dimension of the Christian faith. Intercultural theology, he continued, offers a way of escaping from our Western religious and academic ghetto and demonstrating theology's place in the world in which we live.[1]

This could be read as a manifesto for Western theology. It calls for conversion from a monocultural to an international approach, from a sectarian to an ecumenical outlook, and from intra-institutional reflection to contextual engagement. It is not surprising that it should come from a missiologist, but it is significant that the paper was given to a conference in Cambridge on the study of theology. The conversion called for is clearly responsive to the perceived realities of the twentieth century—post-colonialism, the 'global village', with its culturally and religiously pluralistic societies, the changing profile of the Christian *oikoumene*, combined with increasing awareness of the significance of concrete historical situations for theological reflection.

These realities are now generally acknowledged, but the implications have been only slowly taken into account in the Western theological academy. An 'international ecumenical' symposium held at Tübingen gathered Catholic and Protestant participants to consider some of the

1. Hollenweger, 'Intercultural Theology' (1978), pp. 101-102. The paper forms ch. 1 of Hollenweger's first volume of *Intercultural Theology* (*Erfahrungen der Leibhaftigkeit*), where he notes that the paper was given at the Conference of the Society for the Study of Theology in Cambridge on 6 April 1978 and was also published in *Theological Renewal* 10 (October 1978), pp. 2-14.

issues. In their editorial introduction to the 1989 English edition of the collected papers, *Paradigm Change in Theology*, Hans Küng and David Tracy suggested that the motivation for attendance was 'the sense that we are living in a "time of troubles", a time when old certainties are breaking up, a post-modern era, an era post-Auschwitz and post-Hiroshima'. They continued, 'New natural and humane sciences, democratically pluralistic societies, liberation movements of every kind—all have consequences for theology especially. These consequences have as yet hardly been clearly seen let alone absorbed.'[2]

The 64 eminent participants of the symposium, 29 of whose papers or responses are published in the collection, are, with only a few exceptions, from Europe or North America; only a handful are women; there are no Orthodox or Pentecostal voices. 'International and ecumenical' is an over-statement as a description of the symposium. The two papers by non-Westerners (Leonardo Boff and Mariasusai Dhavamony) are, together with the one paper by a woman (Anne E. Carr), placed in a section of their own entitled 'Particular and Global Aspects of the New Paradigm'. This despite Matthew Lamb's statement in the section 'Retrospects and Prospects' that:

> This symposium…should clearly go on record as repudiating the domi-native tendency of treating theologies elaborated in solidarity with the victims of imperialism, of patriarchy, of racism, or of technocentrism as though they were only partial or particular aspects of dominant first world or western theologies.[3]

Küng noted the general acknowledgement among participants that the paradigm changes in theology are to be seen in the context of the church and against the background of society in general and that 'the thinking subjects of theology and the places where theology is pursued can change'. 'The place where people do theology is not necessarily a university. It can also be a basic community. And it can be pursued not only by academics (let alone male academics) but also by women and non-academics.'[4] Yet the format, tenor and material of the symposium were unmistakably academic.

---

2. Hans Küng and David Tracy (eds.), *Paradigm Change in Theology: A Symposium for the Future* (Edinburgh: T. & T. Clark, 1989), p. xv.

3. Matthew Lamb, 'Paradigms as Imperatives Towards Critical Collaboration', in Küng and Tracy (eds.), *Paradigm Changes in Theology*, pp. 453-460 (455).

4. Hans Küng, 'A New Basic Model for Theology: Divergencies and Convergencies', in Küng and Tracy (eds.), *Paradigm Change in Theology*, pp. 439-52 (443).

These observations are not made in criticism: the book offers the tren-
chant and stimulating enquiry one would expect of the contributors; the
crises in academic theology are continually related to the challenges of the
contemporary world. For example, Leonardo Boff and Johann Baptist
Metz drew attention to the relatedness of the histories of theology, church
and world and the need for analyses from standpoints other than the
Western one.[5] Jürgen Moltmann favoured a move from 'controversial' to
ecumenical theology:

> The person who thinks schismatically considers his own part to be the
> whole. The person who thinks ecumenically considers his own whole to be
> part of the coming community. What happens within the ecumenical
> community of Christians in this way can also have an exemplary effect on
> the ecumenical community of religions and cultures, and on the economic
> and political habitability of our globe.[6]

Responding to Langdon Gilkey and Johann Baptist Metz, John Cobb
drew attention to the need for the theologian to be an advocate for those in
need, not an 'observer of the human condition', while also pointing to the
radically divergent stances which could be generated in practice in response
to a particular situation.[7] For Cobb, all the tasks to be taken on board by
contemporary theologians should be seen in the light of the global issues of
nuclear threat, humanly detrimental development policies in the Third
World and ecological damage caused by policies in the First World.[8]

The observations on the symposium are made to highlight the extreme
difficulty of escaping from the Western religious and academic ghetto

---

5.   Leonardo Boff, 'The Contribution of Liberation Theology to a New Paradigm',
in Küng and Tracy (eds.), *Paradigm Change in Theology*, pp. 408-23 and Johann
Baptist Metz, 'Theology in the New Paradigm: Political Theology', in Küng and Tracy
(eds.), *Paradigm Change in Theology*, pp. 355-66.

6.   Jürgen Moltmann, 'The Interlaced Times of History: Some Necessary Differentiations and Limitations of History as Concept', in Küng and Tracy (eds.), *Paradigm
Change in Theology*, pp. 320-39 (336).

7.   John Cobb, 'Response to Johann Baptist Metz and Langdon Gilkey', in Küng
and Tracy (eds.), *Paradigm Change in Theology*, pp. 384-89 (387). The example he
gives, with reference to Metz's section 'Auschwitz—or theology after the end of
idealism', is that in remembering Auschwitz some theologians would be moved to
support the state of Israel to secure the future of Jews and therefore support its
aggressive policies while others would 'resolve that never again should Christians
stand silently by as a powerless people are oppressed and abused' and criticize the
Jewish State's treatment of West Bank Arabs (pp. 387-88).

8.   Cobb, 'Response', p. 389.

even when the problems have been so ably identified and courageously faced by some Europeans and North Americans. If changing circumstances point to the need to take account of particular cultures, the plurality and divergence of Christianity, global awareness and the contextualized nature of all thinking and action, and the non-exclusivity of academic theologizing, then the issue becomes: 'How can all these constituencies be brought into meaningful relationship?' This is a question which Hollenweger has actively addressed for decades.

The significance of even asking this question should not be underestimated. For many Western theologians engaged with the traditional academic disciplines, it is a new question. For theologians of ecumenism and missiologists it has emerged from at least a century's reflection, tension and debate. In a brief overview of twentieth-century ecumenism introducing a collection of key texts, Michael Kinnamon and Brian Cope helpfully draw out the theology/world/church connections characterizing each of the ecumenical movement's three periods. From 1910–48, in the historical context of the final years of colonial expansion, the First World War (a 'Christian civil war'), the German Church struggle of the 1930s and the Second World War, the church—the whole church—was rediscovered as an essential component of the gospel. 1948–68, 'an era of astonishingly rapid transition', was marked by the cold war, the end of colonialism and rise of self-consciousness of newly independent nations and their churches. Concerns about the unity of the Christian faith (prompted in part by new Orthodox and Roman Catholic involvement) were not a priority shared by others stressing solidarity in the social-political crises of the times (the foundation of liberation theology). These two periods were strongly Christocentric, emphasizing the divinity of Christ. By the late 1960s increasing emphasis was placed on the Trinitarian nature of God and the humanity of Christ in the situation of a global church and awareness of a North–South divide of wealth and poverty. Until around 1968 Christian diversity was seen as a problem rather than as a characteristic of genuine unity, with development programmes and mission directed from the North Atlantic towards Asia, Africa, the Pacific and Latin America.[9]

The point which the modern ecumenical movement takes as its origin was the (Protestant) World Missionary Conference held at Edinburgh in

---

9.   Michael Kinnamon and Brian E. Cope (eds.), *The Ecumenical Movement: An Anthology of Key Texts and Voices* (Geneva: WCC; Grand Rapids: Eerdmans, 1997), pp. 3-4. This book is an invaluable resource on the movement.

1910.[10] Responding in part to the tensions that emerged there—relations between the Western missions and local churches, the relationship of Christianity to traditional religions and other world faiths, and the sometimes conflicting national and individual demands of Christianity, a continuation committee, which became the International Missionary Council, was set up and was important for the formation of the WCC (1948), which the IMC joined in 1961.[11] The study of mission this century has therefore had to try to keep pace with changes in the church, that is to say, has required an awareness of the changes taking place in the practice of and reflection about Christianity among the former recipients of the Western missionary enterprise. This has involved a shift from seeing mission as the expansion of Western Christianity to discussion of accommodation, inculturation and indigenization, reflecting the relevance of diverse cultural settings to the appropriation of Christianity, and more recently (1970s onwards), the development of contextual theologies.[12] Werner Ustorf has referred to the present as the 'polycentric epoch of Christian history'.[13]

10. This conference of 1,200 delegates from Protestant Missionary Societies was significant, not only for the breadth of its considerations (8 commissions carried out an enormous amount of preparatory work on particular topics prior to the presentation of reports and discussions at the conference), but also because the existence of non-Western traditions became apparent and challenged the West for the first time. Only 18 people from non-Western countries were present, but their influence far exceeded their numbers. See particularly *World Missionary Conference 1910. IX. The History and Records of the Conference together with Addresses delivered at evening meetings* (Edinburgh: Anderson & Ferrier, 1910).

11. See Philip A. Potter, 'Mission', in Lossky *et al.* (eds.), *Dictionary*, pp. 690-96.

12. Useful resource books include Norman Thomas (ed.), *Readings in World Mission* (London: SPCK; Maryknoll, NY: Orbis Books, 1995), which has texts from the second century to 1991; James A. Scherer and Stephen B. Bevans (eds.), *New Directions in Mission and Evangelism 1: Basic Statements 1974–1991*, and *New Directions in Mission and Evangelism 2: Theological Foundations* (Maryknoll, NY: Orbis Books, 1992, 1994). The term 'contextualization' was coined in 1972 in a report issued by the WCC Theological Education Fund entitled 'Ministry in Context' according to Thomas in *Readings* (170). It was defined by Robert W. Pazmino in Max L. Stackhouse, *Apologia: Contextualization, Globalization, and Mission in Theological Education* (Grand Rapids: Eerdmans, 1988), p. 237, as 'The continual process by which God's truth and justice are applied to and emerge in concrete historical situations'.

13. Werner Ustorf, *Christianized Africa—De-Christianized Europe? Missionary Enquiries into the Polycentric Epoch of Christian History* (Seoul, Korea: Tyrannus Press, 1992). See particularly ch. 6 'The West—A 'Mission Field'? and ch. 9 'Missiology in View of 1 John 3, 2'.

Catholic writers responding to developments since the Second Vatican Council (1962–65), which also recognized the increasing importance of the local church, have likened their contemporary situation to 'a vast laboratory' with diverse cultural expressions in uneasy tension with the unity of faith,[14] or to both Catholic and Reformed Churches as experienceing 'a movement of incarnation in thousands of different cultures, languages and customs'.[15]

The 1970s were a time when the tide, rising since the beginning of the century, began to turn with an increasing plurality of churches (or cultural pluralism within the Catholic Church) and shift in numerical weight from North to South.[16] It was precisely at this time that Hollenweger, established as a leading authority on the worldwide Pentecostal movement and fresh from experience with the World Council of Churches, assumed his academic role as Professor of Mission and proceeded to develop intercultural theology. There are two major thrusts to his explorations. One is the replacing of mission studies with intercultural theology as a more appropriate approach for the contemporary world, in which Western Christian practice and reflection could no longer be taken as normative. The second is the relevance of particular contexts to theologizing, which, having been recognized and articulated, should then be brought into dialogue with other particular articulations. In an article 'Kultur und Evangelium: Das Thema der interkulturellen Theologie' he wrote that the theme of intercultural theology is that those outside our own circle are important for our theology because there is no universal ecumenical theology and no pure biblical belief.

> The theology of women is important for the theology of men. It is not simply a side-theme of mainline theology. The theology of Blacks is

14. See, e.g., Christoph Theobald, 'The "Definitive" Discourse of the Magisterium', in *Concilium 1999.1, Unanswered Questions* (ed. Christoph Theobald and Dietmar Mieth; London: SCM Press, 1999), pp. 60-69 (66) and the Editorial, pp. vii-ix.

15. José Oscar Beozzo, 'Documentation: The Future of Particular Churches', in *Concilium 1999: 1*, pp. 124-38 (127). For recent short considerations of the subject see *Concilium 1994: 2, Christianity and Cultures,* Norbert Greinacher and Norbert Mette (eds.); and S. Wesley Ariarajah, *Gospel and Culture: An Ongoing Discussion within the Ecumenical Movement* (Geneva: WCC, 1994).

16. Beozzo writes, 'At the beginning of the twentieth century, four-fifths of Catholics lived in Europe. As the twenty-first century appears on the horizon, the proportion is virtually inverted, with only a quarter in Europe, with the rest spread over Latin America, where nearly half the world's Catholics live, the Caribbean, North America, Asia and Africa', 'Documentation', p. 127.

important for Whites. It is not simply under-developed theology. Oral theology is important for literary theologians. It is not simply theology which cannot yet think abstractly. All cultures have something to bring to the church and theology... We must therefore structure our church and theology so that all can bring their charisms...[17]

In the academic arena it is only since the mid 1960s that the contribution of non-Western theologians has begun to be generally accessible to Westerners. There is, for example, a growing literature on Christology. The articles and bibliographic references in *Asian Faces of Jesus* and *Faces of Jesus in Africa* are good examples.[18] They are interesting for their emphasis on context. Commenting on the proliferation of images of Jesus in Asia ('ranging from Jesus as pure consciousness to Jesus as a social activist') Surgirtharajah suggests that:

> the task is not to identify those that represent correct Christological formulations, as the old church councils used to do, but to look afresh at the contexts that bring forth these sketches of Jesus and to find appropriate ways to transform them.[19]

Similarly, Charles Nyamiti, in his paper 'African Christologies Today', writes of the new African categories employed by other contributors to express 'the mystery of our Saviour': 'Christ the *integral healer, chief, elder brother, master of initiation, ancestor, black messiah* (liberator), *plenitude of human maturity*', adding that they should be seen 'from the perspective of the African social cultural background from which they are taken'.[20] Priscilla Pope-Levison and John R. Levison in *Jesus in Global*

17. Walter J. Hollenweger, 'Kultur und Evangelium: Das Thema der inter-kulturellen Theologie', *Evangelische Mission Jahrbuch 1985*, vol. 17 (ed. Verband Evangelischer Missionskonferenzen; Hamburg: Missionshilfe Verlag, 1985), pp. 52-60 (56-57): 'Die Theologie der Frauen ist wichtig für die Theologie der Männer. Sie ist nicht einfach ein Seitenthema zur Haupttheologie. Die Theologie der Schwarzen ist wichtig für die Weissen. Sie ist nicht einfach unterentwickelte Theologie. Die mündliche Theologie ist wichtig für die schriftlichen Theologen. Sie ist nicht einfach Theologie derer, die noch nicht abstrakt denken können. Alle Kulturen haben zu Kirche und Theologie etwas beizutragen... Wir müssen daher unsere Theologie und unsere Kirche so gestalten, dass alle ihr Charisma einbringen können...'

18. R.S. Sugirtharajah, *Asian Faces of Jesus* (London: SCM Press, 1993); Robert J. Schreiter (ed.), *Faces of Jesus in Africa* (Maryknoll, NY: Orbis Books, 1992).

19. R.S. Sugirtharajah, 'Epilogue', in R.S. Sugirtharajah (ed.), *Asian Faces of Jesus* (London: SCM Press, 1993), pp. 258-64 (258, 259).

20. Charles Nyamiti, 'African Christologies Today', in Schreiter (ed.), *Faces of Jesus in Africa*, pp. 3-23 (14).

Contexts provide one instance of Western theologians engaging in 'conversations' with Christologies from Latin America, Asia, Africa and North America.[21]

Ecumenical and mission studies have had a longer period of (painful) sensitization to the breaking-up of Western Christian academic, cultural and institutional hegemony than the traditional theological disciplines, a process which is by no means complete.[22] Intercultural theology can assist the Western academy to escape from its cultural ghetto and to relocate itself in the contemporary world. The pivotal question is 'how can the different constituencies be brought into meaningful relationship?'

Hollenweger's Intercultural Contribution to the Academy

When he assumed his academic role in 1971 Hollenweger responded positively and supportively to growing awareness that all theologies are contextually conditioned and that work was needed to redress the balance for so long tipped in favour of the West.[23] Utilizing the promise given to

21. Priscilla Pope-Levison and John R. Levison, *Jesus in Global Contexts* (Louisville, KY: Westminster/John Knox Press, 1992). 'Conversations', they note, 'can be unsettling' (11).

22. David Bosch's *Transforming Mission* (Maryknoll, NY: Orbis Books, 1991) is a case in point. Already something of a Western classic in its competent analysis and discussion of paradigm shifts in mission over the centuries, colleagues have observed, for example, that his missiology is not contextual (Frans J. Verstraelen); that his omission of consideration of Pentecostalism and women's liberation is conspicuous (William Saayman); and that, regarding the Catholic paradigm in Latin America, Bosch regarded the intellectual and theological currents as more causally significant than the realities they grew out of (Curt Cadorette). See William Saayman and Klippies Kritzinger (eds.), *Mission in Bold Humility: David Bosch's Work Considered* (Maryknoll, NY: Orbis Books, 1996).

23. Hollenweger on several occasions refers to the statements made by Charles Kraft (who in turn quoted Robert McAfee Brown) in Kraft and Tom N. Wisely (ed.), *Readings in Dynamic Indigeneity* (Pasadena, CA: William Carey Library, 1979). In brief, as Hollenweger presents them in 'Intercultural Theology', in *Theology Today* 43.1 (1986), pp. 28-35 (29) these were: '1. All theologies are contextually conditioned. 2. There is nothing wrong with theology being contextually conditioned. 3. It may take others to show us how conditioned, parochial, or ideologically captive our own theology is. 4. Even if once we could ignore such voices, now we can no longer do so. 5. The point of contact between our traditions and the new theologies from the Third World is Scripture. 6. Only in creative tension with the widest possible perspective can we develop theologies appropriate to our own particular situations. 7. Since within the

him that he could experiment with a new type of theological education, Hollenweger's redefinition of 'mission' as 'intercultural theology' emphasized a concern for fully international participation in theological reflection. It also indicated a new emphasis on the significance of contemporary questions and issues, which he considered were an important source for reflection alongside biblical, historical and systematic material.[24] As many of the students were from the Third World, the need to produce work that was relevant to their own context and also comply with the research conventions at a European university could be in conflict. The difficulty of combining these objectives was to Hollenweger one that had to be overcome because the alternative would be the continuance of Western-dominated theology in the Third World.[25] The undesirability of this was twofold. As he put it in a subsequent article:

> if we educate African theologians according to our literary understanding of theology and we are successful in this, we do not only make them useless in their African context but we also lose the possibility for true dialogue, since then they only mirror our thinking.[26]

church the ultimate loyalty is not simply to nation, class or culture, the universal church is uniquely suited to provide the context in which the task of creative theologizing can take place.' See also Hollenweger's review of *Readings in Dynamic Indigeneity* (and two other books) in 'Monocultural Imperialism vs Intercultural Theology', *International Review of Mission* 73.292 (1984), pp. 521-26.

24. See above, Chapter 1 'Professor of Mission'; and Walter J. Hollenweger, 'Chair of Mission', pp. 13-17. The motivation for this article can be found on p. 16: 'The future of Mission Studies in Birmingham is by no means secure. I consider this most unfortunate for financial, social and missiological reasons.' On 1 August 1999 management of the federal institutions of the Selly Oak Colleges, including the joint Chair, the School of Mission and its staff, were transferred to the University of Birmingham. (Letter from Revd Dr Michael Taylor, President of the Selly Oak Colleges, to Friends of the Selly Oak Colleges, July 1999.) In the 28-year history of the Chair, Mission Studies had moved to full academic standing.

25. Hollenweger, 'Chair of Mission', pp. 14-15. Hollenweger writes in support of Kwesi Dickson, whom he quotes from his 1984 book *Theology in Africa*: 'African theologians continue to mouth the theological platitudes they have picked up in universities, theological seminaries and colleges abroad or parade their erudition by quoting the latest theological ideas in Europe and North America. In consequence, theological education in Africa has generally had the effect of producing theologians who are more at home in Western theological thought even if such thought pertains only to a certain level of their consciousness.'

26. Hollenweger, 'The Ecumenical Significance of Oral Christianity', *Ecumenical Review* 41.2 (1989), pp. 259-65 (260).

In an extensive review article entitled 'Towards an Intercultural History of Christianity' Hollenweger referred to the works of 28 different authors from a variety of countries. He pointed out that mission history had in the past been written only by the missionaries and was inevitably biased, employed the priorities and categories of the 'sending' culture and usually underrated the theological status of the pre-Christian context. Now the 'underside' of history was beginning to find expression: 'This is a much needed correction, although it has not yet reached the mainstream of historiography and theology.'[27] Many of the works referred to, some by his own former research students, had been published in the series 'Studies in the Intercultural History of Christianity' by Peter Lang.[28]

The whole area of Pentecostal and charismatic studies, and its general neglect until very recently, is an obvious example of the 'underside' of history struggling to find its place in the academy. Hollenweger recalled that when he came to England he approached Oxford University Press with a plan for an *Oxford Dictionary of Pentecostalism*. 'I received a rather rude letter telling me that the OUP could not possibly provide dictionaries for every conceivable sect.'[29] His personal efforts through writing and teaching have done much to correct this misjudgment of the significance of the movement worldwide, and more particularly through his own research and encyclopaedic knowledge of the research of others he has disclosed the diversity of belief and practice within Pentecostalism (cf. Chapter 1 above). As Martin Conway has observed, the awareness of diversity Hollenweger learnt in his studies of the Pentecostals was carried on 'through all the different ideas and experiences chronicled in his volumes of *Intercultural Theology*'.[30] A major focus of Hollenweger's own interest has been the discernment of the significance of the move-ment's black oral roots, which have given it the following characteristics: orality of liturgy; narrativity of theology and witness; maximum partici-pation at the levels of reflection, prayer and decision making; inclusion of dreams and visions into personal and public forms of worship; and an understanding of the body–mind relationship which is informed by experiences of correspondence between body and mind—applied, for

27. Hollenweger, 'Towards an Intercultural History', p. 526.
28. See Chapter 1 above, pp. 19-20.
29. See his review of Burgess and McGee (eds.), *Dictionary of Pentecostal, International Bulletin of Missionary Research* 13.4 (1989), p. 181.
30. Conway, 'Helping the Ecumenical Movement', p. 279.

example, in the ministry of healing by prayer and in dance in worship.[31] His criticism of the Western academic neglect of Pentecostalism has been equalled by his criticism of Pentecostalism for its slowness to recognize the value of scholarship and for the movement's neglect of the growing number of scholars from within its own ranks.[32]

For Hollenweger the facilitation of new voices and cultural perspectives was only one aspect in an evolving situation. Referring to the growing number of new churches (many belonging to the Pentecostal family) he commented:

> They want to throw off the missionary tutors and produce their own theologians... It is vital for these churches that they develop their own indigenous theology without breaking away from the tradition of European church history, because that would destroy the ecumenicity of the church both abroad and here.[33]

This view was further endorsed in a 1990 article 'The Theological Challenge of Indigenous Churches', where he stated that 'the non-white indigenous churches will have to work together with the rest of the churches for a common future'.[34]

He also pointed out that many Western biblical scholars are ignorant of the hermeneutical tools used in black churches in the USA and Britain;

31. For Hollenweger on this subject see, e.g., 'Priorities in Pentecostal Research', from which the above summary is taken, pp. 9-10; 'Pfingstkirchen', in Ekkehard Starke, Birgit Bender-Junker and Notger Slenczka (eds.), *Evangelisches Kirchenlexikon: Internationale Theologische Enzyklopädie* vol. 3 (Göttingen: Vandenhoeck & Ruprecht, 1992), pp. 1162-1170; 'Verheissung und Verhängnis der Pfingstbewegung', *Evangelische Theologie* 53.3 (1993), pp. 265-88; and *Pentecostalism: Origins*, chs. 3–11.

32. See, e.g., Hollenweger, 'After Twenty Years'; 'Pentecostalism and Academic Theology'; and 'The Critical Tradition of Pentecostalism', *Journal of Pentecostal Theology* 1 (1992), pp. 7-17. He concludes the latter article with the statement: 'In all these fields [ecclesiology, pneumatology, hermeneutics and historiography] a massive shift in positions which were once considered rock-solid is taking place. Pentecostalism has come of age. It is now possible to be filled with the Spirit, to enjoy the specific Pentecostal charismata and Pentecostal spirituality, to believe in Pentecostal mission, and at the same time to use one's critical faculties, to develop them and to use them—as any other charism—for the kingdom of God.'

33. Hollenweger, 'Chair of Mission', p. 17.

34. Walter J. Hollenweger, 'The Theological Challenge of Indigenous Churches', in A.F. Walls and Wilbert Schenk (eds.), *Exploring New Religious Movements: Essays in Honour of Harold Turner* (Elkhart, IN: Mission Focus Publications, 1990), pp. 163-67 (164). NB Hollenweger notes the differences in terminology: Harold Turner uses 'new religious movements' and David Barrett 'non-white indigenous churches'.

many pastoral theologians are unaware of the processes of communication or liturgical traditions of Zionist or Cherubim and Seraphim Churches; and that 'too many systematic theologians are unaware that there are ways of expressing the coherence of the Christian witness other than those we have developed in the West'.[35]

Hollenweger is not alone in perceiving the importance of the universal church and diverse cultures for Western theology. Richard Friedli of the University of Fribourg, for example, has pointed out that the divergence of themes given priority in different contexts has stimulated the need for a change in emphases in theology, of which he highlights the following: 'Intercultural theology is that scientific discipline concerned with God and the offer of salvation which operates in a given culture without absolutising it.' 'The method of intercultural theology depends on the social context.' 'The research methods and community models of Western academic theology can and must be enriched by alternative forms of doing theology.' 'It demands…that this critical examination [Western analysis] be applied also to the total process of intercultural, inner-ecclesiastic, and inter-religious communication in which the West is only one of the participants.' Intercultural theology would lead to the liberation of Christ and his gospel from their 'Western captivity'.[36]

Andrew Walls, of the Centre for the Study of Christianity in the Non-Western World in Edinburgh, has also stated that 'contemporary theology needs renewal by mission studies', among other things for the regular critique of cultural assumptions which they encourage.[37] Hollenweger is

35. Hollenweger, 'The Theological Challenge', p. 165.

36. Richard Friedli, 'Intercultural Theology', in Karl Müller *et al.* (eds.), *Dictionary of Mission: Theology, History, Perspectives* (Maryknoll, NY: Orbis Books, 1997 [German orig. 1987]), pp. 219-22 (221-22). See also Theo Sundermeier, 'Inkulturation als Entäusserung' ('Inculturation as Self-Emptying'), pp. 209-14.

37. Andrew F. Walls, *The Missionary Movement in Christian History: Studies in the Transmission of Faith* (Maryknoll, NY: Orbis Books; Edinburgh: T. & T. Clark, 1996), 'Structural Problems in Mission Studies', p. 147. Walls goes on to comment, 'The nineteenth century…saw scholarship immensely enriched by the missionary movement in (one is tempted to say) every department of learning except theology. The legacy passed to the learned world in various ways; it helped to create new sciences (linguistics), helped to shape or was absorbed into new ways of organizing knowledge (anthropology), contributed to new clusters of subjects that brought the non-Western world within the parameters of Western learning (Oriental and African Studies). But the other great modern religious development—the recession from the Christian faith in Western lands and the consequent marginalization of theology—has intervened' (149-50).

equally direct in his statement that, 'Either theology is universal and inter-cultural or it does not deserve the title of an academic discipline'.[38] Like Hollenweger, Walls is aware that academic theology has either not come to terms with the shift of the centre of gravity of the Christian world, or if it has recognized the change, it has not realized that a 'conversion' in theological discourse is needed. Walls commented:

> It is the very concept of a fixed universal compendium of theology, a sort of bench manual which covers every situation, that mission studies challenge. In mission studies we see theology 'en route' and realise its 'occasional' nature, its character as response to the need to make Christian decisions.[39]

From the recognition of the contextual and particular nature of Christianity follow further implications for Western theologizing. Hollenweger included within the embrace of intercultural theology the relationship of the church to industry, management, economy, medicine and literature,[40] areas which he described elsewhere as 'functional mission fields'.[41] His article 'Efficiency and Human Values: A Theological Action-Research-Report on Co-Decision in Industry' published in the *Expository Times* in 1975 is one example of his own engagement as a theologian, on this occasion responding to the breakdown of relationships in industry.[42]

---

38. Hollenweger, *Pentecostalism: Origins*, the section 'A Quest for an Intercultural Theology', in ch. 10, p. 131.

39. Walls, *The Missionary Movement*, pp. 149, 146.

40. Hollenweger, 'Chair of Mission', p. 16.

41. Hollenweger, *The Future of Mission*, p. 8. See also, 'The Discipline of Thought and Action in Mission', *International Review of Mission* 80.317 (1991), pp. 91-104, which is based on the farewell lecture.

42. Hollenweger, 'Efficiency and Human Values: A Theological Action-Research-Report on Co-Decision in Industry', *Expository Times* 86 (May 1975), pp. 228-32. Hollenweger wrote: 'This is very much more a human, cultural and indeed a theological problem than just—as some superficial observers might assume—a technical problem of management, wages and the distribution of wage packets.' He drew on a recent book by the Swiss theologian, Arthur Rich (*Mitbestimmung in der Industrie, Probleme, Modelle, kritische Beurteilung: Eine sozialethische Orientierung* [Zürich: Flamberg Verlag, 1973]) and other sources such as Fred Blum, *The Scott Bader Commonwealth* (London: Routledge & Kegan Paul, 1968); and Bobbie Wells Hargleroad (ed.), *Struggle to be Human: Stories of Urban-Industrial Mission* (Geneva: WCC, 1973). See also Hollenweger's earlier paper, 'Does Efficiency Imply the Destruction of Human Values? A Theological Action-Research-Report on Co-Decision in Industry', in J.G. Davies (ed.) *Research Bulletin 1974* (Birmingham: University of Birmingham), pp. 114-18.

Another example, and a more extended one, is his scholarly work in relation to Karl Marx. His inaugural lecture as Professor at Birmingham, 'Marxist and Kimbanguist Mission' has already been mentioned; there are also two specific articles 'Karl Marx (1818–1883) and his Confession of Faith' and 'Marxist Ethics' in English and two chapters in the first volume of *Intercultural Theology*.[43] In the review article referred to above, he drew attention to some of his students' researches in these 'functional' areas.[44] Furthermore, the search for an intercultural theology needed the contribution of 'the silenced and silent people of our countries'—like the non-churchgoing working men interviewed in Roger Edrington's research, who shared their religious experiences, their private prayers, their 'lostness', and for whom being listened to was a new experience.[45]

Within the academic realm, then, Hollenweger pursued a course thoroughly in keeping with the global pluralist realities of churches and cultures, where histories are re-examined, Western hegemonies challenged, Christian faith and practice is inextricable from context, and the previously marginalized are allowed a voice. But Hollenweger believed this was not simply an issue for the academy; it involved churches and societies.[46] The objective of intercultural theology is not the creation of meta-concepts but facilitation of the expression of the universality of the church for the sake of a future which the world holds in common. Analysing and discussing the WCC's search for a confession of faith in a two-part extended article in 1975, he similarly drew attention to the limitations of 'definitions and abstractions' at international, ecumenical level:

43. See chapter 1, p. 16 above and *Expository Times* 84 (February 1973), pp. 132-37 and 85 (July 1974), pp. 292-98, respectively; and *Erfahrungen der Leibhaftigkeit*, chs. 2 and 3, pp. 267-98.

44. In 'Towards an Intercultural History', pp. 553-56, Hollenweger reviewed Harold Tonks's *Faith, Hope and Decision-Making: The Kingdom of God and Social Policy-Making* (Frankfurt am Main: Peter Lang, 1984), and Patrick O'Mahoney's *Swords and Ploughshares: Can Man Live and Progress with a Technology of Death?* (London: Sheed & Ward, 1986).

45. Hollenweger, 'Towards an Intercultural History', pp. 551-53. See Roger B. Edrington's *Everyday Men: Living in a Climate of Unbelief* (Frankfurt am Main: Peter Lang, 1987). The Foreword by Hollenweger entitled 'Religion in a Silenced Culture' is based on the article.

46. As Edward Schillebeeckx observed, the theologian is always the latecomer in respect of Christian practice. Practice is preceded by faith but not by theology. *Ministry: A Case for Change* (London: SCM Press, 1981), pp. 101-102.

The task becomes all the more important when a common basis is sought
with those churches who do not know a theology in the Western sense, who
have not developed a system of terms and definitions and do not want to
develop them, not only because this language is foreign to their world but
also because they suspect Western concepts of a pseudo-consensus which
camouflages the vital disagreements and agreements.[47]

Hollenweger was of the opinion that, given the plurality of biblical
confessions and the plurality of situations into which the gospel message is
given, it was impossible to make a confession 'which is valid for all and
always'. Unity of Christians could not be made visible by logical formulas:

> We Europeans have taken a one-sided stand for Paul's argumentative
> approach and have neglected the style of the other Biblical writers. The
> independent Christians from the Third World tell us stories, they celebrate,
> dance, eat, sing, work, laugh and pray together. Only afterwards do they try
> the interpretative reflection.[48]

Seventeen years later, commenting on the writings of two European
contextual Pentecostal theologians, Miroslav Volf and Peter Kuzmic,
Hollenweger made a statement which would seem to reflect his own
position: 'Both understand truth as something which happens. Truth is not
something which simply exists but which emerges. Both therefore are in
opposition to objectivism and idealism.'[49]

Having the perspective of an ecumenical missiologist, Hollenweger saw
the necessity to move beyond conceptual Western consideration of the
postmodern situation to the issue of how the different constituencies living
within the situation could be brought into dialogue with each other for
their mutual enrichment and critique. This demanded a radical shift—not
in paradigms in the first instance, but in theological communication and
theological method. All Hollenweger's knowledge, professional and
personal experience pointed cumulatively in the direction of oral and
narrative categories—the Bible (as discussed in the previous chapter), his

---

47. Walter J. Hollenweger, 'The "What" and the "How": Content and Communication of the One Message. A Consideration of the Basis of Faith, as formulated by the
World Council of Churches. Part 1', *Expository Times* 86 (August 1975), pp. 324-28
(324). Part 2 (September 1975), pp. 356-59.

48. Hollenweger, 'The "What"', Part 2, pp. 358, 359.

49. Hollenweger, 'The Critical Tradition', p. 13, referring to Miroslav Volf,
'Divine Spirit and New Creation: Toward a Pneumatological Understanding of Work',
Pneuma 9.2 (1987), pp. 173-93, and Peter Kuzmic 'Pentecostal Ministry in a Marxist
Context', *EPTA Bulletin* 9.1 (1990), pp. 4-32.

Pentecostal background and the phenomenal growth of Pentecostal and charismatic movements, the de facto, if not de jure limitations placed on non-Western participation at international level by Western academic discourse, and postgraduate Third World researchers studying in Western universities. Oral categories were important, according to his understanding, because 'the Church of Jesus Christ is the place where cultural, academic, political and theological conflicts become organised in such a way that new insights emerge for all participants', and narrative forms enable the 'ruling language' to be brought into intercultural dialogue as one possible language next to other possible languages.[50]

Oral and narrative categories of theology offered a 'language bridge', a way into presenting the value of dreams and interpretation, visions and analysis, storytelling and critical exegesis—a way of escaping from the academic ghetto.[51]

Narrative Exegesis—One Way to Escape the Ghetto

If Hollenweger had confined himself to writing about oral theologies and narrative exegesis then he would have remained clearly within the norms and expectations of the academy. But he did not. He chose the radical course of actually using narrative forms for theologizing. His warrant was, as we have seen, the model of Scripture. His motivation was to present the search for intercultural theology 'in a way that is understandable both to black and white theologians, to academic theologians and to people who want to contribute to the theological decision making process without being forced to use the jargon of theological academia'.[52]

The piece of narrative exegesis that follows this statement is especially

50. Hollenweger, 'Kultur', p. 58. 'Nach meinem Verständnis ist die Kirche Jesu Christi der Ort, wo die kulturellen, wirtschaftlichen, politischen und theologischen Konflikte so organisiert werden, dass daraus für die Beteiligten neue Einsichten entstehen. Die narrative Form wählte ich, weil ich so die Sprache der Herrschenden als eine mögliche...neben anderen möglichen Sprachen in den interkulturellen Dialog einbringen kann.' The editor of the *Jahrbuch* notes that Professor Hollenweger had given a lecture on a similar theme at the 65th anniversary of the Westphalian Mission Conference in Iserlohn on 2 March 1985, which had been documented.

51. Hollenweger, 'Kultur', pp. 57-59.

52. Hollenweger, 'Intercultural Theology' (1986), p. 29. An abbreviated version of this article in German, 'Was Bonhoeffer von den Negern lernte' can be found in Madeleine Strub-Jaccoud and Hans Strub (eds.), *Wegzeichen gelebten Evangeliums* (Festschrift Marga Bührig; Zürich: TVZ, 1985), pp. 78-83.

interesting, not only because of the method and the audience, but because
the subject is a Western theologian—Dietrich Bonhoeffer, whom Hollenweger presents as a striking example of the value of intercultural theology
for Western theologians:

> The decisive insight for Bonhoeffer was his discovery that the church
> transcends the boundaries of class, race, and nation. He came to this insight
> through his negative experience in a nationalist German church (which in
> his view was a contradiction in terms) and through the positive experience
> of his ecumenical contacts, among them his discovery of the black churches
> in New York City. Bonhoeffer was the first—and, for at least forty years,
> the only—theologian who saw the political and theological relevance of the
> spirituality of these black churches.[53]

The 'midrash' tells the story of Bonhoeffer's visit to a black church service in New York—the singing taken up by the choir, musicians and
congregation, interspersed with solo verses or verbal comments inviting
responses and affirming the ability 'to smile' in the face of life's difficulties when filled with the Holy Spirit; the welcome to Bonhoeffer and
invitation to speak, which he, taken by surprise, lamely and inadequately
responded to; words of the pastor taken up spontaneously by the
trombonist with the tune of 'When the Saints', to which the choir danced;
the questions of a member of the congregation. 'When the saints march
into the new Jerusalem do you think there will be Catholic saints, Lutheran
saints, Pentecostal saints…black saints, white saints?' and the shouted
response of the congregation, 'No, No'; the preacher, 'You know, in
heaven it will be become very, very clear indeed what we worship.
Whether we worship Jesus, the manual worker, Jesus our savior, or
whether we worship our own fears and our own impulses… I wouldn't be
surprised in the least if all white people would be confronted with a black
Jesus, and all black people with a white Jesus'; Bonhoeffer not knowing if
white Christians would meet a black Christ, but if they did, Aryan
Christians would meet a Jewish Christ.[54]

This 'midrash', continued Hollenweger, was one way of describing how
Bonhoeffer reached the certainty that 'the church is a community which

---

53. Hollenweger, 'Intercultural Theology' (1986), p. 29.

54. Hollenweger, 'Intercultural Theology' (1986), pp. 30-32. An earlier experiment
with narrative form on the subject of a visit to a black church by 'Mr Chips' and a
colleague was presented to the 1976 Pastoral Studies Spring School at the University
of Birmingham. Some of the material is used in the 'midrash'. Manuscript 76.20,
Hollenweger Papers, Orchard Learning Resources Centre, University of Birmingham.

stands against all human divisions', a conviction evident in the catechism he wrote on return to Germany, his involvement in the German Church struggle and finally in subversive revolutionary action.

The simplicity of the narrative is deceptive: in about 1,000 words Hollenweger portrays key features of black spirituality (see p. 76 above), makes clear the German Lutheran pastor's liturgical 'culture shock'; raises the issue of racism in its concrete realities of 1930s USA and Germany and challenges the reality of the church in the light of its unrealized possibilities. The narrative, in other words, presents important theological subjects in an accessible way to non-academics, concretizes theological reflection, and highlights the functionality of intercultural encounter and dialogue (in this instance for the development of Bonhoeffer's theology and praxis). Its general accessibility is evident in its publication in April 1995 by a Swiss newspaper to recall the fiftieth anniversary of Bonhoeffer's death.[55]

The secret of its effectiveness lies, of course, in the scholarship that lies behind the narrative: an exegesis such as this depends on considerable research and reflection. Hollenweger's familiarity with Bonhoeffer's writings is amply demonstrated in his chapter on Bonhoeffer in volume 2 of *Intercultural Theology, Umgang mit Mythen*. Here Hollenweger focused on the relationship between Bonhoeffer's ecumenical praxis and his political resistance and the relationship between his ecclesiology and his politics, and referred to Bonhoeffer's *Gesammelte Schriften, Widerstand und Ergebung, Ethik, Nachfolge*, and *Sanctorum Communio*, as well as to secondary literature.[56] It is possible to see from this earlier work how Hollenweger's grounding of Bonhoeffer's theological insights in his personal, social and political context facilitated the development of the fully narrative presentation of the 'midrash'.[57]

---

55. Walter J. Hollenweger, 'Was Bonhoeffer in Harlem lernte: Eine frei gestaltete Reminiszenz zu Bonhoeffer's Umgang mit den Schwarzen Amerikas', *Der Kleine Bund* (8 April 1995), *Kultur-Beilage*, p. 6. A further full-page (broadsheet) article by Hollenweger on Bonhoeffer was published by *Der Kleine Bund* on 9 September 1995, p. 5: 'Aus christlicher Verantwortung lügen: Eine Würdigung von Dietrich Bonhoeffers nachgelassener "Ethik"' ('Out of Christian Responsibility to Lie: An Appreciation of Dietrich Bonhoeffer's Diminished "Ethics"').

56. *Umgang mit Mythen*, p. 15: '…konzentriert sich das erste Kapitel dieses Buches auf das Verhältnis zwischen Bonhoeffer's ökumenischer Praxis und seinem politischen Widerstand, auf das Verhältnis zwischen seiner Ekklesiologie und seiner Politologie'.

57. Hollenweger explores Bonhoeffer's family and social background, finding there

The critical insight that intercultural experience was formative for Bonhoeffer's understanding of the church as universal, transcending boundaries of race, class and nation, was further developed by Hollenweger in
an article comparing two ecumenists, Bonhoeffer (using the 'midrash')
and William J. Seymour, the son of former slaves, whose preaching of the
baptism of the Spirit and incorporation of black spirituals and oral liturgy
in worship led to a revival in 1906 in Los Angeles—the 'cradle of
Pentecostalism'. In this revival black and white, men and women, Asians
and Mexicans, educated and uneducated met together as equals. Hollenweger again pointed out the need to find a theology 'which will not be
conceptually uniform but will nevertheless provide the basis for a mutual
process of learning and recognition'. 'There is no reason', he concluded,
'why black and white, Seymour and Bonhoeffer, should not meet in prayer
and in theology.'[58]

And to a large extent this is what Hollenweger achieved a few years
later with the *Bonhoeffer Requiem*, first performed at the Berlin *Kirchentag* in 1987.[59] To the element of story Hollenweger added drama, dance,
music, song and audience participation. The drama in three acts—Bonhoeffer's Life, Bonhoeffer's Death and Bonhoeffer's Words—is presented,
in effect, within a framework of black American Pentecostal liturgy. For
example, Bonhoeffer's liberating 'discovery' of the Sermon on the Mount
is followed by some verses from the Beatitudes:

> Jesus Christ says 'Blessed are they which do hunger and thirst after
> righteousness: for they shall be filled. Blessed are the peacemakers: for they
> shall be called the children of God. Blessed are they which are persecuted
> for righteousness' sake: for theirs is the kingdom of heaven'.

Music, song and dance follow immediately, taking up the theme, with
'By an' by I'm goin' to lay down my heavy load. I know my robe's goin'
to fit me well, I tried it on at de gates of hell...' There is Bonhoeffer's

---

no explanation for the understanding of Christianity he came to, and continues by
describing his visit to the USA and analysing the complex debates of the mid 1930s
among European churchmen responding to the rise of Hitler and the situation in
Germany, focusing on Bonhoeffer's part in these debates (see also 'The "What"').

58. Walter J. Hollenweger, 'Dietrich Bonhoeffer and William J. Seymour: A
Comparison between Two Ecumenists', *Norsk Tidsskrift for Misjon* 39.3-4 (1985)
(Festschrift for Nils Bloch-Hoell), pp. 192-201 (199, 200).

59. *Requiem für Bonhoeffer* was published in German by Metanoia Verlag. In
manuscript form only in English, from which the following is taken.

account of his observations in New York and his new catechism question 'What is the church's position on family and nation?' and the answer:

> The church recognises them as gifts from God but she also knows that the Holy Spirit is a stronger bond than the bonds of blood, of a common heritage, of national interest. In the church there is neither master nor slave, neither man nor woman, neither Jew nor German.[60]

Bonhoeffer's decision to return to Germany on the last boat from the USA in 1939, aware of what that course would mean, is followed by the spiritual 'Go down Moses, way down in Egypt land. Tell ole Pharaoh to let my people go'. Bonhoeffer's statement to fellow Christians 'Cry out for the Jews, then you can chant plainsong' is sung by the whole audience at several points.[61] The drama closes with Bonhoeffer reciting his now famous poem/hymn written in prison, 'With Every Power for Good to stay and Guide Me' and the choir singing Brahms' 'Selig sind die Toten' (Blessed are the Dead).

Since its public debut with semi-professional actors, musicians and singers in the Deutschlandhalle in Berlin before an audience of thousands, *Requiem für Bonhoeffer* has been performed many times in Germany and

60. Eberhard Bethge (ed.), *Bonhoeffer: Gesammelte Schriften*, 6 vols, Munich, 1958–74. Notes on the visit to the USA from vol. I, 97: Hollenweger's excerpt in the Requiem ms (it is quoted in full in *Umgang Mit Mythen*, p. 18) reads: 'One can hear preaching in New York on almost everything except for the Gospel of Jesus Christ, his cross, sin and forgiveness, life and death. But in the negro churches I hear the Gospel. Wherever the Gospel is preached the negroes join in with shouts and prayer. Unlike the detached and formal "white sermon", the "black Christ" was preached with passion and the power of imagination. If you have understood the Negro spirituals, you will appreciate the strange mixture of subdued sadness and exploding joy in the negro soul.' Bonhoeffer's catechism is in vol. III, p. 362.

61. Hollenweger does not reference this particular quotation in the ms. Renate Wind, *A Spoke in the Wheel: The Life of Dietrich Bonhoeffer* (trans. John Bouden; London: SCM Press, 1991 [German original 1990]), uses it and expands on the context as follows: 'The public church repudiation of the opposition church also consolidated the Finkenwald community. Their communal form of life together, which meant "not monastic segregation but innermost concentration for service outside", was above all to strengthen readiness to resist. It was not an aim in itself or a flight from reality, as in other groups which came into being at this time and which attempted to get over the wretchedness of church politics by retreating into new liturgical forms, religious aesthetics, meditation and song. To these Dietrich objected, "Only those who cry out for the Jews may sing Gregorian chant" ' (81). Her source is Eberhard Bethge, Renate Bethge and Christian Gremmels (eds.), *Dietrich Bonhoeffer: A Life in Pictures* (London: SCM Press, 1986), p. 133.

Switzerland by different groups of people.[62] An advertising flier for two performances in June 1998 in Zürich, for example, described it as, 'A project with students of the Theological Faculty and other Faculties of the University of Zürich, in cooperation with the church community of St Jakob am Stauffacher and interested people from a great variety of other places'.[63] To which, of course, would be added the participating audiences at the performances.

Hollenweger's introduction of narrative exegesis into academic discourse grew out of his experiments at international ecumenical level, as observed in Chapter 2.[64] It was at the WCC Assembly of the Commission for World Mission and Evangelism at Bangkok in December 1972 and January 1973 that 'Mr Chips' entered the institutional arena. The theme of the Assembly was 'Salvation Today' and sections addressed the topics 'Culture and Identity', 'Salvation and Social Justice', and 'Churches Renewed in Mission'. Hollenweger, having left his position as Secretary of the Department of World Mission and Evangelism in 1971, not only was present in the category of 'Consultants and Fraternal Delegates', but also submitted a report entitled 'Evangelism Today: Mr. Chips goes back to Philadelphia' for the Committee on 'Evangelism and Relationships'.[65] The report was the story of a delegate returning home from Bangkok; meeting a variety of people, Mr Chips asks himself whether and how he should put into practice what has been said at the Conference. A member

62. Many of the young people who took part in the *Requiem* at the *Kirchentag* found the Bonhoeffer story hard to believe. Hollenweger took them to Flossenberg, where Bonhoeffer was executed, and a local pastor guided them around and told them of the treatment many had received in the prison. Their response was to make sure the story was heard more widely, and the drama was performed in many other places in Germany.

63. 'Ein Projekt mit Studierenden der Theol. Fakultät und anderen Fakultäten der Uni Zürich, in Zusammenarbeit mit der Kirchgemeinde St. Jakob am Stauffacher und Interessierten aus verschiedensten Orten.' For this particular occasion Hollenweger had been invited to contribute to an introductory evening on Bonhoeffer a week before (also open to the public), his time and the *Requiem*. The session was entitled, 'Die Kirche war stumm, wo sie hätte schreien müssen' ('The church was silent when she should have cried out').

64. See the sections 'Flowers and Songs' and 'Saints in Birmingham', in Chapter 2.

65. *Minutes and Reports of the Assembly of the Commission for World Mission and Evangelism of the World Council of Churches December 31 1972 and January 9-12 1973* (Geneva: WCC, 1973), pp. 3-4; list of delegates, p. 48; 'Evangelism Today', pp. 15-17.

of his church, for example, is an estate agent preventing black people from buying houses in the white areas of Philadelphia. When Mr Chips challenges him, 'Mr Rothschild' defends his actions by saying he has to please his customers and stay in business, adding that he gives generously to evangelistic and missionary programmes. Mr Chips suggests he get together with other estate agents (Christian and non-Christian) to change the situation, and perhaps some Bible study might help, but 'Mr Rothschild' disapproves of 'horizontalizing' the gospel, preferring the gospel of God's judgment. 'How can I tell him that a Christian is "saved" to do the unexpected, that he can take great risks and live more dangerously and thus more creatively?' wonders Mr Chips, concluding that it is more difficult to speak to a friend about judgment than to put it on paper or to preach it from the pulpit. The report was formally accepted 'with the suggestion that every delegate read it on the plane returning home'.[66]

This presentation in narrative form of some of the major issues addressed apparently grasped the imagination of colleagues. Mr Chips had arrived and Hollenweger found a persona and a method of combining fact and fiction through which to express not only the issues, but divergent responses to the question of, as J.H. Oldham had phrased it, 'what the Church of Christ was meant to be and to do in the world'.[67] A few months after the conference Hollenweger shared his experiences with a wider audience in 'Mr Chips Goes to Bangkok'.[68] The article is a mixture of Mr. Chips's description of some events, quotations from section reports, responses of participants (many named) in the sessions and private conversations, and Hollenweger's own thoughts. The result is a perceptive,

---

66. World Council of Chuches, *Minutes*, p. 15.

67. J.H. Oldham, *The World and the Gospel* (London: Church Missionary Society, 1916), p. 146. Oldham was the first Secretary of the Continuation Committee of the World Missionary Conference in Edinburgh in 1910, Secretary of the International Missionary Council formed in 1921, Chairman of the Research Committee for the Universal Christian Council on Life and Work and organizer of its Oxford Conference on 'Church, Community and State', in 1937, and was involved with the plans for the formation of the WCC, being made an Honorary President at its first assembly in 1948. His influential book *Christianity and the Race Problem* was published in 1924 by SCM Press, London. See Kathleen Bliss, 'Oldham, Joseph Houldsworth', in Lossky *et al.* (eds.), *Dictionary*, pp. 746-47.

68. Walter J. Hollenweger, 'Mr. Chips Goes to Bangkok', *Frontier* 16.2 (1973), pp. 93-100. The article first appeared in the conference newspaper according to Gerhard Linn in his Review of Hollenweger's *Glaube, Geist und Geister* in *International Review of Mission* 65.260 (1976), pp. 461-63 (461).

lively, 'warts and all' account of the conference proceedings which not only imparts the vital issues debated, but also keeps them grounded in reality—concepts are not divorced from people in concrete situations, be they from the northern or southern hemisphere. The response to the suggestion of R.J. Van der Veen in an open hearing that a hundred Christians from the conference should go to Hanoi, inform the American President they were going to put their bodies between the American bombers and North Vietnam, and make sure the action was interpreted clearly before the world public, caused Mr Chips considerable disquiet:

> Thinking very hard how he could avoid a decision without making it obvious he found a solution: 'I've got it,' he said, 'somebody must make it clear that the issue is very unclear. And then we can appoint a committee which will look into this very complex matter and that gets us off the hook.' He was relieved but not happy.

> 'Incidentally, that is exactly what happened', added Hollenweger.[69]

The following year in 'Mr. Chips Reviews Bangkok' Hollenweger considered 11 publications about the Bangkok Conference.[70] Finding most of the publications were not in English, Mr Chips enlisted some of his teacher colleagues to read the French, German, Swedish and Dutch books (no one could be found to translate the Polish articles and the British report had not yet been published) and they gathered to discuss them. Thus four characters compared and contrasted elements of the various reports, with an opportunity to voice different queries and reservations. The subjects selected naturally reflect Hollenweger's main interests. He includes how delegates responded to the issue of the relationship between personal salvation of the soul and social salvation of the body, in which debate the expected polarization did not materialize, either between Westerners and Third World delegates, or between evangelicals and liberals. The Bible studies led by Hans-Ruedi Weber, criticized by some evangelicals because of his method of taking contemporary situations and leading from there to the theological and hermeneutical questions are discussed, as is the inclusion in some of the publications of reports and evaluations by non-Westerners.

69. 'Mr. Chips Goes to Bangkok', p. 96. For a brief summary of the Bangkok conference see Ans J. Van Der Bent, 'Ecumenical Conferences', in Lossky *et al.* (eds.), *Dictionary*, p. 332.

70. Hollenweger, 'Mr. Chips Reviews Bangkok', *International Review of Mission* 63.249 (1974), pp. 132-36.

For German-speaking readers 'Mr. Chips' became 'Professor Unrat', with the particular associations of Heinrich Mann's novel of that title.[71] Mr Chips and Professor Unrat went on to explore other issues during the next two years. 'Saints in Birmingham' is available in English (see Chapter 2 above), as is 'Mr. Chips looks for the Holy Spirit in Pentecostal Theology'.[72] In this article Hollenweger addressed the academy and the church on pneumatology, a subject he considered in the mid 1970s not to be strong in classical Pentecostalism or neo-Pentecostalism (the charismatic movement) and to be in need of rethinking by others.[73] Most of the narrative used in the first part of 'Saints in Birmingham' concerning Mr Chips's visit to 'an evening of spirituality' introduces Hollenweger's discussion of charismatic ecclesiology, hermeneutics and parapsychological phenomena. The topics raised in story form—the presence of Christians of different denominations and backgrounds; the hospitable, informal and participative nature of the meeting ('Well,' thought Chips, 'is this a party or a prayer meeting?');[74] the 'litany of saints' which included St Francis, Gandhi, Dag Hammerskjold, George Fox, Karl Marx and Bach; the despair voiced at the impenetrability of academic theology and hope that the Holy Spirit would assist in casting light on what was important or false; medical healing and prayer for healing—form the basis of critical analysis of Pentecostalism in the 1970s.

'Mr. Chips in Switzerland' is the third narrative exegesis available in English.[75] Mr Chips engages as an outsider (!) with Swiss and Swiss

71. See Gerhard Linn's Review of *Glaube, Geist und Geister*.

72. Walter J. Hollenweger, 'Mr. Chips Looks for the Holy Spirit in Pentecostal Theology', *Journal of Theology for Southern Africa* 12 (1975), pp. 39-50, and *Theological Renewal* 4 (1976), pp. 12-20.

73. In *Theological Renewal*, p. 12. Two decades later he believed this was was still an important area for further work. See 'Towards a Pentecostal Missiology', in T. Dayanandan Francis and Israel Selvanayagam (eds.), *Many Christian Voices in Christian Mission: Essays in Honour of J.E. Lesslie Newbigin* (Madras: The Christian Literature Society, 1994), pp. 59-79 (71): 'Pentecostalism has so far not developed a pneumatology which fits its experience. That is all the more astonishing since one would expect Pentecostals and Charismatics to be strong on pneumatology. This is not the case. They are strong on experiences of the Spirit, on pneumapraxis, but weak on the interpretation of these experiences.'

74. Hollenweger, 'Mr. Chips looks for the Holy Spirit', *Theological Renewal*, p. 14.

75. Hollenweger, 'Mr. Chips in Switzerland', in J.G. Davies (ed.), *Looking to the Future* (Institute for the Study of Worship and Religious Architecture, University of

Christian responses to the presence of foreign workers, the country's arms trade, experimental eucharistic and Christmas liturgies (three black kings who arrive empty-handed remind Chips of the angry words of Africans at the Bangkok Conference to the continuation of colonial missionary attitudes), the role of the church in the world, and banking. In a footnote Hollenweger says that a theological title for the essay could be 'The Process of *leitourgia* in a Given Social and Political Context' but 'In this piece of narrative theology I try *to do* what others are *writing* about', that is doing theology and liturgiology in a style that makes it possible for lay people to contribute.[76] The narrative takes the now familiar form of a combination of 'invented' people and meetings and accounts of actual events, which are documented from independent sources in the footnotes.

The 'Professor Unrat' versions of all these, and another narrative not available in English, 'Professor Unrat in Paris', where he attends a spiritualist meeting and encounters parapsychological phenomena, were published in German in the book *Glaube, Geist und Geister: Professor Unrat zwischen Bangkok und Birmingham* in 1975.[77] The book was quite widely reviewed in German, Dutch, Spanish, French and English, almost entirely favourably.[78] Many reviewers commented on the accessibility of the narrative form, including David Bosch: 'His light-hearted—sometimes even flippant—style is deceiving... Almost without noticing it, the reader is being introduced to serious theology. It is done in such a way that the reader cannot but feel himself involved.'[79] 'A delicious little book which doesn't lack depth', concluded the reviewer for a Benedictine publication.[80] Gerhard Linn observed that although the book is composed of

Birmingham, Papers read at an international symposium on prospects for worship, religious architecture and socio-religious studies; Birmingham: University of Birmingham, 1976), pp. 13-33.

76. Hollenweger, 'Mr. Chips in Switzerland', p. 29 n. 1.

77. Frankfurt am Main: Otto Lembeck, 1975. Professor Unrat in Paris is also included in vol. 3 of *Intercultural Theology*, *Geist und Materie*, Hollenweger's search for an intercultural and ecumenical pneumatology, pp. 69-86.

78. An exception was the review by Peter Beyerhaus in *Theologische Blätter* 3 (1977), pp. 139-40, whose antipathy to the dominant trends of the Bangkok Conference at which his proposal for the acceptance of his 'Frankfurt Declaration' had been rejected had been noted by Hollenweger in 'Mr. Chips Goes to Bangkok' and 'Mr. Chips Reviews Bangkok'.

79. David Bosch, Review of Hollenweger, *Glaube, Geist und Geister*, *Missionalia* 4.1 (1976), pp. 43-44.

80. 'Petit livre délicieux qui ne manque pas de profondeur', NE in *Irénikon* 4,

separate articles, unity is to be found in the theme which they all address—the possibility of experiencing the presence of the Spirit'—and the 'sub-theme'—that this theological question is of shared importance to the Third World and the West. Linn continued, 'The book's pleasing style is combined with a surprisingly high level of information', not only in the bibliography, which demonstrates that it is a scholarly book, but in the way in which the theological information is communicated to the theologically untrained reader, for example on Old Testament understanding of the Spirit, Paul's view of the Lord's Supper, and church history (about Zwingli and Fox), 'to the extent that this information is needed to understand the present time and the decisions to be taken by Christians today'.[81]

Comment

The concerns of intercultural theology arose primarily through twentieth-century ecumenical and mission studies, which have yet to impinge on the traditional theological disciplines—at least to the extent and in all the ways Hollenweger has perceived necessary. It is interesting that, born of modernity, they have been more responsive to the situations that typify postmodernity (see Introduction) than the older disciplines, still perhaps more geared towards dealing with the scars of the church's intellectual struggle with the Enlightenment than with Christianity in the contemporary world. Ustorf has commented on Hollenweger's inclusion of what was normally omitted from academic theology:

> the Christian experience in the diversity of its oral and often non-western expression, the theological quality and structure of charismatic phenomena, the marxist critique, the usage of art, drama, narrative and music as 'theological' languages, and his abandonment of watertight theological systems

and sees in this 'not a return to a past naivity or to a pre-enlightened simplicity', but 'an attempt to leave the narrow confines that theological discourse has erected in order to get out of the troubled waters of the post-Christendom era'.[82]

Hollenweger's intercultural approach is an attempt to put into practice

Prieuré Bénédictin Chevetogne, Belgique (1978), p. 596.
    81. Gerhard Linn, Review of Hollenweger, *Glaube, Geist und Geister*, p. 462.
    82. Ustorf, 'The Magpies', p. 28.

what many of the participants in the symposium on 'Paradigm Change in Theology' considered should be the way forward. He in fact shows great confidence in the Western academy's specialized expertise and knowledge by acting on the insights that have arisen from its endeavours, but his contribution in this regard has not yet been generally recognized. This is partly, I suggest, because the wide variety of material he considers and the variety of methods he employs (as shown in Chapter 2) do not place him easily within the ambit of any of the traditional theological disciplines. Moreover, his academic articles, as the footnotes indicate, have been mainly for Pentecostal, missiological and ecumenical publications so that those in general theological journals have largely reached an audience unaware of the extent of his scholarship in the areas which nurtured the development of his intercultural approach. The intimate relationship he has perceived between Pentecostalism, ecumenism and intercultural theology does not fit the categorization and increased specialization of the academy. It is also partly because his deliberate efforts to communicate the fruits of scholarship to non-academics can easily be viewed as simplifying complex subjects by those who consider the academy to be the arbiter of correct Christian thinking and practice. To those, however, who consider the academy to be one contributor among others to the ongoing process of Christian faith and life, Hollenweger's approach is a necessary step towards opening a meaningful dialogue between the academy and the world for the benefit of both. Of course, this means power-sharing and will evoke resistance from those who have enjoyed unquestioned, if increasingly marginalized, authority.

Hollenweger's extensive writings show how stimulating intercultural encounter and dialogue can be. The 'others' are necessary for insights and correction that 'insiders' cannot, without difficulty, obtain themselves, and for this they need to retain their 'otherness' but find a way of communicating it. That is why the search for 'Truth' cannot be short-circuited by a ruling group, be it from the Western academy, church and culture, or any other, by imposing a norm to which others are expected to conform and by which they are judged.

In his characteristic role as a frontier-crosser, Hollenweger as Professor of Mission moved back and forth, mediating between the Western academy and the academies developing in other parts of the world: to the West he counselled cognisance of diversity and the potential field of study of oral, as distinct from literary cultures; to the others he counselled the need for analysis and reflection and the need to relate to the history of the church. To everyone he stressed the need for sensitive, appropriate and critical Christian response to the concrete realities of local and global, historical and contemporary, contexts.

This was thoroughly in keeping with his understanding of the Bible; the connection between authors and their contexts giving rise to the plurality of biblical writings was extended to the contemporary diversity of Christianity and cultures. Just as he found myth to be a useful content and method in the Bible and today, so he recognized syncretism as belonging to the Bible and contemporary Christianity. Hollenweger, against the flow of Western attitudes to this issue, was less concerned about preserving Christian identity expressed in traditional Western terms than to point out the realities of the situation for churches everywhere. Thus he affirmed Leonardo Boff's view that syncretism is a normal step in any creative encounter of the gospel in a local context.[83] Christopher Duraisingh in an extended editorial on themes for the forthcoming Salvador World Mission Conference in 1996, commented that many Christians in the West are frightened by the term, though processes of syncretism are evident in the Bible. He sees this as related to religion being 'reduced to a set of doctrinal beliefs and fixed liturgical practices' rather than an ongoing process in dynamic cultural situations, in which scenario syncretism can be positive or negative. He noted that:

> Such a process of integration has gone on throughout the history of Christianity both in the east and west. It is only recently, as churches in the third world seek to integrate their religious-cultural memories and their Christian identity, that such a process has become intensely controversial. Unfortunately, as Boff rightly claims, 'our understanding of syncretism has come from those who have been afraid of it: the defenders of theological and institutional knowledge'.[84]

83. On each occasion when he addresses the issue of syncretism Hollenweger refers to Leonardo Boff, *Church, Charism and Power* (London: SCM Press, 1985). See *Pentecostalism: Origins*, p. 132; 'Towards a Pentecostal Missiology', p. 70; 'Theology and the Future', p. 1028; 'A Plea for a Theologically Responsible Syncretism', *Missionalia* 25.1 (1997), pp. 5-18 (7); 'Syncretism and Capitalism', *Asian Journal of Pentecostal Studies* 2.1 (1999), pp. 1-16 (a different form of the previous article).

84. Christopher Duraisingh, 'Editorial', *International Review of Mission* 85.337 (1996), pp. 155-70 (165, 166). Boff reference, *Church*, p. 89. See Juan Sepúlveda, 'To Overcome the Fear of Syncretism: A Latin American Perspective', in Lynne Price, Juan Sepúlveda and Graeme Smith (eds.), *Mission Matters* (Frankfurt am Main: Peter Lang, 1997), pp. 157-68, for a Pentecostal consideration in relation to Chile.

Hollenweger's position developed both from his biblical scholarship and from his long study of the worldwide diversity of Pentecostalism and it is not until the 1990s that he writes explicitly on the subject. Considering the oral roots of Pentecostalism in the USA, South Africa, Zaire, Mexico, Korea, England and Chile in Part I of *Pentecostalism: Origins* (1997), he concludes with a chapter entitled 'A Plea for a Theologically Responsible Syncretism'.[85] 'The question is not "syncretism, yes or no", but what kind of syncretism? Already the Bible is an example of theologically responsible syncretism.'[86] In two journal articles he added that all forms of Christianity, including the Western ones, are syncretistic; the problem is that we do not recognize our own syncretisms.[87] Writing for a general theological encyclopedia he averred:

> Not only must the church be syncretistic, it must produce different syncretisms in different cultures. The touchstones for a theologically responsible syncretism—over and against a theologically irresponsible syncretism—are first, the willingness to learn from the biblical authors the methodology of such a theologically responsible syncretism… [Second] a willingness to enter into dialogue with Christians from other syncretistic backgrounds.[88]

85. Summarizing his conclusions from this extensive survey in the articles in 'A Plea', p. 7 and 'Syncretism', p. 3, Hollenweger wrote: 'There is… no question that the different forms of Pentecostalism are syncretistic: the transformation of Shamanism into Korean Pentecostalism, the black and African roots in American Pentecostalism, the Africanization of Christianity in Congolese Kimbanguism and in South African Zionism, the excavation of old Mexican cultural elements in Mexican Pentecostalism, the integration of popular religion in Chilean Pentecostalism etc.'

86. *Pentecostalism: Origins*, p. 132. 'A Plea', p. 7; 'Syncretism', p. 3.

87. In both articles he draws on the research of one of his post-graduate students, Jane Collier, whose book *The Culture of Economism: An Exploration of Barriers to Faith-as-Praxis* was published in the Studies in the Intercultural History of Christianity Series (Frankfurt am Main: Peter Lang, 1990). Collier, a lecturer in economics at Cambridge University, argued that economics was not a neutral science, but one that uses prejudices and value judgments, that is, decisions are determined by faith options and this should be recognized by economists. There are other faith options that could be taken—an opportunity, as Hollenweger notes, for a theologically responsible syncretism. 'A Plea', pp. 15-17; 'Syncretism', pp. 13-15.

88. 'Theology and the Future', pp. 1028-1029. Hollenweger observes that the Western churches 'probably owe more to their Celtic and Germanic ancestors and to Greek and Roman culture than to the Bible (think of our burial rites, some of our buildings, our liturgies, our liturgical vestments, our church music)…' See also Walter J. Hollenweger, 'Pluralismus als Gabe und Aufgabe: Die Zukunft des Christentums in

Hollenweger's 'touchstones' have not been considered stringent enough by Lesslie Newbigin. Responding in a private letter to Hollenweger's contribution to the book produced in his honour, Newbigin wrote:

> I agree with you that there is a sense in which Christianity must always be syncretistic. You rightly ask for a 'responsible' syncretism, but you do not indicate the criteria for responsible judgment. In my view the criterion can only be Christological.

Hollenweger replied,

> Responsible syncretism is not learned by learning a few criteria. It is rather learned like playing the violin. One goes to a maestro… Our maestros are the biblical authors. They show us standards and patterns. That is why we learn Greek and Hebrew, the art of exegesis so that we get a glimpse of their craftsmanship, their workmanship, their method on how they transform pagan material so that it becomes transparent for the Kingdom of God.[89]

In this brief exchange we glimpse the different approaches of a systematic and an intercultural theologian. Hollenweger values method, with all its attendant risks, above imposing typically Western dogmatic arbitration before, as it were, the story is finished.

Turning to his use of narrative exegesis, Hollenweger developed a corrective to the Western tendency to abstraction by concretizing and personalizing the process of theologizing, thus making it more accessible for all to participate. The use of narrative also, as he himself recognized, created questions rather than providing answers to theological issues, in that the complexities and uncertainties of theological decision making were laid bare for all to see. That was the price to be paid for a 'body-of-Christ' theology, a more precarious, yet realistic and responsible, state of affairs.[90]

multireligiöser Gesellschaft' ('Pluralism as Gift and Task: The Future of Christianity in Multi-Faith Society') in Johannes Lähnemann (ed.), *Das Wiedererwachen der Religionen als pädagogische Herausforderung* (Hamburg: E.B. Verlag Rissen, 1992), pp. 65-76; and Hans Norbert Janowski and Michael Straus, 'Glauben lernen wie das Violinspiel: Gespräch mit Professor Walter Hollenweger' ('Learning to Have Faith Like Playing the Violin: Interview with Professor Walter Hollenweger'), *Evangelische Kommentare* 6 (1993), pp. 343-47.

89. Hollenweger's article 'Towards a Pentecostal Missiology'. Newbigin's letter is undated. Hollenweger's reply, 25 January 1995. Copies of correspondence courtesy of Walter Hollenweger. In the other articles by Hollenweger where he discusses syncretism, concrete examples are given on how biblical authors transform existing material.

90. 'Body-of-Christ' theology, see Chapter 3.

The next chapter addresses the other side of the relationship: Hollen-weger's attention to the local Western churches and people outside the ghetto. Like the theological academy, the church does not exist for itself but, as Bonhoeffer clearly understood, for others.[91]

---

91. Dietrich Bonhoeffer, *Letters and Papers from Prison* (ed. Eberhard Bethge; London: SCM Press, enlarged edition 1971), p. 382: 'The church is the church only when it exists for others.'

Chapter 5

PARTICIPATING IN MISSION

It is 10 o'clock in the evening of 14 June 1998. An animated crowd of
people are arriving, laughing and chattering, at a pub in Bayreuth to celebrate the performance they have just taken part in. Some of them are
Protestant, some Catholic, some with no church affiliation. Some belong to
an amateur dramatic group, some to a church choir or a concert choir,
some to a student orchestra; family and friends accompany them; there are
a few people from the district church adult education organization which
facilitated the event. Everyone is in high spirits, for the performance has
been well received by a capacity audience of 500 people of all ages in the
church where it took place.[1] In the middle of the crowd is Professor Walter
Hollenweger, co-author with Estella Korthaus of *Eine 'Unerhörte' Frau:
Maria von Wedemeyer—Bonhoeffer's Braut,* the drama featuring the
'unheard' fiancée of Dietrich Bonhoeffer, which has just been acted out
with music, song, dance and visual effects.[2] The local daily newspaper
will subsequently give a lengthy and favourable account of the play, the
love story of Maria and Dietrich, recounted through excerpts from Maria's
recently published diary and letters, punctuated with the haunting refrains
of a folk song, 'Wenn ich ein Vöglein wär' ('If I were a little bird'), and
hymn, Bonhoeffer's 'Von guten Mächten wunderbar geborgen' ('With
every power for good to stay and guide me').[3] The reporter thanks heaven

1.   Erlöserkirche Altstadt, Hans-Meiser Strasse. The event was organized by
Evangelisches Bildungswerk Bayreuth/Bad Berneck. Two further performances took
place in Bischofsgrün and Weiden on 28 June and 5 July.
2.   The group had worked with a manuscript. The drama was published in 1998 by
Metanoia Verlag, Kindhausen, Switzerland as *Hommage an Maria von Wedemeyer—
Bonhoeffers Braut.*
3.   Ruth-Alice von Bismarck and Ulrich Kabitz (eds.), *Love Letters from Cell 92:
Dietrich Bonhoeffer and Maria von Wedemeyer 1943–1945* (trans. John Brownjohn;
London: HarperCollins, 1994 [German original 1992]).

for a message understood and highly valued on this side of the Rolling Stones and Guildo Horn.[4]

Walter Hollenweger at the beginning of a visit to Bayreuth where he was also to lecture, take part in a panel discussion 'Healing as gift and task for doctors and pastors', and lead a workshop for the group who had planned a Service of Anointing at which he was to preach, was in his element. Despite his 71 years and having driven 800 km from his village home in Switzerland that same day he was telling stories, answering questions, making jokes.[5] I note his involvement with an institutional church organization does not confine him to formal church settings. I observe the ecumenical nature of the group of people and the presence of non-Christians. The means of evangelistic communication being celebrated is not a sermon, but a drama that has involved participants physically and emotionally as well as cognitively. The subject matter of the drama, a counterpart to *Requiem for Bonhoeffer*, is the real-life, contextually situated, human and religious story of the relationship between Dietrich Bonhoeffer, and his fiancée, Maria von Wedemeyer, told from her perspective. She was a woman 18 years younger than Bonhoeffer, from a German military family, whose father and older brother both died fighting for their country in the 1939–45 war, almost at the end of which Bonhoeffer was executed as a traitor. I note both the liturgical and academic elements of Hollenweger's visit, the interest in healing, the willingness to engage in dialogue with those outside the church.

This snapshot of Hollenweger, theologian and evangelist, in 'retirement' provides an introduction to our consideration of his understanding of mission, and therefore also of the church.[6] In contrast to the previous chapters where the academy has been the starting point for our reflections, this chapter begins with the public in the world. *Maria von Wedemeyer*

4.   Eva Bartylla, 'Der leise Laut der Liebe: Beeindruckende Premiere des Theaterprojekts "Eine unerhörte Frau"', *Nordbayerischer Kurier* (Tuesday 16 June, 1998), p. 11: 'dem Himmel sei Dank—... eine Message jenseits von Rolling Stones, Guildo Horn oder FWM gehört, geschätzt und verstanden wird.'

5.   The panel discussion on 17 June, 'Heilung als Gabe und Aufgabe für Ärtze und Seelsorge', with two doctors, a psychologist and Hollenweger as theologian, was open to the public and advertised in the Evangelisches Bildungswerk programme for March to August 1998. The Service of Anointing on 16 June at which Hollenweger preached was also open to the public and had been planned by the workgroup 'Salben und Segnen' ('Anointing and Blessing') of the Evangelisches Bildungswerk.

6.   I accompanied Walter and Erica Hollenweger on this visit to Bayreuth and was present at all the events mentioned.

brings Hollenweger's interest in Bonhoeffer to attention again and is most appropriate for introducing our topic: participating in mission. Bonhoeffer's thinking and action was a key factor in the development of Hollenweger's interpretation of Christian participation in God's (or Christ's) mission in the world, summed up in Bonhoeffer's beliefs that 'the church is the church only when it exists for others' and therefore that it should respond to the agenda of the world.[7] From the sometimes narrow concerns of Swiss Pentecostalism in the 1940s and 1950s,[8] Hollenweger entered the international ecumenical arena at a time when mission was a contentious issue.

The Church for Others

Debate on relations between (mainly Western) missionary societies and local churches, the relationship of Christianity to traditional religions and other world faiths and the conflicting national and individual demands of Christianity—tensions which had been signalled at the International Missionary Conference in Edinburgh in 1910—became increasingly pressing by the middle of the century. In the context of the transfers of political control, the relinquishment of Western hegemony, the rise of communism and fascism and the question of Christian loyalties in relation to church and state policies in Europe during the 1939–45 war, J.C. Hoekendijk, in preparation for the International Missionary Conference at Willingen in 1952, had launched an attack on a church-centred approach to mission which separated salvation history from world history. The subject of evangelism is, he said, the Messiah, and the aim of evangelism is to do what Israel expected the Messiah to do, establish shalom (peace, integrity, community, harmony, justice). Mission, he stated, was God's mission, and the church is a function of mission; the order should be God–

---

7.   Bonhoeffer, *Letters*, p. 382.
8.   Addressing the European Pentecostal Theology Association in 1999, Hollenweger recalled this period: 'When I was a young Pentecostal pastor, my ministry was questioned because my wife used nail-varnish and wore a wooden necklace. My ministry was put at risk because I refused to criticise young female converts who wore short hairstyles… A Prophecy by a woman, who had even put rouge on her lips would have been outright rejected in the Swiss Pentecostal movement in the fifties. We may laugh nowadays at such childish prohibitions. At that time it was a dead-serious affair. It was the topic of night-long theological debates amongst the Swiss Pentecostal pastors.' See 'The Challenge of Reconciliation', *Journal of the European Pentecostal Theological Association* vol. 19 (1999), pp. 5-16 (13-14).

World–Church, not God–Church–World.[9] Hoekendijk's perspective was influential in ecumenical circles during the following years and is associated with what is commonly referred to as *missio Dei* thinking.

At the WCC Assembly in Delhi in 1961, the year the International Missionary Council merged with the WCC, a major study on the Missionary Structure of the Congregation was authorized under the auspices of the Department of Studies in Evangelism. Hans Jochen Margull who was a key figure in influencing the direction of the Study wrote:

> 'What must the structure of a congregation be like so as not to hinder the proclamation of the gospel?' This is the first question in the introduction to the study... Once we have acknowledged that structures condition the congregation's life and witness, we must face the fact that they can distort or veil the gospel...structures are heretical when they prevent the congregation from penetrating every geographic and social realm, thus standing between the gospel and the world.[10]

9.   See J.C. Hoekendijk, 'The Call to Evangelism', *International Review of Missions* 39 (1950), pp. 167-75. For the Willingen Report and addresses see Norman Goodall (ed.), *Missions Under the Cross* (London: Edinburgh House, 1953). Hoekendijk was Professor of Modern Church History at Utrecht 1953–65 and Professor of Mission at Union Theological Seminary 1965–75. For Hollenweger on Hoekendijk see, 'Hans Hoekendijk: Ein ökumenischer Souffleur' ('an ecumenical prompter'), *Leben und Glauben* 52.15 (1977), p. 10; review of Gianfranco Coffele's book *Johannes Christiaan Hoekendijk: Da una teologia della missione ad una teologia missionaria* (Rome: Universita Gregoriana Editrice, 1976), *International Review of Mission* 66.262 (1977), pp. 192-93. Here Hollenweger wrote 'Coffele does not attempt to portray Hoekendijk as a scholar, a Christian, a translator, an incorrigible humanist, a marxian Bible expositor, an artist, and ecumenical operator and university teacher. Instead he describes Hoekendijk as he appears in his writings and books. It is a very detailed and competent presentation of Hoekendijk's *thinking*...' Hollenweger, having known Hoekendijk personally, described him as 'a pious radical, an agent of the Dutch and French resistance against the Germans and for the Jews...' (p. 192). See particularly the section 'Hoekendijk', in *Umgang mit Mythen*, pp. 45-62, where Hollenweger gives extended consideration to Hoekendijk's life and work: he was not only knowledgeable in Bonhoefferian theology, said Hollenweger, through his participation in the Dutch resistance movement, he lived it ('Hoekendijk war nicht nur ein Kenner der Bonhoefferschen Theologie, er hat als Theologe in der holländischen Widerstandsbewegung die Spannungen und Verheissungen der Bonhoefferschen Theologie gelebt') (p. 45). This article was first published as 'Johannes Christian Hoekendijk: Pluriformität der Kirche' ('The Pluriformity of the Church') *Reformatio* 16.10 (1967), pp. 663-77.

10.   Hans Jochen Margull, 'Structures for Missionary Congregations', *International Review of Missions* 52.208 (1963), pp. 433-46.

Hollenweger, who succeeded Margull as Executive Secretary of the Department of Studies in Evangelism, paid tribute to his colleague and friend's leadership in the decisive years of the study. Margull's understanding of mission, he said, was not the transfer of ideology but the disclosure of freedom in the light of biblical and Christian tradition.[11] Hollenweger briefly summarized the study as follows:

> [it] has tried to understand afresh the meaning of 'mission' and the meaning of 'church', how the Christian message (*Evangelium*) should be included in 'the agenda of the world', and which of the church's structures are obsolete and need changing. It has directed its attention especially to the forms of worship, to the parochial system, and to the pastoral ministry. It has proposed far-reaching and bold experiments.[12]

A number of working groups were set up to carry out research on the missionary structure of congregations. The Western European Group met first in 1962 and, under the chairmanship of Professor J.G. Davies of the University of Birmingham, proceeded by producing individual papers and

11. 'Im Ökumenischen Rat der Kirchen leitete Margull in entscheidenden Jahren das Referat für Fragen der Verkündigung, das den Sammelband *Mission als Strukturprinzip* und den Schlussbericht *Die Kirche für andere* herausgab. Beide Publikationen spielten sofort in allen Kirchen und in der Ökumene eine grosse Rolle.' In 'Als die Ökumene noch jung war und die Studenten die Welt gewinnen wollten...: Versuch über Hans Jochen Margull, der 1995 70 Jahre alt geworden wäre' ('When ecumenism was still young and students wanted to win the world... An attempt [to write] about Hans Jochen Margull, who would have been 70 years old in 1995') in *Jahrbuch Mission 1995* vol. 27 (ed. Verband Evangelischer Missionskonferenz; Hamburg: Missionshilfe Verlag, 1995), pp. 175-86 (177). An editorial introduction to the article describes the two men's professional careers and Margull's proposal that Hollenweger take over from him as Executive Secretary (175-76). Hollenweger's previous article on Margull in *Jahrbuch Mission 1993*. *Mission als Strukturprinzip*: *Ein Arbeitsbuch zur Frage missionarischer Gemeinden* (Genf: RK, 1965), was edited by Margull. The English version, re-edited and translated by Thomas Wieser was published the following year by Epworth Press, London as *Planning for Mission* and includes Margull's article 'Gathering at the Point of Mission', pp. 146-48. A selection of Margull's writings and introduction to his thinking, *Hans Jochen Margull, Zeugnis und Dialog*, edited by Missionsakademie an der Universität Hamburg, was published by Verlag an der Lottbek in 1992.

12. Hollenweger, 'A Church for Others', *Study Encounter* 3.2 (1967), pp. 84-99 (85). In this article Hollenweger correlated findings from enquiry made through questionnaires in Portugal, Belgium, France, French-speaking Switzerland and Italy on responses to the French version of *Planning for Mission*, *Vers une église pour les autres* (cf. n. 22), including a whole section of criticisms (pp. 91-95).

then incorporating them into preliminary reports representing the agreement of participants. The North American Working Group, taking a more sociological than theological approach, responded to new forms of missionary action taking place and a sense of urgency about issues such as Civil Rights in the United States. The Eastern European Group was similarly concerned with specific practical issues.[13] The Western European Group submitted its final report, *The Church for Others*, in 1966. It was adopted by the Working Committee of the Department of Studies in Evangelism, together with the resolution that the WCC be asked to publish it, as recorded by Hollenweger in the Minutes.[14] *The Church for Others* was published the following year, together with the report of the North American Working Group, *The Church for the World*.[15] The subsequent WCC Department report 'Renewal in Mission' for the Assembly in Uppsala in 1968 relied heavily on the two regional reports so far completed as part of the Study on the Missionary Structure of the Congregation.[16]

13. Introduction to *Planning for Mission*, pp. 5-11. This book brought together a number of the contributions and papers produced in the course of the study, almost entirely from the Western European and North American Working Groups, with the aim of sharing the insights so far gained with a larger audience. A preliminary report by the DDR group drawn up in Spring 1966 was published in *Study Encounter* 3.2 (1967), pp. 100-108, under the title 'The Congregation for Others'.

14. Minutes: Session of the Working Committee of the Department on Studies in Evangelism, Boldern, Männerdorf, August 22-26, 1966, p. 4.

15. *The Church for Others and The Church for the World* (Geneva: WCC, 1967). Another resolution seeking the production of 'a film to present central themes of the Missionary Structure of the Congregation study for possible presentation to the 4th Assembly of the WCC and for subsequent use across the world' did not reach fruition. *The Church for Others and The Church for the World* was also published in German (1967), Spanish (1967) and Portuguese (1969).

16. *Drafts for Sections: Prepared for the Fourth Assembly of the World Council of Churches, Uppsala, Sweden, 1968* (Geneva: WCC, 1967). The report itself is brief— less than 5 pages, 28-32; the commentary, which quotes extensively from the *The Church for Others and The Church for the World* (and from other recent ecumenical discussions) is lengthy—32-51. In a later article, 'The Church for Others—Ten Years After', in Davies (ed.), *Research Bulletin 1977*, pp. 82-96, Hollenweger noted: 'The draft of that section report was hotly contested in Germany and Scandinavia and also in the Anglo-Saxon world. Some Norwegian delegates went so far as to threaten the resignation of the Norwegian Church if this draft were not withdrawn' (85). He continued by referring to Jörg Müller's explanation of the wide-ranging discussion and contestation of 'Renewal in Mission': it was understood and it questioned normal church routine see *Uppsala II. Eine redaktionsgeschichtliche Studie zu Sektion II der*

The Church for Others, its mixed reception, responses to 'Renewal in Mission' at Uppsala, and subsequent debates demand more attention than can be given to them here—attention which is certainly warranted: *The Church for Others* makes remarkably refreshing and stimulating reading even 30 years or so after it was produced.[17] Although it provoked wide interest when published, it seems that its proposals and their implications were too radical to be adopted. Dietrich Werner suggests that, with hindsight, the report was too optimistic about Western secularization and not concerned enough with worship and spirituality for the renewal of congregational life.[18] However, it is not entirely forgotten: extracts appear in the collections of international ecumenical and missionary documents recently published and referred to in my previous chapter.[19] Thomas commented:

> Both groups began with the premise that the main task of mission is to discern God's presence in the world. The aim and goal of mission was

4. Vollversammlung des Oekumenischen Rates der Kirchen Uppsala 1968 (Frankfurt am Main: Peter Lang, 1977).

17. Jongeneel and van Engelen comment that 'After Willingen the concept of *missio Dei* conquered the ecumenical world' but received severe criticism from some evangelicals, including Arthur Glasser, who stated that 'the WCC secularized version of *missio Dei* had gained the upper hand and that the concept had degenerated into a green light for revolutionary thought and action'; In their article 'Contemporary Currents in Missiology', in F.J. Verstraelen *et al.* (eds.), *Missiology: An Ecumenical Introduction* (Grand Rapids: Eerdmans, 1995), pp. 438-57 (448), Jongeneel and van Engelen comment that 'After Willingen the concept of *missio Dei* conquered the ecumenical world' but received severe criticism from some evangelicals, including Arthur Glasser, who stated that 'the WCC secularized version of *missio Dei* had gained the upper hand and that the concept had degenerated into a green light for revolutionary thought and action'. Kinnamon and Cope (eds.), note in *The Ecumenical Movement*, that 'Willingen, coming at the end of the colonial period, represents a turning point in ecumenical reflection. Its attack on a church-centred view of mission…led gradually to significant differences between "evangelical" and "ecumenical" approaches' (p. 339). Efiong Utok suggests that one of the currents which led to the organization of international evangelical conferences in the 1960s (Wheaton and Berlin) was growing uneasiness with conciliar missiology and states that 'Wheaton was billed as a Counter-World Council of Churches movement'. E. Utok, 'From Wheaton to Lausanne', in Scherer and Bevans (eds.), *New Directions*, 2, pp. 99-112.

18. Dietrich Werner, 'Missionary Structure of the Congregation', in Lossky, *et al.* (eds.), *Dictionary of the Ecumenical*, pp. 699-701 (700-701).

19. Kinnamon and Cope (eds.), *The Ecumenical Movement*, pp. 347-50; Thomas (ed.), *Readings*, pp. 91-92.

described as 'shalom' by the European group and as 'humanization' by the
North Americans. Existing forms of parish life were severely criticized as
'come structures'. Favored were 'go structures', through which the church
could help victims of injustice, racial hatred, loneliness, and other personal
crises... the congregation in mission was to be a flexible structure evolving
around specific needs of people in the world.[20]

Hollenweger was closely involved with the preparation of *The Church
for Others* and 'Renewal in Mission' and had been a participant at the
Western European Group meetings from the outset. That he was also
personally committed to the approach and recommendations of the reports
is clear from his own writings. Two of his contributions to the ongoing
deliberations of the Western European Group are included in the pre-
report publication *Planning for Mission*. One is a short piece entitled 'A
Reminder from Church History', in which he drew attention to the new
structure of proclamation and mission introduced by the arrival of Irish
missionary monasteries in sixth- and seventh-century Switzerland among
the Alemmanic tribe, which operated outside the parochial system of the
Latin church.[21] The other is a theological sketch of reflections on the God–
world–church relationship under the title of 'Christus extra et intra muros
ecclesiae'. In a somewhat polemical vein Hollenweger argues that the
history Christ initiated does not repeat the past but creates new things.
From the Old and New Testaments he demonstrates that God is neither to
be confounded with the natural world and religious rites nor entirely
separated from them. This, he suggests, allows the world to be viewed as
secular, and therefore sanctified. Those outside the walls of the church and
those inside have been redeemed, even if the former do not recognize it,
therefore structures are needed that allow those inside and outside to
express their joint concern and action for new relationships with neigh-
bour, the created world and God—understood by those inside as a theological expression and by those outside as a human expression ('profane
sacraments').[22] These themes—God being active in history, allowing the
'world to be the world', seeing Christ's presence outside as well as inside

20. Thomas (ed.), *Readings*, p. 90.

21. Hollenweger, 'A Reminder from Church History', in Wieser (ed.), *Planning for
Mission*, p. 153.

22. Hollenweger, 'Christus extra et intra muros ecclesiae', in Wieser (ed.),
Planning for Mission, pp. 56-61. Also included in George Casalis, Walter J.
Hollenweger and Paul Keller (eds.), *Vers une église pour les autres: A la recherche de
structures pour des communautés missionaires* (Geneva: WCC, 1967), pp. 32-35.

the church, partnership between those inside and outside—were central to *The Church for Others*.[23]

More particularly, his commitment can be seen in the energy with which he fulfilled his secretarial and editorial roles at the WCC by furthering the dissemination not only of the study reports, but also of responses to them, through a constant stream of articles between 1965 and 1969 in the WCC publications *Concept* and *Study Encounter*.[24] He also spoke on the subject. *The British Weekly* of 1 December 1966 described Hollenweger in an article headed 'Agenda of the World' as 'a dedicated enthusiast, whose unconventional methods of approach are perhaps as striking as the message that he brings'. Visiting a number of cities in Wales at the invitation of the Council of Churches for Wales, he had been talking about the church not as the 'private hobby of a local congregation' but the place where worship and service were held together and life conducted according to the 'agenda of the world' (p. 14).

This second key phrase borrowed from Bonhoeffer was the subject of an article Hollenweger wrote for *Concept* a month after *The Church for Others* had been adopted by the Department of Studies in Evangelism. ('The World Provides the Agenda' was another subtitle of the report, referenced to Hollenweger's article.[25]) Presented also as a lecture in Birmingham and Wales, the article set out to show that taking the agenda of the world seriously was part of the church's tradition. First taking examples from the Old Testament, he pointed out how the authors were responding to the agendas of their times.[26] The Apostolic Creed was

23. The sections of the report were headed 'Secular Society', 'World as History', 'God and World', 'A Church for the World', 'Reasonable Service', 'Christian Presence', 'Reform and Renewal' and 'Recommendations'. The influence of Hollenweger's article 'Christus extra et intra muros ecclesiae' is evident in the subsections 'Secularization, A Fruit of the Gospel', pp. 9-10, and 'The Christ Outside', pp. 11-12.

24. In addition to articles referred to here, see Bibliography in Jongeneel *et al.* (eds.), *Pentecost, Mission and Ecumenism*. A substantial article in *Study Encounter* 5.1 (1969), for example, 'The Church for Others: Discussion in the DDR' (pp. 26-36) opened with 'The Study "The Missionary Structure of the Congregation" has evoked wide interest in the DDR. It has been and is discussed in many committees and consultations. The following article is intended to introduce readers who do not read German to this fascinating theological discussion in a socialist country'.

25. World Council of Churches, *The Church for Others*, p. 20.

26. Hollenweger, 'Agenda: The World', *Concept* 11 (September 1966), pp. 19-20 (19). The commandment 'Honour thy father and thy mother' (Exod. 20.12) was one which arose from the agenda of the nomadic time in the wilderness: instead of leaving

formulated in specific situations—against Marcion and other Gnostics it testified against the splitting up of God the Creator and God the Saviour and declared Jesus, not Caesar, was Lord.

> If we recite a Creed, which spoke precisely to the agenda of the third or fourth century, we must not wonder, if nobody finds it neither exciting nor helpful. It is deadly for the Church, if she confuses the helpful testimony to *yesterday's agenda* with revelation because she misses the courage to engage herself in *today's* agenda.[27]

In this agenda of the world, Hollenweger continued, 'the Church has to confess Christ, she has to participate in the *missio Dei*, to proclaim and identify the *shalom* of God'.[28] The traditional means of doing this were the sermon, liturgy and sacraments and the sermon in particular belonged to the 'pre-Gutenbergian' world and no longer functioned efficiently as public proclamation or teaching medium. Sympathy for the parish pastor, in some churches a highly trained specialist whose training is not wanted ('It hurts when he realises that he is only a badly paid and wrongly prepared entertainer for a religious club'), is Hollenweger's prelude to the closing appeal: 'Find out the agenda of the world! Ask the people outside the Church: What are the issues of today? Where does it hurt? Do you expect something from us, and what?'[29]

Another article, first published in 1965, 'A Vision of the Church of the Future', focused on the laity, emphasizing the ideas of partnership and

the infirm elderly behind if they could not keep up, the author instructed them to be taken along. Among the exiled Jews in Babylon, Hollenweger 'imagines' three parties: the conservatives who clung to 'the old-time religion' and had a 'back to the Bible programme', the modernists who wholeheartedly accepted Bablylonian religion and culture, and the authors of the Priestly Code, Ezekiel and Second Isaiah, who accepted the agenda of their world and challenged the Babylonian belief in nature gods, that is 'secularized' the world.

27. Hollenweger, 'Agenda', p. 20. Revd Dr Leslie Weatherhead, the well-known Methodist evangelist and psychologist, in his own inimitable style, commented in his popular book *The Transforming Friendship* (London: Epworth Press, 1928), p. 56, that words can become prisons which prevent people from entering the friendship of Jesus: 'we ought to have a reverence for creeds and confessions of faith. My own regard for them is a regard for very interesting and impressive museum specimens.' Quoted in Lynne Price, *Faithful Uncertainty: Leslie D. Weatherhead's Methodology of Creative Evangelism* (Frankfurt am Main: Peter Lang, 1996), p. 64.

28. See *The Church for Others*, the sub sections 'Partnership with God in History' and 'The Church Witnessing to Shalom', pp. 13-15.

29. Hollenweger, 'Agenda', p. 20

community in church structures.[30] It opened with a direct criticism of the central and dominant position of the clergy. 'We are a Church of yesterday in the world of today.' The charge, he acknowledged, was a serious one, but justified because he considered the church was 'standing in its own way'.[31] The church claimed that the gospel was for the whole world, but stifled the Holy Spirit by excluding everyone who did not 'fall into line with a particular form of worship'. The words 'whosoever loses his life for my sake shall save it', also, he said, held true for the church. The church of the future would be a serving church, one which served those outside rather than counting on drawing people in, a 'church for others'.[32]

Under the heading 'What is such a church-for-others like?' Hollenweger drew on the church community described in 1 Corinthians 12–14, where the outsider is made the judge of style for prayers, hymns and sermons, to argue that, instead of making them 'churchy', ways should be sought for the outsider to use his or her gift of impartiality, his or her ability to speak for the non-church people; journalists, poets, dramatists, teachers, painters and so on can help the church.[33] Equally important, Paul's letter to the Corinthians showed a community in which the existing gifts of the people were taken seriously—he did not create them, he found them there. Moving effortlessly from Corinthians to *My Fair Lady*, with Professor Higgins as the church and Eliza as the outsider being corrected in her pronunciation, Hollenweger made a sustained plea for a place for emotion and spontaneous expression in worship services, facets of human existence as important as the rational ones: 'emotion without interpretation has no direction. But interpretation without emotion has no power'.[34]

---

30. Hollenweger, 'A Vision of the Church for the Future', *Laity* 20 (November 1965), pp. 5-11. German version in *Reformatio* 15.2 (February 1966), pp. 90-98, reprinted with the title 'Kirche und Charisma', in R.F. Edel (ed.), *Kirche und Charisma* (Ökumenische Texten und Studien Nr. 35; Marburg: Edel, 1966), pp. 191-99. The WCC also published the article in French, an abridged version of which appeared in *La Vie Protestante* 29.6, p. 3.

31. See Hans Jochen Margull, 'We Stand in our Own Way', *Ecumenical Review* 17.4 (1965), pp. 321-31.

32. Hollenweger, 'A Vision', p. 6.

33. Hollenweger, 'A Vision', p. 7.

34. Hollenweger, 'A Vision', p. 8. Hollenweger returned later to further reflection arising from the film *My Fair Lady* (a musical based on George Bernard Shaw's play *Pygmalion*) developing his theme of intercultural theology between men and women and between social classes. An article 'My Fair Lady—ein theologisches Gleichnis' (a theological allegory) was published in *Kunst und Kirche* 4 (1976), pp. 161-64, and

Hollenweger's practical suggestions are radical. In keeping with *The Church for Others*, he challenged the 'fiction' that the parish is the only form of church organization and suggested local groupings could support new full-time ministries.[35] Those he suggested were 'celebrators' to encourage musical and linguistic innovation, 'theologians' to help with biblical exegeses, 'teachers' to pass on what they have studied with theologians, 'co-ordinators' with management, organizational and resource-gathering capabilities, and 'discussion leaders'. Worship services would be planned by groups of such ministers, preferably in suitably designed buildings.[36] Addressing the question of church structure, he stated in his 1973 Audenshaw Paper that 'the church is the place where social, racial and political differences are overcome in the celebration of the presence of the One who is greater than all our differences'.[37]

Finally, the church of the future would not only be 'for others' in its worship service, but in its prophetic dimension regarding the 'ills of our troubled world'.[38] This prophetic dimension was one Hollenweger developed more fully in an article, 'The Common Search—Experiment and Tradition', for the Roman Catholic journal *Pax Romana*.[39] Here he

included in vol. 1 of his *Intercultural Theology, Erfahrungen der Leibhaftigkeit*, pp. 106-11.

35. World Council of Churches, *The Church for Others*, pp. 29-30.

36. Hollenweger, 'A Vision', pp. 9-11. Hollenweger returns to this theme in *The Christian and the Church of the Future*, *Audenshaw Papers* 39 (November 1973), where he suggests these new structures will meet the needs not only of church-based Christians but also of 'floating' Christians of the future—who are less likely to attend Sunday services, but who have 'learnt to pray, either in an ecumenical retreat centre, or in a lay training institute or in a monastery'—will contribute to relief agencies or directly to people in need, and will witness as a journalist or artist or office clerk in the work situation, not failing to speak about Jesus of Nazareth (p. 1).

37. Hollenweger, 'The Christian', p. 2.

38. Hollenweger, 'The Christian', p. 11. The example given is an American steel company which asked a city mission to study the consequences for individuals and families in Chicago of changes in working hours and automation in the factories.

39. Hollenweger, 'The Common Search—Experiment and Tradition', *Pax Romana* 4 (1966), pp. 19-21 (also in the French edition of the journal). Hollenweger here uses the writings (5 different works are referred to) of Emil Brunner, a 'conservative' theologian, who already 30 years before had 'measured the authenticity of theological work by its helpfulness in dealing with the troublesome controversies of its time' (p. 19). For Hollenweger on Brunner see 'Aus dem weltweiten Echo auf Emil Brunners Theologie' ('On the Worldwide Echo of Emil Brunner's Theology'—a consideration of 17 responses to Brunner's work) in *Reformatio* 12.8 (1963), pp. 441-48, and

pointed out that 'the world provides the agenda' does not mean to make compromises with the world but to act and speak on, for example, the controversial matters in Mississippi: 'Almost nobody in Mississippi will contradict a trinitarian theology...almost everybody believes in the inspiration of the Bible... Here "the world's agenda" is made up by the cries of our black brethren, who freeze and starve to death. Here the world's agenda is written by the Ku-Klux-Klan...'[40] It is responded to by an ecumenical task group, the Delta Ministry, which supports (with 'blood, sweat and tears') voter registration, education, community organization and welfare programmes for the black population. Another example given is of two Roman Catholic priests in Callampaya, Bolivia, who moved into average accommodation in the barrio to work with people who did not identify themselves with the church. Yet another refers to a South London parish which rebuilt its premises for dual use as a community centre (with altar and crucifix firmly fixed to 'demonstrate that the cross is not shamefully hid when people are laughing, eating or dancing').[41] These, and other concrete examples gathered through the WCC, provide the basis for Hollenweger to spell out trends and experiments involved in the two-pronged thrust of *The Church for Others*: change in attitude to the world and change in church structures to match.[42] The significance of the laity, team work across confessional boundaries, discovery of charismata, the conviction that God speaks to Christians in their encounters with others and with events and not only in worship, recognition of contemporary changes, the experimental nature of responses and the risks involved are all noted. The journal editors, while not sharing all the ideas in Hollen-weger's article, commend the reflection of the WCC on the relevance of religion to everyday life and suggest the article will be of benefit to those who have read the Vatican II documents, particularly *Gaudium et Spes* and *Lumen Gentium*.[43] The 1960s was indeed a remarkably fertile decade.

'Wurzeln der Theologie Emil Brunners: Aus Brunners theologischer Entwicklung von ca. 1913 bis 1918' ('Roots of Emil Brunner's Theology: On Brunner's Theological Development from c. 1913 to 1918'), *Reformatio* 12.10 (1963), pp. 579-87. Some of this material is also incorporated in Hollenweger, *Evangelism Today*.

40. Hollenweger, 'The Common Search', p. 20.

41. Hollenweger, 'The Common Search', pp. 20, 21.

42. Several of these experiments are referenced to the WCC *Monthly Letter on Evangelism*, which Hollenweger edited from 1965–71.

43. Insert in 'The Common Search', p. 19. These documents dealt with the Pastoral Constitution of the Church in the Modern World, and Dogmatic Constitution on the Church respectively.

In a paper 'The Church for Others—Ten Years After' Hollenweger reflected that 'on the whole the theological significance of the Bonhoefferian testimony of *The Church for Others* was quickly forgotten' and 'no ecumenical life-inspiring and forward-pointing vision has so far emerged which can successfully compete with the still prevailing superstition of the Church as depicted in the [1974] *Oxford Dictionary of the Christian Church*'.[44] This volume had no entries on economics, capitalism, technology, contemporary science, Karl Marx, trade unions, liberation theology, or African Independent Churches, to mention but a few omissions. 'Thirty years after Bonhoeffer's martyrdom, the *Oxford Dictionary of the Christian Church* conveys the picture of an irrelevant church, a Church turned in on herself, a Church with a pathological relationship to the world...'[45]

Hollenweger has not wavered from his understanding of the church as existing for others and therefore as necessarily responsive to the agenda of the world. We noted in the last chapter that in academic terms this was embraced in his reinterpretation of mission studies as intercultural theology and the necessity for research into 'functional' mission fields. In ecclesiological terms he has expressed it as the requirement of the church to exercise its prophetic function in society. In a 1999 paper given to European French-speaking Pentecostals and charismatics on this subject he drew attention to the adverse effects of aspects of global capitalist economics and contemporary Western medicine.[46] The former issue was again raised the same year at the Conference of the European Pentecostal Theological Association at Erzhausen with his question, 'What do we say to the syncretism between capital and Christianity with its devastating effects for our world?'[47] Appropriately for the turn of the millennium, his challenge is based not only on the realities of life but also on his reading of the book of Revelation, the subject of his most recent drama published in 1999, co-authored with Estella F. Korthaus, *Neuer Himmel—neue Erde: Die Visionen der Offenbarung* (*New Heaven—New Earth: The Visions of Revelation*). John described the fusion of religious, political and economic power in the Roman Empire. Here the 'crash of the whole system'

---

44. Hollenweger, 'The Church for Others—Ten Years After', p. 82. The exceptions, he said, were the churches in East Germany and Czechoslovakia.

45. Hollenweger, 'The Church for Others—Ten Years After', p. 84.

46. 'La Fonction prophétique de l'Eglise dans la société', *Hokma* (Special issue: 72 (1999), pp. 109-23.

47. Hollenweger, 'The Challenge', p. 12.

described in ch. 18 is seen to have parallels with our present time.[48] Hollenweger contrasts the present general obsession with immediate results and short-term goal-setting in the business world with the example set by the Quaker Cadbury family, who involved employees in decision making on terms and conditions of work, ran a very successful business that outlasted many others and donated much of their wealth to a variety of socially beneficial projects.[49]

In his contribution 'Prophecy' to the *Dictionary of Mission*, Hollenweger had also referred to the Quakers, observing that they:

> have prophesied in important instances against the text of scriptures but in the spirit of the gospel. I mention only their policy of peace…and their fights against slavery…against the death penalty…against the exclusion of girls from schools, against economic exploitation of American Indians, and against persecution of those of other faiths…[50]

Concluding the article, in which he discussed prophecy in the Old and New Testaments, the early church, church history and today (where it seems to be absent in the Western churches but not elsewhere), Hollenweger selects 'lived theology of the cross' as the preferable criterion for ascertaining 'true prophecy'. Drawing on Gerd Theissen's analysis of the Jesus movement in the New Testament as 'the reworking of aggression', he comments, 'Instead of understanding themselves as censors of the prophets, church institutions should understand themselves as hosts for the reworking of aggression for a new vision of love and reconciliation'.[51]

---

48. 'Revelation was written for the seven churches in Asia Minor. Nevertheless, its structural analysis also has value for our prophetic ministry. I have discussed the text of Revelation with laypeople who do not usually go to church. They immediately saw the parallels between John's era and our own. To begin with, John described the fusion of religious, political, and especially economic power in the Roman Empire… It says to us, for example, that globalisation and fusion are necesary for survival. In certain areas that is the case. In others it is a disaster.' 'La Fonction prophétique', p. 113. See also 'The Challenge', pp. 11-12.

49. Hollenweger, 'La Fonction prophétique', pp. 113-16.

50. W. Hollenweger, 'Prophecy', in Karl Müller *et al.* (eds,), *Dictionary of Mission*, 368-72 (370). For an extended discussion see *Geist und Materie*, pp. 316-24. See also on prophecy and the Quaker example of practical response, *Geist und Materie*, pp. 121-33, and 'Ripe for Taking Risks?', *Pneuma* 18.1 (1996), pp. 107-12.

51. Hollenweger, 'Prophecy', pp. 371-72. Hollenweger refers to Theissen's description in *Urchristliche Wundergeschichten* (1974) of the Jesus movement in the New Testament as 'unstable', having resistance fighters and collaborators with the Roman occupying power. The latent aggression against the Romans was 'transferred'

In the 1970s and 1980s, commented Hollenweger in 1999, the World Council of Churches had played a prophetic role. 'Now it has fallen into a sort of hibernation.'[52]

Non-colonial Evangelism

At the time when the WCC Department of Studies in Evangelism was focusing attention on openness, mission in life context and appropriate church structures, Donald McGavran at Fuller Theological Seminary was spearheading an influential movement focusing on strategies for church growth. Invited by the *International Review of Missions* (*IRM*, published by the WCC), he wrote an article for the October 1965 issue criticising mission which did not have church growth as its primary aim or 'require the baptism of bodies, the salvation of souls and the building of new visible churches'. Recalling this three years later, in a further article in the *IRM*, he expressed surprise at the negative response received.[53] He concluded the article with strong criticism of 'Renewal in Mission', about to be discussed by the Fourth Assembly of the WCC:

> It says precisely nothing about presenting the Gospel to the two billion who now owe Jesus no allegiance… The DWME in session at Uppsala should remedy this tragic lack in her preparatory documents. Uppsala should make plans for church growth and the evangelization of earth's myriads to match God's mandate.[54]

This July 1968 issue of the *IRM* was devoted entirely to discussion of the church-growth movement. Hollenweger, now Secretary for Evangelism of the Division of World Mission and Evangelism, was the guest editor. Copies of McGavran's second article had been sent to a number of

---

in the reworking of the death of the movement's leader. The guilt of the Romans is projected onto the Messiah as 'scapegoat'; the movement then identified itself with the 'scapegoat' and celebrated him in the Lord's Supper, and 'turned human relationships upside down from within'. 'This reworking of aggression created space for the new vision of love and reconciliation, whose central point was the new command to love one's enemies.'

52. Hollenweger, 'La Fonction prophétique', p. 121. 'Le C.O.E. a joué un rôle prophétique dans les années 70 et 80. Maintenant, il est tombé dans une sorte d'hibernation.'

53. Donald McGavran, 'Church Growth Strategy Continued', *International Review of Missions* 57 (July 1968), pp. 335-43 (336).

54. McGavran, 'Church Growth', 342-43.

different people; Hollenweger, by choosing to 'reveal some points where the lines of different commentators have converged' and finding that 'most of them criticize McGavran' managed to make clear his own position purportedly without entering the debate.[55] He concluded, in agreement with one of the contributors, that it would be a mistake to pit church-growth strategy against 'Christian presence thinking' but added the salutary warning, 'What will it profit a church, if it gains the whole world and forfeits its life?'[56]

As observed earlier, it has not been Hollenweger's habit to engage in point-by-point argument with those with whom he disagrees, but rather to offer examples of what he considers good practice. His opportunity came in the same edition of the *IRM* through his review of Eberhard Bethge's recently published book on Bonhoeffer.[57] The review was entitled 'Church Growth or Political Prophecy: The Question of Priorities'. Using Bethge's biography as a basis and with constant references to particular events and Bonhoeffer's writings contained in it, Hollenweger suggested what Bonhoeffer might contribute to the discussion of church growth. This included the church being silent until asked to speak, avoiding propaganda, and Bonhoeffer's view that '*we* have to be converted not Hitler' while involved in the conspiracy to remove him, contrasted with Frank Buchman's thanking heaven for Hitler, 'who built a front line of defence against the anti-Christ of Communism' ('No doubt for Buchman, Hitler was a means of church growth', commented Hollenweger).[58] Bonhoeffer's daily discipline of prayer, meditation and Bible reading was the source of his 'genuine worldliness', 'existing for the world'. Hollenweger concluded his review by pointing out that the majority of German Christians withheld their protest against the persecution of the Jews and against the government's foreign policy 'lest it impede their opportunities for church growth

55. Hollenweger, 'Guest Editorial', *International Review of Missions* 57 (July 1968), pp. 271-77 (271-72).

56. Hollenweger, 'Guest Editorial', p. 277. References to Herbert Neve's observation in 'Christian Presence and One of its Critics', p. 329 and Mt. 16.25. In April 1987 (76.302) the *International Review of Mission* marked its 75th anniversary by publishing a selection of articles (or parts of them) from its publications over the years. Hollenweger's guest editorial on church growth was one of these (pp. 207-212).

57. Hollenweger, 'Church Growth or Political Prophecy: The Question of Priorities', review of Eberhard Bethge, *Dietrich Bonhoeffer: Theologe, Christ, Zeitgenosse* (Munich: Chr. Kaiser Verlag, 1967), *International Review of Missions* 57 (July 1968), pp. 377-80.

58. Hollenweger, 'Church Growth or Political Prophecy', p. 379.

and evangelism'. For Bonhoeffer and his friends the question was 'how can we evangelize if at such crucial moments our unqualified silence betrays the Gospel?'. 'Today', said Hollenweger, 'it has become clear for everyone what the priorities should have been'.[59]

Timothy Yates, in his recent survey of twentieth-century mission, draws attention to the institution of world evangelical conferences in the 1960s and 1970s and the 'growing distrust, even hostility, to the WCC in the evangelical world'. He continues:

> At the Berlin Congress on Evangelism in 1966 this was so marked that W.J. Hollenweger, then study secretary of the WCC, sought out Billy Graham, whose evangelistic organisation had mounted the meeting, to remonstrate. He was assured that confrontation and polarisation was not the intention of the evangelical leaders.[60]

It certainly would not have been Hollenweger's, as he made very clear in his most sustained publication on evangelism, written after he left the WCC. *Evangelisation gestern und heute* ('Evangelization Yesterday and Today') was published in 1973; the English version *Evangelism Today: Good News or Bone of Contention?* appeared three years later.[61] Here he commented that while evangelical observers at the WCC ecumenical

59. Hollenweger, 'Church Growth or Political Prophecy', p. 380. For an analysis of handwritten and confidential Minute Books of the Council and Federation of German Protestant Missions 1924–49, see Werner Ustorf, 'The Documents that Reappeared', in Price *et al.* (eds.), *Mission Matters*, pp. 63-82. Ustorf considers the discussions and positions of the chief participants on issues such as the situation of overseas missions, mission publications, missions to the Jews, and ecumenical or colonial mission models. He suggests that the Minute Books (given to the Archive of the Evangelisches Missionswerk in Deutschland in Hamburg in 1989 and accessed by Ustorf in 1993) not only raise questions about leading representatives of the Protestant missionary movement in Germany during Nazism, but also 'whether there were cultural and theological foundations within the Protestant missionary movement which made it plausible to some degree (and for some) to support Nazism rather than the social and cultural traditions opposed to Hitler' (p. 82). A wider-ranging investigation and discussion can be found in Ustorf's *Sailing With the Next Tide: Missions, Missiology and the Third Reich* (Frankfurt am Main: Peter Lang, 2000).

60. Timothy Yates, *Christian Mission in the Twentieth Century* (Cambridge: Cambridge University Press, 1994), ch. 7 'Mission as Proclamation and Church Growth 1970–1980', here p. 195, with reference to *Ecumenical Review* 19.1 (1967), pp. 88-89.

61. The English book omits the detailed footnotes included in the German version. The following references are to the English book.

councils 'voiced their criticism loudly', at the evangelical congresses (Wheaton, Illinois; Berlin; Singapore; Amsterdam) non-evangelical observers were prohibited from participation. The reason, he said, was:

> the fear of Evangelical leaders that their own constituency might find out that their attacks against the ecumenicals are ill-founded or, even worse, that Evangelicals and ecumenicals are stuck with an identical problem, namely the end of traditional missionary and evangelistic sermonizing.[62]

No Christian would deny that evangelism and diakonia belong together, he pointed out, the controversy is about *how* they belong together.[63] Despite the charged atmosphere of the time, *Evangelism Today* is something of a tour de force in its clear communication of Hollenweger's own viewpoint without being aggressive or confrontational. Three factors contribute to this outcome: it is grounded in biblical material, written in narrative and discursive form, and draws heavily on evangelical authors expressing minority perspectives to substantiate his views.[64]

The study begins with an examination of the account of the conversion of Cornelius, which Hollenweger points out is equally the account of the conversion of the evangelist, Peter. The text is scandalous, said Hollenweger, 'if it were not in the Bible, its author would risk being branded as a dangerous heretic, who distorts biblical conversion into a friendly interreligious dialogue over the fence'. Peter learnt something in the course of his evangelism; modern preachers who consider they have nothing to learn about Christ from 'the heathen, the agnostics, the indifferent or—*horribile dictu*—the communists' are not evangelists, they are only propagandists. 'The real evangelist cannot help but take the risk that in the course of his evangelism his understanding of Christ will get corrected.'[65] Moving then to three examples from church history, Hollenweger reinforces his insight

---

62. Hollenweger, *Evangelism Today*, pp. 39-40. He continues by giving three examples of evangelical inconsistency to support his contention that there exist meeting grounds for evangelicals and ecumenists—no difficulty in having 'open-hearted and sincere' private conversations with evangelicals at their congresses but only the 'all too well-known slogans' being published; evangelical condemnation of the Orthodox churches at one congress and then inviting Haile Selassie to open the next congress in Berlin; calling Bishop Lilje, a president of the WCC, a real evangelist and at the same time pretending that evangelicals are not represented in the WCC.

63. Hollenweger, *Evangelism Today*, p. 34.

64. *Evangelism Today* is a short book—118 pages in all. The Bibliography, however, consisting of a general list and chapter lists, is substantial (19 pages).

65. Hollenweger, *Evangelism Today*, p. 17.

that the gospel is 'objective'—that is, the gospel stands over against both the evangelist and the evangelized.[66]

The English edition of *Evangelism Today* appeared after the important 1974 International Congress on World Evangelization at Lausanne, Switzerland, and contained a Preface entitled 'The Spirit of Lausanne'. Here Hollenweger quoted Billy Graham, who had stated in his opening address that 'evangelism and the salvation of souls is the vital mission of the church... Thus, while we may discuss social and political problems, our priority for discussion here is the salvation of souls.' Hollenweger pointed out that this was not his approach, nor was it the approach of some of the major speakers at Lausanne.[67] Returning to the subject a further 20 years on in *Pentecostalism: Origins* in a chapter entitled 'Mission: What Kind of Missionaries?', Hollenweger quoted two such speakers who argued that only a truncated gospel could be concerned with the numbers who died without Christ and not concerned with the numbers who died from hunger.[68] Where Yates sees the growing evangelical social awareness as internally generated and the Lausanne Conference successful in holding together proclamation and social justice, Hollenweger claims some influence for *The Church for Others* and is more impressed by the fact that there was, on this occasion, open debate.[69]

Hollenweger does not question whether Christians should share their experience of Christ with others: that is assumed. The critical questions are, as he succinctly put it, 'How will this sharing take place? And what

66. The examples are Belgian missionary Placide Tempels and the African Jamaa movement, the failure of dialogue between Ram Mohun Roy and missionaries in India, and John Wesley.

67. Hollenweger, *Evangelism Today*, p. 6. See also 'The Church for Others—Ten Years After', 89-90; this article is incorporated in *Umgang mit Mythen*, pp. 29-45. Hollenweger's concern with the Lausanne Conference in this article is to demonstrate the pluriformity of the evangelical movement within a broader consideration of the nature and future of the church. He draws extensively on the writings of Wolfhart Pannenberg.

68. Hollenweger, *Pentecostalism: Origins*, pp. 304-306. The speakers were Samuel Escabar and Réne Padilla. Hollenweger notes that in Bruce Kaye's account, Padilla received warm applause at the Conference while the speeches of his opponents McGavran and Lindsell 'were greeted with stony silence', and that Graham himself was persuaded by Padilla's paper. See also Hollenweger's, 'Evangelism: A Non-Colonial Model', in *Journal of Pentecostal Theology* 7 (1995), pp. 107-28 (110-13).

69. Yates, *Christian Mission*, p. 200; Hollenweger 'The Church for Others—Ten Years After', p. 82.

should we avoid if we do not want to run the risk that the way of sharing contradicts the content of what we want to share?'[70] His answers are that the sharing should, following the example of Jesus and the New Testament, be dialogical and situational (the Peter and Cornelius story remains paradigmatic[71]); and that a colonial approach, assuming the form of Christianity presented by the evangelist is the only form, should be avoided.

Clearly, by 'colonial' evangelism, Hollenweger is not only referring to overseas mission undertaken by Westerners. The non-colonial or biblical evangelism he advocates applies within geographical areas. Drawing together insights from study of the Bible, mid twentieth-century European historical realities and experiences of international Christianity in the 1960s, Hollenweger has increasingly focused his own efforts on the transmission of Christianity in the West. Not only does he understand mission as participating in God's mission—establishing the salvific messianic shalom in the world—as an activity in which all (Christians and non-Christians)—are participants, but he understands the very transmission of Christianity as an activity in which all who are willing (Christians and non-Christians) can be involved.

The dramas, which were analysed in Chapter 3 as Hollenweger's vehicle for imparting critical biblical scholarship to non-specialists in narrative form, are also his prime medium for non-colonial evangelism. 'Better Played Than Preached' is the title of an article by Fritz Imhof in *Leben und Glauben* of 3 March 2000 describing Hollenweger's narrative exegetical method and announcing three performances of *Maria von Wedemeyer* by the church and Jazz-Gospel choirs of Huttwil, Bern.[72] As indicated in the description of the Bayreuth production of *Maria von Wedemeyer* which opened this chapter, a key factor is the participation of actors, musicians, singers and dancers who had no church affiliation and yet were involved in the interpretation of the script. My personal experience of co-facilitating and participating in the production of *The*

---

70. Hollenweger, *Evangelism Today*, p. 5.

71. It is referred to again, with all its provocative implications, in 'Evangelism: A Non-Colonial', pp. 116-21.

72. Fritz Imhof, 'Besser gespielt als gepredigt', *Leben und Glauben* 75.10 (2000), pp. 32-37. This project was initiated by Simon Jenny, a Bern pastor and musician, who was inspired by hearing Hollenweger lecture at the university on narrative exegesis. The article includes colour photographs of Hollenweger in his study and Simon Jenny and participants rehearsing. Performances 31 March, 2 April at the Reformed Church, Huttwil, Bern, and 7 April at the French Church, Bern.

Adventure of Faith in Birmingham in 1996 convinced me of the work-ability of the method. A number of those who took part were non-church-goers, uninterested or disaffected, and also one Jew, but all were pleased to contribute to this creative venture. Comments made by these colleagues included finding the biblical material interesting, being excited by the event, feeling comfortable, finding the interaction of imagination and faith helpful, being surprised at Christianity grappling with contemporary issues, and enjoying the feeling of community and mutual support generated among a very diverse group of people. Several participants said they were drawn to reassessing their own faith and life situations.[73]

In two recent articles Hollenweger makes it clear that the dramatic form invites participants to examine themselves and their own political, social and religious context. At the same time, the dramas communicate nar-ratives from the Bible or Christian tradition, and the faith and hopes of Christians.[74] The general formula that emerges from study of Hollen-weger's dramas is that he presents the points of debate on belief or practice within the spoken words, while the affective dimensions of the story are contained in the instrumental music, dance and movement, and faith expressed through the hymns and songs.

Maria von Wedemeyer was a particularly poignant and meaningful drama for Germans to participate in. For the many young people involved in the Bayreuth production, it portrayed a part of their history with which they were unfamiliar. For the older generation in the audience, and for older participants and audience at another production at Berneuchener Haus in Kloster Kirchberg, southern Germany in August 1997, there were the difficulties of facing anew a history with which they were familiar and uncomfortable.[75] At the week-long conference during which the play was

73. For a full account see Lynne Price, 'Scholarship and Evangelism: Oil and Water?', in Anderson and Hollenweger (eds.), *Pentecostals after a Century*, pp. 197-208.

74. Hollenweger, 'Evangelism: A Non-Colonial', and 'Theology and the Future'.

75. Berneuchener Haus is a former Dominican monastery acquired in 1958 and run by the Community of Saint Michael. It offers a varied programme run by visiting specialists, which during the year 2000 included Bible studies and Bible dramas, various forms of meditation and quiet days, art and dance workshops and exploration of liturgies, as well as providing meeting facilities and offering visitors a quiet and comfortable retreat house. Regular prayer meetings during each day feature a sung liturgy. The Berneuchen Movement originated in the 1920s as a spiritual renewal movement. Ruth-Alice von Bismarck, Maria's sister, writes about it in the Notes to *Love Letters*, pp. 262-64, where she records that their father was involved in the

rehearsed by amateurs guided by artistic specialists at Berneuchener Haus, tensions were evident. As the only English participant, I found the experience personally challenging; living in community for a week gave opportunity for personal conversations and moments of reconciliation, within and outside the drama. As Hollenweger pointed out in his introductory session, the theme of a 'community of opposites' was a central one in the story of Maria and Dietrich. This was, incidentally, the only time he gave a formal presentation on the drama, though he was present throughout and was repeatedly asked to give a theological exposition. To the annoyance of some participants, this he resolutely refused to do, insisting that their participation in the drama was the most important factor. Further reflection and reading could be done after they had emotionally, physically and intellectually engaged with the narrative.

Hans Werner von Wedemeyer, Maria's younger brother, was also a participant at Berneuchener. He paid tribute to Hollenweger and Korthaus for their distinctive appreciation of his family history and presented them with pieces of the von Wedemeyer silver, which Maria had taken with her when the family fled their home at Pätzig just before the Russian Army invaded the village in January 1945. The public performance of *Maria von Wedemeyer* at Berneuchener was fully reported in the local press, with accompanying photographs.[76]

Besides emphasizing the involvement of lay people and non-church-goers in this form of evangelism, Hollenweger particularly points out the importance of enlisting the help of people with expertise in the arts: quality sensory input and interpretation is considered vital for a holistic approach to the matters of faith and life introduced in the dramas. Estella Korthaus is herself a theatre director and has worked with Hollenweger in this capacity on a number of productions.[77] Another example of collabora-

beginnings of the movement and provided it with a base at Pätzig in the early 1920s. Their grandmother, however, was committed to the Confessing Church with its concern for social and political responsibility, when it was established in response to National Socialism. Von Bismarck continues: 'There thus arose between the two reformist movements a field of tension into which Maria herself was drawn. In saying "Only those who cry out for the Jews have the right to sing the Gregorian chant", Dietrich Bonhoeffer vehemently dissociated himself from the Berneucheners' (p. 263). See pp. 83-84 above.

76. *Schwarzwälder Bote* (11 August 1997); *Südwest Presse* (11 August 1997). Hans Werner von Wedemeyer also attended the performance at Bayreuth, to the delight of all the participants, Walter Hollenweger and myself.

77. For Korthaus's account (in German) of their three-week visit to Fuller

tion between theologian and artists can be found in the performance of *Im Schatten Seines Friedens: Ein Weinachtsoratorium* (*In the Shadow of His Peace: A Christmas Oratorio*) in Württemberg in 1985. The text was written by Hollenweger, music by Hans-Jürgen Hufeisen and the drama and dance performed by the Stuttgarter Theater der Bilder with the support of the district church youth pastorate.[78] (The oratorio was also performed by local participants in four Swiss villages during Advent 1999.)[79] The four gospel authors' different attitudes to Christ's birth scripted by Hollenweger in Part III were distinctively expressed musically, artistically, dramatically and choreographically by the other artists. The diversity of the gospel writers' handling of the Christmas story is the basis for the 'message': we live in the shadow of his peace, a contemporary Christian suggested near the climax of the oratorio, when we take pleasure in those who are different from us.[80] *Der Knabe und die Mondin* (*The Boy and the Moon*) grew out of the 1991 *Kirchentag* Bible study project Hollenweger engaged in with Bodo Leinberger and others. Based on the narrative in Mk 9.14-29, the visualization is here chiefly through ballet dancing and the dramatic portrayal of the story is followed by the invitation to the audience to receive anointing with oil from stations around the room. Bodo Leinberger's book *Getanztes Leben: Heilende Liturgie* (*Danced Life: Healing Liturgy*) contains the script they co-authored, exegesis on the Bible text by Hollenweger (and another on Num. 11), and articles by Leinberger and Peter Bubmann, the composer, describing how they have developed the use of drama and music drawing on church and non-church resources.[81]

Theological Seminary in Pasadena in 1995 to conduct a practical course on narrative exegesis, see her 'Sprechende Bilder: Wie die Bibel in Kopf und Herz dringt', *Evangelische Kommentare* 7 (1995), pp. 404-407.

78. Information taken from the programme—a beautifully produced booklet containing the whole script and audience hymns, short articles and photographs.

79. Correspondence Erica Hollenweger, December 1999.

80. Part III, No.12: 'Im Schatten seines Friedens leben wir, wenn wir Freude haben an denen, die anders sind als wir?' Part I, 'The Participants', contains short speeches by Joseph, Mary, an angel, the hotel manager, a soldier's wife and a shepherd. Part II is 'The Birth', and Part III 'The Interpreters'. The Oratorio included 12 well-known hymns sung by the audience.

81. Bodo Leinberger (ed.), *Getanztes Leben: Heilende Liturgie* (Hammersbach: Verlag Wort im Bild, 1993). For the origin of the piece see the Foreword. Hollenweger's exegesis of Num. 11 contains a story of the author of John's Gospel undertaking a Bible study on this passage with his contemporary community. Hollenweger's drama on this, *Fontana: Die Frau am Brunnen und der siebte Mann* ('Fontana: The

Hollenweger also demonstrates how it is possible for the evangelist to contribute to occasions planned by others in his collaboration with a performance of Bach's *Saint John Passion* in 1998. Through conversations with the producer (a lapsed Christian) about Bach's interpretation of the text of John's Gospel, the conductor decided to begin the event with the foot-washing of the musicians and choir at several places around the church. This was followed by a reading of John 13 before the oratorio began. Hollenweger was invited to deliver a sermon in the middle of the Passion. He drew attention to John's Gospel having been written at a time when the Christians were at loggerheads with the Jewish religious authorities and were excluded from the synagogues, giving rise to subsequent anti-Jewish polemic; and to Bach's influence by Reformation concern with sin, so that he blames not the Jews, but contemporary Christians for Christ's death. Finally he suggested what 'new life' might mean for people today. The concert audience applauded the sermon, affirming Hollenweger's conviction that, 'The general public and our communities can bear the truth'.[82]

Non-colonial evangelism is also possible, according to Hollenweger, in church services. In the entry 'Community and Worship' in *A New Dictionary of Liturgy and Worship* published in 1986, he began: 'In early Christianity worship was in general intended for the faithful. Nevertheless, already in the earliest liturgical regulations we find an unexpected pre-occupation with the outsider, the "idiotes" (1 Cor. 14.24, 25).'[83] The uncertainty about who worship is intended for continues, he claimed, and suggested that 'one way forward might be to invite outsiders and non-Christians to participate in the process of preparing specific experimental liturgies'. Worship, he considered, should not be geared totally to the needs of insiders; cultural, religious and theological outsiders should

woman at the Well and the Seventh Man') is published by Metanoia Verlag together with *Herr, bleibe bei uns, denn es will Abend werden: Salbungsliturgie zu Lukas 7, 36-50* ('Master, Stay with Us for Evening is Coming: Anointing Service on Luke 7.36-50').

82. Interview, 11 June 1998; article by W.J. Hollenweger, 'Im Gottesdienst Zärtlichkeit und Lebenskraft feiern' ('Celebrate tenderness and vitality in worship'), *Wendekreis* (6/1998), pp. 18-19; and detailed account of the preliminary discussions and performance in *Der Klapperstorch*, pp. 25-30. The quotation is from *Der Klapperstorch*, p. 30: 'Das allgemeine Publikum und unsere Gemeinden können die Wahrheit ertragen.' The concert was performed twice in the Stiftskirche at Gandersheim, Germany, on 4 and 5 April 1998.

83. W.J. Hollenweger, 'Community and Worship', in Davies (ed.), *A New Dictionary*, pp. 183-84. See also Hollenweger, 'A Vision', p. 7.

receive preferential treatment.[84] Clarifying 'experimental liturgy' in another entry as making an experience which includes the risk of an experiment, he described several liturgies where 'the whole people of God shared their Christian and non-Christian traditions including their personal and collective sufferings and joys'.[85] Addressing the Hymn Society of Great Britain and Ireland in 1986, he had specifically extended this collaborative approach to music as a productive field of reconciliation between those inside the churches (mostly white and middle class) and those outside, like the non-churchgoing, working-class men Edrington interviewed in Birmingham, who were uncertain of what they believed, or whether they were Christians, or who prayed in secret to a God they had no words to describe. The memories, visions and songs of these men were important, declared Hollenweger, as was their search for ways to articulate their life experiences and longings. 'This search for the names is called theology. The celebration of this search is called church music.' He recommended that church musicians put themselves at the disposal of the wider community, using people's gifts as the starting point and medium of communication.[86]

84. Hollenweger, 'Community and Worship', p. 184. Other entries by Hollenweger in Davies (ed.), *A New Dictionary*: 'Camp Meetings'; 'Experimental Forms of Worship'; 'Liturgies: Pentecostal'; 'Open Air Meetings'; 'Ordination; Pentecostal'; 'Spirituals'; and 'Pentecostal Worship'. With the exception of 'Community', all these were also in Davies (ed.), *A Dictionary of Liturgy and Worship* (London: SCM Press, 1972).

85. Hollenweger, 'Experimental Forms of Worship', pp. 231-36. One example was a Thanksgiving Day (roughly approximating to Remembrance Day) in a Geneva church, where Spanish and Italian waiters served coffee to the arriving congregation, took coffee beans to the altar with the bread and wine and spoke of the plight of Brazilian coffee workers and poverty of farmers in southern Italy (related to the bread). A Swiss parishioner introduced the wine, the cup of the new covenant, with the story of the writer of the hymn just sung: J.C. Lavater died protecting a man persecuted by a French soldier of the occupying army. A very short sermon spoke of the story of Jesus and Levi, the outsider who made Jesus the occasion of a feast. During the distribution of the Lord's Supper, cards were distributed asking what people could do about fair trade, poverty and the inclusion of outsiders—Swiss or foreigners—and what things are changed in the world by the Lord's Supper. The account of this liturgy is also to be found in Hollenweger, *Umgang mit Mythen*, pp. 130-32. See also 'Gottesdienst mit Nichtchristen' ('Worship with Non-Christians') in *Geist und Materie*, pp. 188-92.

86. Hollenweger, 'Music in the Service of Reconciliation', *Theology* 92.748 (1989), pp. 276-86 (281). For reference to Roger Edrington's *Everyday Men*, see Chapter 4 n. 45 above.

Comment

Hollenweger has applied himself wholeheartedly to the understanding of mission and evangelism hammered out in the international arena of the mid twentieth century. For him, collaborative participation in God's mission, in the life of the world, together with others (Christian and non-Christian) who differ in beliefs, gifts and insights is reconciliatory and salvific in its contributions to the realization of shalom. This he has put into practice in the academic context by, for example, teaching Christology with a Jewish rabbi and Muslim theologian.[87] In *Evangelism Today: Good News or Bone of Contention?*, a deceptively unassuming book written in popular style, he addressed the relation of word and deed. 'Jesus did not merely describe the new man. Where Jesus appeared, the new man became *visible*.' Jesus broke the social and political taboos of his time by mixing with sinners, prostitutes and publicans, he celebrated with them, and opened closed doors by healing on the sabbath. The Eucharist of the early church broke down barriers by celebrating agapes which included free and slaves, rich and poor, men and women in worship. 'An experience of salvation was made which the world did not know.' It is this 'revolutionary freedom' which could lead Christians today to work with media specialists, dramatists, architects and so on to create 'visible alternatives to the *status quo*, a lived gospel' rather than persist in offering 'the disembodied word or the uninterpreted, unimaginative so-called practical deeds'.[88]

Hollenweger's approach to mission and evangelism has its own inner coherence: it is participatory engagement—with God, with life contexts, with the Bible, with people who are not Christians. This coherence, however, results not in consistency and uniformity but in diversity and risk taking. The Good News is a bone of contention according to Hollenweger because it is an event not a statement.[89] Because it is Good *News* it cannot be repetition of something seen before; it is *Good* News because it is about God's goodness, not humanity's. 'A Christian's understanding of the Good News is always in the making, fundamentally in the making.'[90]

Anthony Gittins, CSSp, more recently and from a Roman Catholic

---

87. In 1988, for example, a module 'One Jesus—Many Christologies' included sessions by guest lecturers Rabbi Norman Solomon and Dr M. Surty, with a panel discussion to conclude the module (author's personal records).

88. Hollenweger, *Evangelism Today*, pp. 42-43.

89. Hollenweger, *Evangelism Today*, p. 93.

90. Hollenweger, *Evangelism Today*, p. 94.

perspective, has also explored the need for mission and missioners to be transformed in his 1993 book *Bread for the Journey*. Because mission has in the past been understood as a one-way process, he argues that what is needed now is 'Mission in Reverse':

> If God universally calls and invites to conversion, then the church and missioners are not exempt. And unless we ourselves are committed to the kind of dialogue that is open to changing the hearts of all parties, evangelism is no better than proselytism.

He continues with a lengthy quotation of Hollenweger, from an article written for a 1979 edition of *Concilium*:

> Evangelization is *martyria*. That does not mean primarily the risking of possessions and life, but rather that the evangelist gambles, as it were, with his understanding of belief in the course of evangelizing. He, so to speak, submits his understanding of the world and of God and of his faith to the test of dialogue. He has no guarantee that his understanding of faith will emerge unaltered from that dialogue. On the contrary. How can any one expect that the person who is listening to him should be ready in principle to change his life and way of thinking if he, the evangelist, is not notionally prepared to submit to the same discipline?[91]

Like Hollenweger 20 years earlier, Gittins is inspired by the gospel accounts of Jesus' dialogical and situational ministry, refers to the *Missio Dei*, 'God's mission to love and save all humankind', as the 'unbounded, unlimited dimension of mission that makes mission so challenging' and further affirms:

> A person committed to mission in reverse is not lacking in faith or uncommitted to seeking the truth, but in Hollenweger's word, he or she 'gambles' with a personal, limited, current understanding of faith, trusting that this is no less than Jesus asks'.[92]

The church that is inward-looking and primarily concerned about its institutional survival, whose structures are designed for maintenance and the imperial expansion of its members' own beliefs and practices, which believes it has a package of truth to be handed out, has in Hollenweger's

---

91. Anthony J. Gittins, *Bread for the Journey: The Mission of Transformation and the Transformation of Mission* (Maryknoll, NY: Orbis Books, 1993), p. 24, quoting from Hollenweger 'Evangelization in the World Today', *Concilium* 114 (1979), pp. 40-41. Cf. Hollenweger's *Evangelism Today*, ch. 4. See also Gittins, 'Missionary Myth Making', in Scherer and Bevans (eds.), *New Directions*, 2, pp. 143-57.

92. Gittins, *Bread*, pp. 61-63.

perspective ceased being the bearer of good news. The church that accepts its own limitations of knowledge of God and the world and recognizes its need to learn from outsiders, that is alert to its need to engage prophetically with its contexts, that is willing to engage in 'the adventure of faith', is 'fundamentally good news in the making'. As he put it three decades after the publication of *The Church for Others*:

> Everybody else wants to sell something which is finished—either a piece of art or a commercial product or political programme, it is all finished and they want to sell it as a good thing. We can say we have something, but this thing only comes to light, becomes visible, if we produce and construct it together.[93]

As with his approach to interpreting the Bible, it seems that in mission and evangelism also, content and process are inextricably interwoven. Hollenweger's commitment to Hoekendijk's God/world/church prioritization and understanding of mission as the establishment of the messianic shalom, and his support for Bonhoeffer's prophetic stance rather than church-growth strategies, continue to challenge an overestimation of the importance of the church. Today, as with the general reluctance to take up the recommendations of *The Church for Others* after the flurry of debate, many prefer the safety of a clerically dominated church intent on bringing people in, rather than the danger of the laity venturing precariously into the world to establish shalom together with the 'others'.

What, it may be asked, of the saving of souls for the hereafter? Is this not the essential missionary burden laid upon the church, the reason why it should look first to its own safety and growth? Hollenweger, it seems, would say that only God saves souls; apart from setting out the different traditions on life after death in the Bible in the drama *Neuer Himmel— neue Erde*, it is a subject he rarely refers to. When asked his views in interview he replied:

> The images and theories in the New Testament are not harmonizable. But on one thing they are clear—that we are in the hands of God and he is probably doing what he thinks best... I believe there is life after death but what happens after death who knows? All that I know is that the one who is my judge is also my saviour, he is the one who gave his life. But that is true for the others too... For me it's enough to know that we are in God's hands—what else can I wish for?[94]

93. Interview, 29 October 1997.
94. Interview, 29 October 1997.

Salvation, he wrote in the context of Pentecostalism, is in experience diverse and inadequately integrated in soteriology. It encompasses the personal-spiritual, personal-physical and socioeconomic aspects of life; it is to be freed from fear of life and from fear of death, to experience liberation and become a human person.[95] Eschatology is not among the theological issues explored in this most recent extensive survey of the origins and developments of worldwide Pentecostalism. For Hollenweger, belief in God's goodness is sufficient for the next life. God's goodness is also the basis of Christian tolerance in this life, he wrote in a 1995 article for the journal *Die Politische Meinung* (*Political Opinion*), adding that Zwingli (in contrast to Luther) expected to find non-Christians, pagans and Muslims in heaven.[96]

His prime missionary concern, as we have seen repeatedly in this chapter, is with Christian responsibility now, in this present life: continuing Jesus' announcement of the kingdom of God, motivating people to see that the world can be changed for the better, discerning where change is necessary inside and outside the churches, and practising shalom. All of which involves participation, dialogue and collaboration in the broadest intercultural and ecumenical perspectives—and, consequently, a reappraisal of pneumatology.

95. Ch. 19, 'Soteriology: Who is Saved?', in Hollenweger, *Pentecostalism: Origins*, pp. 246-57. Though written in the context of Pentecostalism, Hollenweger's different 'expressed' and 'lived' examples of salvation draw from a wide ecumenical and intercultural field.

96. 'Toleranz im Islam und im Cristentum', *Die Politische Meinung* 310 (September 1995), pp. 90-95: 'Grundlage der christlichen Toleranz ist der Glaube an Gottes Güte... Darum glaubte auch Huldreich Zwingli, der Züricher Reformator, im Himmel Nichtchristen, Heiden und Muslims anzutreffen, weswegen er von Luther arg beschimpft wurde' (p. 95). In this article, and also in an interview for *Itinéraires* July–September 1994: 8 (a French-Swiss publication), Hollenweger emphasized the positive contribution of critical biblical and Koranic scholarship to interfaith dialogue, noting, however, that because of its longer period of intercultural formation, the Bible was more pluralistic than the Koran. He makes particular reference to the work of the Sudanese Muslim scholar Mahmud Muhammed Taha (1908–85), who distinguished differences between the Mecca and Medina periods.

Chapter 6

RUACH YAHWEH—HOLY SPIRIT: PNEUMATOLOGY

From Life to Theology

Hollenweger's thinking about the Holy Spirit is appropriately addressed at this juncture—the last topic of his work to be examined. It is only after having some appreciation of his Pentecostal scholarship, his methodologies, his understanding of the Bible, his intercultural approach to theology and missiology, his international ecumenical experience, and his dialogical model of evangelism, that his approach to pneumatology can be appreciated. I am of the opinion that this very unusual combination of knowledge and experience is what makes Hollenweger's contribution to pneumatology of value not just to Pentecostalism but to the wider theological academy. In this chapter, therefore, it is not intended to follow the specialist debates within Pentecostalism in which Hollenweger has been an active and controversial participant for 40 years.[1] Rather, the intention is to demonstrate through Hollenweger's writing how his study and understanding of some of the realities of life—biblical, historical and contemporary—have informed his theological position. The 'from life to theology' rather than 'from theology to life' approach is a central interest. We have encountered it repeatedly in Hollenweger's work. Here it is brought more sharply into focus on a specific dogmatic subject: the Holy Spirit.

Questionable Doctrine

Hollenweger's foundational research on the worldwide Pentecostal movement in the 1960s demonstrated the variety of twentieth-century experiences, beliefs and practices within it, not least in regard to the doctrines of

---

1. Readers unfamiliar with the academic study of the Pentecostal and charismatic movements may find it helpful to refer again to Chapter 2, 'Pentecostal Scholar' and Chapter 3, 'Pentecostal Boundaries', with their attendant bibliographical references.

the Holy Spirit and the Trinity.[2] That 'the most difficult point of Pentecostal theology is, astonishingly, their pneumatology' was an observation
he made in his contribution to the Fifth Oxford Institute on Methodist
Theological Studies in 1973.[3] In 'Creator Spiritus', an article for *Theology*
in January 1978, he wrote:

> It is no secret that the Pentecostal churches have so far not produced a
> charismatic theology. Even their doctrine of the Spirit is nothing new and
> often only a weak rehash of the position of the Holiness Movement of the
> nineteenth century, dressed up with the doctrine of the 'initial sign' (speak-
> ing in tongues), which characterizes the baptism of the spirit. It is my con-
> viction that the Pentecostals' theological articulation does not adequately
> represent their practice and experience.[4]

Particularly in Latin America and Africa, indigenous Pentecostal-type
churches communicated their theology largely through contextually rooted
oral categories of story, dance, song, music and liturgy, and, as we saw in

2.   Hollenweger, *The Pentecostals*; the subject is referrred to in 'Part One: History'
in each of the geographical sections (The United States of America, Brazil, South
Africa and Europe) and in 'Part Two: Belief and Practice', in particular in ch. 22, ' "A
Crimson Stream of Blood": The Doctrine of the Trinity and Christology'; ch. 24,
' "Showers of Blessing": The Doctrine of the Spirit'; ch. 25, ' "The Day of Miracles is
Still Here": Healing by Prayer and the Doctrine of Miracles'; and ch. 26, 'Against
Principalities and Powers: Demonology'.

3.   Hollenweger, 'Charismatic and Pentecostal Movements: A Challenge to the
Churches', in Dow Kirkpatrick (ed.), *The Holy Spirit* (Nashville: World Methodist
Council Tidings, 1974), pp. 209-33 (223).

4.   Hollenweger, 'Creator Spiritus: The Challenge of Pentecostal Experience to
Pentecostal Theology', *Theology* 81.679 (1978), pp. 32-40 (34). There is an extensive
literature on the subject of the relationship between the Holiness Movement and the
modern Pentecostal movement. See, for example, Charles Edwin Jones, *A Guide to the
Study of the Holiness Movement* (Metuchen, NJ: Scarecrow Press, 1974) and *A Guide
to the Study of Pentecostalism*; Donald W. Dayton, *Theological Roots of Pentecostalism* (Metuchen, NJ: Scarecrow Press, 1987). The entry 'Holiness Movement', in
Burgess and McGee, *Dictionary of Pentecostal* provides a short introduction and
bibliography by C.E. Jones and opens with the statement, 'The Pentecostal movement
owes its inspiration and formation to the Wesleyan Holiness revival of the nineteenth
century'. For Hollenweger on the subject see, for example, *The Pentecostals*, ch. 24;
'Pfingstkirchen', pp. 1162-1170; 'Verheissung', pp. 265-87; 'From Azusa Street to the
Toronto Phenomenon: Historical Roots of the Pentecostal Movement', *Concilium
1996.3 Pentecostal Movements as an Ecumenical Challenge* edited by Jürgen
Moltmann and Karl-Joseph Kuschel, pp. 3-14 (4-5); and *Pentecostalism: Origins*, ch.
12 'Wesley's Catholic Roots'.

Chapter 4, no great efforts had so far been made to build scholarly bridges between oral and literary genres. His expectations that the charismatic renewal movement in the traditional Protestant and Roman Catholic Churches (neo-Pentecostalism) might stimulate new thinking on pneumatology, rather than simply enliven and confirm confessional orthodoxies, were largely disappointed in the 1970s.[5] Only a few, he said, 'understood that "charismatic theology" does not merely mean to introduce a new chapter on "charismata" in an otherwise unchanged theological system', but rather to rethink the doctrine of the Trinity, ecclesiology and the work of the Holy Spirit in the world as well as the church.[6]

This is the enterprise that has engaged Hollenweger. His study of the Bible, his extensive knowledge of the history of the Pentecostal movement and his understanding of the functioning of charismatic experiences in different cultures led him to appreciate the wider significance of charismata for theological reflection.[7]

The criticism of the Pentecostal movement was clearly a double-edged sword. Already, at the conclusion of *The Pentecostals*, Hollenweger had expressed the hope that both the Pentecostal and the historic churches would engage critically with their own traditions as part of a dialogical process.[8] Experiences including speaking in tongues, healing, prophecy and exorcism, and not excluding those 'humanizing' gifts of the Spirit that enabled Pentecostals to engage in political and social reform,[9] presented a direct challenge to the traditional churches in precisely the same areas of

5. See, for example, Hollenweger's Preface, 'Towards a Charismatic Theology', in Simon Tugwell *et al.* (eds.), *New Heaven? New Earth? An Encounter with Pentecostalism* (London: Darton Longman & Todd, 1976), pp. 9-13 (9-10) (Hollenweger found these four authors had wrestled with the important questions). See also 'Creator Spiritus'.

6. Hollenweger, 'Creator Spiritus', pp. 35-36. The third area was the most controversial at the World Methodist Council meeting referred to above. Dow Kirkpatrick wrote in the Preface to *The Holy Spirit*: 'Through ten days of discussion, one central issue divided lecturers and members: whether the Spirit works only in and through the church, or whether the Presence may be discerned in movements outside the People of God?' (p. 6).

7. For a concise recent summary see Hollenweger, 'From Azusa Street'. In German, see 'Pfingstkirchen', and 'Verheissung'. Primarily, see *The Pentecostals* and *Pentecostalism: Origins*.

8. Hollenweger, *The Pentecostals*, p. 508.

9. Hollenweger, 'Creator', pp. 38-39; see also *Pentecost between Black and White*.

unresolved conceptual debate. This is reflected in a more recent World Council of Churches Faith and Order Commission publication *Confessing the One Faith*, published in 1991. The outcome of a ten-year study consultation involving theologians from various confessions (though not, apparently, any Pentecostals) prompted by 'the conviction that the coming together of Christians in an authentic communion of faith and life calls for the common confession of the apostolic faith', it stated in the preamble to the section 'The Holy Spirit':

> There are many challenges to the confession of the Holy Spirit today. Among them the most pressing are: the conflict between East and West as to the *filioque*; the relation of the divine Spirit to the human spirit, consciousness and conscience; the relation of the Holy Spirit to the prophecy of the Old Covenant and the gift of prophecy in the Church; the criteria for the discernment of the activity of the Spirit within the Church; and the question of the activity of the Spirit outside the Church.[10]

It is the challenges which have interested Hollenweger, not the call for a common confession of the apostolic faith. Before the WCC even started its study he had signalled areas of uncertainty to be of key importance—not to be suppressed, but responded to creatively. He had suggested, for example, that the Mediterranean language and thought-forms of traditional Trinitarian doctrine could not provide universal answers to the question behind the doctrine—the relationship between creation, revelation and salvation. He pointed out the similarity between the oral functioning of Pentecostal churches and early Christian communities before the split with the Marcionites, the period when 'it was possible to belong to the holy, apostolic, and catholic Church without giving up the pluriformity in soteriologies, ethics, pneumatologies and christologies'. If diversity was taken as a starting point, he observed, then *statements* of faith could be replaced by *questions* of faith. The understanding of the Spirit in the Old Testament and the experience of the Spirit in the non-Western churches,

---

10. WCC, *Confessing the One Faith: An Ecumenical Explication of the Apostolic Faith as it is Confessed in the Nicene-Constantinopolitan Creed (381)* (Faith and Order Paper, No. 153; Geneva: WCC, rev. ed. 1992 [1991]), p. 73. Previous quotation from back cover. Reading the lists of participants in the consultations, including the consultation on the third article of the Creed ('We believe in the Holy Spirit, the Church and the Life of the World to Come') I cannot see any participants at all from Pentecostal churches, though some Latin American and African Independent Churches were received into full membership of the WCC in the 1970s (there are many Roman Catholic participants, though the RC Church was not a full member).

he said, indicated that the Spirit was at work in the world as well as in the church.[11]

It was in the 1980s that Hollenweger began to draw together the threads of his diverse research, observation and practice that bear on pneumatology. A key article first published in German in *Evangelische Kommentare* in 1983, 'All Creatures Great and Small: Towards a Pneumatology of Life', was published in 1984 in English in a book edited by David Martin and Peter Mullen, *Strange Gifts? A Guide to Charismatic Renewal.*[12] In the following summary we can see how his Pentecostal, ecumenical, intercultural and missionary interests are combined in reflection on pneumatology.

In the Introduction Hollenweger says that 'All Creatures Great and Small' examines Western (including charismatic and Pentecostal), Eastern Orthodox, non-white indigenous and Old Testament pneumatologies:

> It reopens the debate on the *filioque* and investigates what these non-western pneumatologies can contribute first to a better understanding of the Charismatic movements and the non-white indigenous churches and secondly to the questions which are asked today by physicists and biologists on the relationships between matter and energy, between life and 'eternal life'. Finally it suggests some practical consequences for evangelism and mission by starting with the belief that every single person (and not merely every Christian) has the Spirit of God.[13]

Affirming again in this article his opinion that the Pentecostal and charismatic movements are not strong in their doctrine of the Spirit, he states that in their writings they adopt a Western pneumatology, viewing the spirit as the Spirit of Christ, and thus follow the Western tradition of the *filioque* clause inserted into the Nicene–Constantinople Creed, which states that 'the Spirit proceeds from the Father and the Son'. The Eastern Orthodox Church retained the original version where the Spirit is said to 'proceed from the Father'. That this is the case he says is borne out in the official documents by and on the charismatic movement published by Kilian McDonnell in *Presence, Power, Praise*, and those of the Pentecostal churches in his own book *The Pentecostals.*[14] The pneumatology of

---

11. Hollenweger, 'Creator Spiritus', pp. 35-36.

12. Hollenweger, 'Pneumatologie des Lebens', *Evangelische Kommentare* 16.8 (1983), pp. 446-48; 'All Creatures Great and Small: Towards a Pneumatology of Life', in Martin and Mullen (eds.), *Strange Gifts?*, pp. 41-53.

13. Hollenweger, 'All Creatures', p. 41.

14. Kilian McDonnell, *Presence, Power, Praise: Documents on the Charismatic Renewal* (3 vols.; Collegeville, MN: Liturgical Press, 1980). In his review of this book

the Pentecostal and charismatic movements shares the deficiencies of the pneumatologies of Western tradition by restricting its doctrine of the Holy Spirit to the realization of a Christ-centred theology and the doctrine of salvation. 'The *creator spiritus*, the life-giving *ruach Yahweh* is a perplexing "lost" entity for the west'; it has become 'a prisoner of the Church and its interpretation of the Bible'.[15]

Turning to the Bible, and deliberately focusing on the Old Testament because he felt it had been neglected in thinking about the Spirit, he points out that in the early Hebrew writings the Spirit is the giver of life, of all life, not just of religious life. All life is sustained by the breath of God, the *ruach Yahweh*, which is feminine in Hebrew. Not only good, righteous and religious life, but the whole of life is sustained by her. This Spirit of God is associated with the *force vitale*, as for example in leadership qualities, ecstatic experience, or extraordinary strength; it does not operate only in God's chosen people. He says that the prophets, whose concerns were ethical, were cautious about the Spirit and did not want to be identified with the ecstatics and wonder-workers of their times. Similarly, Hollenweger suggests, the Roman Catholic Church and the Protestant churches have, with a few exceptions, wanted to guard against a 'free-floating' Spirit and so they developed a pneumatology almost identical to their Christology.

Hollenweger's next step is to suggest that the Old Testament attitude to the Spirit of God is not unlike that held by the non-white indigenous churches of the Third World, which selectively take over religious, political, social and medical traditions of their non-Christian past. This selection is not indiscriminate, he says, but their criteria are mostly not Western ones, and Western theologians have mostly regarded as superstition what is outside their own experience—dreams, visions and healings, for example. They have usually opposed pre-Christian practices introduced by Christians in Western missionary churches and indigenous churches—this despite, he points out, Europeans having introduced features of Roman, Hellenistic, Germanic or Celtic traditions into their

---

in *Worship* 55.3 (1981), pp. 267-68, Hollenweger praised McDonnell's work in collecting, translating and interpreting over a hundred documents from classical Pentecostal, Protestant and Roman Catholic churches. He noted, however, the lack of documentation from African, Caribbean, Indian and Pacific independent churches and from non-Catholic churches in Latin America and pointed out this was an area for future ecumenical research.

15. Hollenweger, 'All Creatures', p. 44.

own liturgy and theology (Western funeral rites, marriage ceremonies, 'the graves of war lords in our cathedrals'). His point is that 'the adoption of thought patterns, liturgical formulations and religious rites from paganism was a continuous process in Israelite religion and in the New Testament and European Christianity'. Therefore the problem is not that Third World churches introduce features from their pre-Christian past, but that Westerners do not have theological tools for understanding the process. 'We were not able to attribute the good and life-giving elements in paganism to the Holy Spirit, therefore our theology came into conflict with the experiences of Christians from other cultures'.[16]

A modern pneumatology, says Hollenweger, would have to deal with scientific enquiry into the world. Einstein's famous formula ($E = mc^2$) states that matter can be understood as a form of energy and energy can be understood as a form of matter; matter can be transformed into energy. With subsequent discoveries of the uncertainty principle and quantum theory, it has become increasingly difficult to define what matter is. Experimental physicist John Hasted found, for example, that metal objects could be bent by the presence, or light touch, of certain people—a structural molecular change occurred in the metal only normally possible under very high temperatures. What are the forces, Hollenweger asks, that heal people by laying on of hands, inside and outside Christianity?[17] The biologists' investigations into evolution also warrant theological reflection. It is the theologian's task to understand the world as well as God and human relationships, he says.

The Spirit of Life, Hollenweger suggests, could be one way of expressing the relationship between matter and energy and approaching the question of creation. In fact, he immediately goes on to adopt his own suggestion and says, 'I rather think it is time to acknowledge that the Spirit is the giver of all life in all cultures and religions and perhaps even the agent which holds our universe together'.[18] A new form of Trinitarian doctrine is needed which links the *force vitale* and the appearance of God's revelation in Jesus of Nazareth, the Spirit of Life of the Old Testament and the Spirit as an aspect of Christ in the New Testament. Theologically, this is the question of the relation between creation and salvation. The doctrine of the Holy Spirit, he says, should be in the form of

16. Hollenweger, 'All Creatures', p. 47.
17. Hollenweger, 'All Creatures', p. 49. John Hasted, *The Metal Benders* (London: Routledge & Kegan Paul, 1981).
18. Hollenweger, 'All Creatures', p. 50.

a question, not an answer: different answers will be given according to different thought-patterns, in different models and on the basis of different experiences: a common question, not a common statement is the basis of ecumenical unity. In a situation where people have all kinds of religious experiences, the primary task of the theologian is to distinguish not so much between the demons and the Spirit of God, as between mani-festations of the Spirit that are 'for the common good' (referring to 1 Cor. 12.7) and those that are not.

Finally, a practical consequence of this understanding of the Spirit as the giver of life is this:

> If we are prepared to include in our understanding of the Spirit, the Spirit as giver of life, then this will have important implications for mission and evangelism. If the Spirit is in all people, we can invite whoever is willing to co-operate with us 'for the common good'. They can co-operate in our churches whether they are baptised or not, whether they sign our credal statements or not, because we know that the Spirit is poured out on all flesh.[19]

In his experience, many unchurched people—artists, actors, writers, musicians, for example, are willing to offer their gifts, their charisms. We (Westerners) ignore these gifts, he says, in the same way that we ignore the gifts of indigenous Christians of the Third World.

In this summary of 'All Creatures Great and Small' readers will readily discern from previous chapters how Hollenweger has arrived at this stage of reflection on pneumatology. Contemporary cultural contexts and life experiences, as well as those in the Bible and the first few centuries of Christianity, are recognized as legitimate resources for theologizing. Further, debate on the doctrine of the Holy Spirit and the interpretation of the experiences of the Holy Spirit are firmly placed in an ecumenical and contextual arena. An exclusively christological pneumatology, whether by choice or default in the Roman Catholic Church, the Western Protestant churches or the Pentecostal churches, simply did not encompass the realities of life or the varied writings of biblical authors. Giving due attention to creation as well as to revelation and salvation provided the framework for an intercultural approach to pneumatology.

Giving Attention to Creation

'All Creatures Great and Small' was followed by an extensive exploration of the potential for an intercultural pneumatology giving due attention to

19. Hollenweger, 'All Creatures', p. 53.

creation, a pneumatology that had relevance to the realities of life. *Geist und Materie* ('Spirit and Matter'), the third volume of Hollenweger's *Intercultural Theology*, was published in 1988.[20] He is here, he says, in search of a doctrine of the Spirit that stands in critical dialogue with his life, with the life of research entrusted to him, with the lives of his friends and colleagues, with the life of communities with which he has been in regular contact.[21] His point of departure, given in the Introduction, is a sharpened analysis of his previous submission: the Pentecostal movement, the charismatic movement and the independent churches of the Third World have no independent pneumatology; this is an observation, not a reproach, for they think strictly within Western pneumatology.

> It is not possible for them to get the whole breadth of human experience within and outside the *oikumene* into the theological field of vision. That would only be possible if Spirit-doctrine were anchored in creation-doctrine. In spite of occasional attempts in the west, until now this has not been taken up. This is in part also the responsibility of we theologians for contributing very little to the Christian experience of healing, similarly to the secular experience of parapsychology, to common religious experiences and to the questions of modern physics.[22]

Hollenweger explores these topics using case studies, narratives and literature drawn from different cultures and material from non-theological disciplines.[23] The 'from life to theology' approach is reflected in the novel

20. See Chapter 1 above, p. 21.

21. Hollenweger, *Geist und Materie*, p. 18: 'Vom Leben zur Theologie' ('From Life to Theology'): 'Ich versuche eine Geistlehre, die in kritischem Gespräch zu meinem Leben steht, zum Leben der mir anvertrauten Forscher, zum Leben meiner Freunde und Kollegen, zum Leben der Gemeinden, mit denen ich regelmässig in Kontakt bin.'

22. Hollenweger, *Geist und Materie*, p. 13. 'Die Pfingstbewegung, die charismatische Bewegung und die mit ihnen verwandten Unabhängigen Kirchen der Dritten Welt haben keinen eigenständigen Beitrag zur Pneumatologie geleistet... Das soll kein Vorwurf, sondern eine Feststellung sein, denn die pfingstlichen Bewegungen denken strikte innerhalb der westlichen Pneumatologie. Est ist ihnen daher nicht möglich, die ganze Breite menschlicher Erfahrung innerhalb und ausserhalb der Ökumene ins theologische Blickfeld zu bekommen. Das wäre erst möglich, wenn die Geistlehre in der Schöpfungslehre verankt würde. Dass dies trotz vereinzelter Versuche im Westen bis jetzt nicht zum Tragen kam, ist zum Teil verantwortlich dafür, dass wir Theologen sowohl zu den christlichen Erfahrungen der Heilung, wie zu den säkularen Erfahrungen der Parapsychologie, zu allgemein religiösen Erfahrungen und zu den Fragen der modernen Physik recht wenig beizutragen haben.'

23. On Hollenweger's methodology see Chapter 2 above.

organization of the book: the sections are 'Spirit and Body', 'Spirit and Spirits', 'Spirit and Religion', 'Spirit and Matter' and 'Spirit and Church'. As one reviewer observed:

> his pneumatology is not a systematic essay of what the Bible says about the Holy Spirit, but a collection of responsible Christian answers to questions people ask when faced with the notion of spirit, no matter whether they are Christian, disciples of another religion, or not religious at all.[24]

Another commented:

> The person who reads it without prejudice will constantly be astonished at what a mass of surprising connections, unfamiliar perspectives and formulations are given us... The person looking for a systematic structure will often be irritated.[25]

I am faced with a considerable challenge at this point. As the book has not been translated into English,[26] its coverage in some detail would be useful. Because of the nature of the book, as indicated by the reviewers, a comprehensive summary is well-nigh impossible. The constant surprises, novel juxtapositioning of topics, variety of source material and wide-ranging discussion are of the essence of the book. The wisdom of trying to convey the contents of 340 pages of text and footnotes (plus 33 pages of bibliography) dealing with unconventional material from unfamiliar perspectives in a few paragraphs is questionable. I am, however, going to take the risk, because although the reader may be (temporarily, I hope) overwhelmed by the ensuing bombardment of ideas, this course seems to be the most appropriate available to communicate faithfully Hollen-weger's approach and thinking.

The first section, 'Spirit and Body' sets the tone of the book by using a praxis orientation to the subject of healing.[27] Hollenweger briefly affirms that whatever the modern conceptual resistance to the biblical healing

---

24. Jean-Daniel Pluess, Review of *Geist und Materie* in *EPTA Bulletin* 7.2 (1988), pp. 70-72 (71).

25. Christoph Müller, Review of *Geist und Materie* in *Reformiertes Forum* 38 (22 September 1988): 'Wer es unvoreingenommen liest, wird immer wieder erstaunt sein, welche Fülle an überraschenden Zusammenhängen, ungewohnten Perpsektiven und Fragestellungen uns begegnet... Wer systematisch Ordnung sucht, wird oft irritiert.'

26. Parts that have been published in English as articles, or related articles, are noted where appropriate.

27. A very condensed version of 'Spirit and Body' can be found in English in 'Healing through Prayer: Superstition or Forgotten Christian Tradition?', *Theology* 92.747 (1989), pp. 166-74. See also *Pentecostalism: Origins*, ch. 18, 'Signs and Wonders'.

miracles, it remains true that the evangelists and the community of Jesus Christ have something to do with service to the sick and that, in practice, prayer with the sick is found to be helpful.[28] This is followed by a text of a Christian liturgy 'with and for the sick'. Having endorsed the Christian practice of prayer for the sick, Hollenweger then presents two case studies of 'spontaneous healing' or 'healing through prayer' known to him personally where medical or psychiatric explanations could be offered. If readers are unsure where they are headed at this point, the next chapter takes another unexpected direction. 'For all the nations were deceived by your *pharmakeia*' (Rev. 18.23) concerns not, as might be anticipated, witchcraft and sorcery (familiar translations of the ambiguous Greek), but the crisis in Western medicine. It is in crisis in the West, Hollenweger says, because of, among other things, unrealistic expectations, because of the pharmaceutical industry, bureaucracy and the passivity induced in patients. Secondly, Western medicine is in crisis because of its 'catastrophic failure' in the Third World—it is prohibitively expensive and inefficient and ignores alternative therapies. Quoting Gerd Theissen's 'Superstition is the faith which is rejected in a society… Faith is the superstition accepted in a society', Hollenweger prepares the way for his discussion of healing outside Christianity and medicine.[29] African traditional healers, Western spiritualist healers, a Hindu in Birmingham who is healed and becomes a Christian, a Korean Buddhist nun who performs operations without instruments or anaesthetics and later joins a Reformed church, a spontaneous healing in a Western charismatic setting, all provide Christians with questions about the classification of alternative healing practices. Hollenweger articulates the dilemma: healing cannot be neatly divided into Christian or non-Christian, medical or non-medical.

> God has made humans (not only Christian humans) so wonderfully that they have in themselves gifts of healing. The Bible says clearly that we live because God breathed his Spirit into us. If he takes back his Spirit, we die. That is to say, all people, not only Christians, live through the Holy Spirit.

---

28. Hollenweger, *Geist und Materie*, pp. 24-28: 1.1 'Die Theorie: Gebet mit Kranken ist überholt' ('The Theory: Prayer with the sick is outdated') and 1.2 'Die Praxis: Gebet mit Kranken ist hilfreich' ('The Practice: prayer with the sick is helpful'). Hollenweger relates the experience of a hospital chaplain, who discovered that prayer with the patient, staff and immediate family before an operation was found helpful, whatever the outcome of the operation.

29. Hollenweger, *Geist und Materie*, p. 45. Gerd Theissen, *Urchristliche Wundergeschichten. Ein Beitrag zur formgeschichtlichen Erforschung der synoptischen Evangelien* (Gütersloh: Chr. Kaiser Verlag, 1974), p. 230.

It is therefore not surprising that this Spirit of God liberates forces of healing in Christians and non-Christians alike.[30]

His final question, 'Is there a specifically Christian encounter with the sick?' is answered positively: it is derived from the belief in God's freedom and sovereignty. Therefore, a causal connection between the sins of the patients or their ancestors and their illness is rejected by the gospel, faith does not automatically lead to health nor is unbelief automatically the cause of illness, faith is not always a condition for healing, and Christians involved in the healing ministry avoid self-propaganda.[31] The purpose of the 'Body and Spirit' section, he says, has not been to prove God's intervention but to embolden the Christian community to take the bodily, material side of their worship and service to God seriously.[32]

The next section, 'Spirit and Spirits', has a lengthy narrative featuring the fictional 'Professor Unrat' attending a séance in Paris.[33] Through the offices of a medium, audio and visual messages are received from dead relatives, including an oblique warning of a plane crash. The group, which includes a politician, a doctor, a musician, an army officer and a Jesuit, meet to discuss the event the following day, allowing Hollenweger to introduce some of the history of church attitudes to, and scientific research into, parapsychological phenomena. After this narrative forming a European experiential and intellectual base, Hollenweger gives the reasons for his interest in parapsychology: (1) his encounters with the healing of the sick; (2) Fritz Blanke, his teacher in church history, had introduced him to phenomena such as stigmatization; and (3) the theological issues raised by his doctoral students from the Third World, for whom the question whether psychic abilities could be put to the service of the kingdom of God is particularly important.[34] In addition there is a general interest evident in the media and current research like that of Hasted referred to above.[35]

30. Hollenweger, *Geist und Materie*, pp. 56-57.

31. Hollenweger, *Geist und Materie*, pp. 57-58. Hollenweger is thus critical of the proponents of 'power' healing like the late John Wimber, of whom he writes briefly in *Pentecostalism: Origins*, pp. 230-32.

32. Hollenweger, *Geist und Materie*, p. 59: 'Die Funktion dieses Kapitels war nicht, Gottes Eingriff zu beweisen, sondern den christlichen Gemeinden Mut zu machen, die leibhafte, materielle Seite ihres Gottesdienstes ernst zu nehmen.'

33. Hollenweger, *Geist und Materie*, pp. 69-86. On 'Professor Unrat' see above, Chapter 4, pp. 89-91.

34. An issue raised by Adolf Köberle in various works, noted 103-4.

35. Hollenweger refers here to Yuri Geller and the research of John Hasted. See *Geist und Materie*, pp. 94-96.

European and South African cases of spirit possession and exorcism are discussed, with social and psychological factors considered. As Hollenweger had earlier commented in an article published in English, 'Roots and Fruits of the Charismatic Renewal in the Third World', whereas demon possession was formerly regarded as Third World superstition, there is now an upsurge of interest in Europe. Referring to a well-documented and debated (by psychiatrists and theologians) instance of exorcism in Germany, he remarks: 'the cultural barriers between Europe and Africa are not insurmountable if we Europeans take serious note of those parts of our history which are out of keeping with our view of Europe as entirely rational and enlightened'.[36] Posing the question 'Are there evil spirits?' in 'Spirit and Spirits' Hollenweger refuses to give a straight answer, suggesting instead that if people believe in them then they have power, and secondly that in the Old Testament Satan is not entirely separated from God: 'He has access to heaven and belonged, so to speak, to the staff of the heavenly spirit. It is possible to imagine of God that all reality is contained in Him, including the shadow side of Creation.'[37] Hollenweger inclines to this perspective rather than the other, later, biblical view of Satan as God's opponent and the dualistic explanation of Good versus Evil. Many Third World theologians also, says Hollenweger, refuse to draw a sharp line between God and the Devil.[38] The attitude of biblical writers is to give little attention to the nature of evil spirits but rather to focus on how to overcome them; there is room for liturgical

36. Hollenweger, 'Roots and Fruits of the Charismatic Renewal in the Third World', in Martin and Mullen (eds.), *Strange Gifts?*, pp. 172-91 (184). A fully footnoted and documented version of this article appeared in *Theological Renewal* 14, (February 1980) and in *International Bulletin of Missionary Research* 4.2 (1980). The need for a multidisciplinary approach to the study of demon possession and exorcism and other 'ecstatic' manifestations had been affirmed by Hollenweger much earlier in a substantial article, 'Funktionen der ekstatischen Frömmigkeit der Pfingstbewegung' ('Functions of the ecstatic religiousness of the Pentecostal movement'), in T. Spoerri (ed.) *Beiträge zur Ekstase. Biblioteca Psychiatrica et Neurologica* 134 (Basel: Karger, 1968), pp. 53-72.

37. Hollenweger, *Geist und Materie*, 'Gibt es Böse Geister?', pp. 113-16 (114): 'Nach dem Alten Testament ist der Satan nicht total getrennt von Gott. Er hat Zutritt zum Himmel und gehört sozusagen zum Stab der himmlischen Geister. [Job 1:6ff] Es ist möglich, sich Gott so vorzustellen, dass alle Wirklichkeit in ihm enthalten ist, auch die Schattenseiten der Schöpfung.'

38. He cites as an example George Mulrain's research *Theology in Folk Culture: The Theological Significance of Haitian Folk Religion* (Frankfurt am Main: Peter Lang, 1984), dealt with earlier in the chapter.

exorcism as well as social, individual psychological and political action to
assist the 'overcoming'.[39]

Hollenweger's persistent boundary-crossing encourages subjects to be
considered together which are not conventionally embraced at the same
level of discourse. This is well illustrated in the next section, 'Spirit and
Religion'. Having addressed healing and parapsychology in relation to the
Spirit of God, he turns attention to religions other than Christianity as
another area of very practical concern to society which requires Christian
response. The foundation here is the 'inner light' of the Quakers.[40] On the
basis of their social-ethical and social-political engagement (which
Hollenweger documents in some detail) the hermeneutic principle of the
inner light can be understood as a cooperative principle in the sense of the
body of Christ.[41] He then proceeds to examine this principle with regard to
Christian relations with non-Christian religions, using new religious movements and the Unification Church, then Jesus in the Koran and Muslim
Christology as 'ways in'. The complexities and possibilities of a 'pneumatology of life' are demonstrated through chapters including religious
pluralism, race, the 1985 Handsworth riots in Birmingham; civil religion,
church and state and cross-cultural evangelists; the church for others; new
patriotism (examples from 5 different countries); the role of outsiders; the
Bible as process (with the example of 'wrestling Jacob')[42]; and elements
of a Christian theology of religion developed from a non-colonial model of
mission.[43] The section closes with a discussion of the necessity of dialogue
with non-Christians, adherents of New Religious Movements and popular
religion, new and old patriotism, and with Hindus, Buddhists and Muslims, summed up with the quotation of Lk. 6.21, 'Blessed are you that
hunger now, for you shall be satisfied', indicating that the subject remains
open rather than concluded.[44]

The term 'Intercultural', as Hollenweger uses it, refers both to encounter

---

39. Hollenweger, *Geist und Materie*, pp. 116-20, 'Nicht Definition, sondern
Heilung' ('Not definition but healing') and 'Elemente einer exorzistschen Liturgie'
('Elements of an exorcism liturgy').

40. Hollenweger, *Geist und Materie*, pp. 123-33.

41. Hollenweger, *Geist und Materie*, p. 133: 'Das hermeneutische Prinzip des inneres
Lichtes, das nicht individuell, sondern kooperativ im Sinne des Leibes Christi verstanden
wird, ist die Grundlage ihres sozialethischen und sozialpolitischen Engagements.'

42. See above Chapter 3, pp. 49-50, 57.

43. See Chapter 5 above, especially the section 'Non-Colonial Evangelism'.

44. Hollenweger, *Geist und Materie*, p. 269. This section, 'Spirit and Religion' is
the longest in the book: pp. 121-269.

and dialogue between Christians with different cultural traditions in different parts of the world and to encounter and dialogue between church cultures and non-church cultures in particular contexts.[45] Thus in Part IV, 'Spirit and Matter', he takes up a conversation with modern physics on the understanding of creation. The summary at the beginning of the section says that with the end of a worldview which thought that things could be observed and written about objectively and that biographical, cultural and social contexts were irrelevant for scientific research, has come the end of the separation of reality into matter and spirit. If scientists want to locate the spirit in matter, this makes work on a theological pneumatology more difficult, rather than easier. If the Spirit of God is in everything, then it is necessary to distinguish between pantheism (which makes everything God) and panentheism, in which the Spirit of God can be seen in everything but this Spirit is not limited to the accessible world.[46] Hollenweger then takes readers through propositions made by W. Heisenberg (Uncertainty Principle and Quantum Theology), Albert Einstein (Theory of Relativity and Formulation of Energy), and Carl Friedrich von Weizsäcker, focusing particularly on von Weizsäcker's book *Der Garten des Menschlichen*. The autobiography of this German nuclear physicist and the reflections on science and religion offered in his book provide Hollenweger with a breadth of material to use for informed and referenced discussion on spirit and matter which range from political power and peace to facts, truth and prayer.

Geist und Materie ends where a book on Christian pneumatology might

---

45. See Chapter 4 above.

46. Hollenweger, *Geist und Materie*, p. 271: 'Das Thema wird durch eine Geschichte eingeführt, die auf allgemein verständliche Weise das beschreibt, was H. Pietschmann "das Ende des naturwissenschaftlichen Zeitalters" nennt. Was zu Ende geht, ist das kausale, determinierte Weltbild, die Illusion, dass wir die Dinge objektiv sehen und beschreiben können, der Glaube, dass der biographische, soziale und kulturelle Kontext des Forschers irrelevant sei für seine wissenschaftlichen Forschungen. [An extensive list of literature is given in the footnote].

Was zu Ende geht, ist die Trennung der Wirklichkeit in Materie und Geist. Darum kommen in Kap. 23 diejenigen Naturwissenschaftler zu Wort, die den Geist in der Materie lokalisieren wollen, was allerdings die Arbeit an einer theologischen Pneumatologie nicht etwa erleichtert, sondern erschwert.

Wenn der Geist Gottes in allem ist, wie vermeiden wir dann einen Pantheismus, der alles zu Gott macht? Wir vermeiden ihn durch einen differenzierten Panentheismus, der zwar in allem den Geist Gottes sieht, aber diesen Geist nicht auf die uns zugängliche Welt beschränkt.'

be expected to begin—with 'Spirit and Church'. By the time we have
arrived at this topic Hollenweger has presented a plethora of material to
illustrate the complexity of experiences and interpretations which can be
set in critical relationship with an understanding of the Holy Spirit in
solely christological categories. Elaborating on the ecumenical diversity of
understandings outlined in 'All Creatures Great and Small', he points out
the resources of the Eastern Orthodox and Old Catholic Churches and
Reformers such as Calvin and Zwingli to mitigate the Western application
of the *filioque* clause which, in practice, regards the Spirit as proceeding
from the Father through the Son and not directly from the Father. 'The
Western doctrine of the Spirit is not in the first instance a doctrine about
the Spirit but about the Spirit's management by the Church.'[47] Under the
heading 'Freedom of the Spirit' Hollenweger draws particularly on Daniel
Lys's classic book *Rûach, le souffle dans l'Ancien Testament* (1972) to
point out the Old Testament understanding of the *ruach Yahweh* as the
giver of all life, an understanding which does not distinguish between
physical and spiritual life, between 'respiration' and 'inspiration'. *Ruach
Yahweh* does not indicate the 'spiritual' side of the creation of humans, but
rather that human beings owe their creation to God.[48] In the New Testament this understanding, though still present, became limited by the assessment of charisms in the letters to the Romans and Corinthians particularly.
On the one hand 'charisma' indicates all of human existence and on the
other it indicates concrete instances like diakonia, teaching, comforting
and exhortation, organization, prophecy, gifts of healing, speaking with
tongues, being married or single, and so on. Paul did not restrict charisms
to the miraculous or spontaneous; he took a functional perspective on the
exercise of the gifts using the criterion of whether they contributed to 'the
common good of the community' (1 Cor. 12.7). Hollenweger draws the
conclusion, holding the two threads together, that whether Christian or not,
all people have God-given charisms which can be used 'for the common
good' of the community. Jesus, he reminds us, sent the disciples to work
before they were really converted, and few of the prophets were theologically and morally flawless when God used them.[49]

---

47. Hollenweger, *Geist und Materie*, p. 305. 'Die westliche Geistlehre ist nicht in
erster Linie eine Lehre über den Geist, sondern über dessen Verwaltung durch die
Kirche.' The foregoing section, 'Die Verwaltung des Geistes' ('The Management of
the Spirit') can be found in English as 'After Twenty Years'.
    48. Hollenweger, *Geist und Materie*, pp. 308-11.
    49. Hollenweger, *Geist und Materie*, pp. 311-14.

Thus he makes the firm statement, 'The spirit is not only at work in the Church, but also in the World'.[50] Speaking in tongues (glossolalia), for example, could be viewed not as a spontaneous occurrence in Christians of power from outside, but as an integral part of creation. It is not supernatural but uncommon, a means of communication found in some social contexts more than others.[51] Similarly, prophecy is a widespread phenomenon found in many historical and contemporary religions.

Finally, in 'The Community of the Spirit', Hollenweger points out that the doctrine of the Trinity has long been and continues to be a 'bone of contention' in the church among lay people, pastors and theologians. His considered position is that the doctrine is a 'monument to archetypal connections', a 'frontier-marker' to a question which because it cannot be answered, must be held open.[52] Its usefulness as a question is that we must continue to address the relationship between God's three modes of being, or roles ('personas'), as the transcendent one (who is not identical with us or with his creation), the immanent one (the *Creator Spiritus* whom we experience in creation, in history and in our lives) and the God who decisively reveals himself in the event Jesus of Nazareth.[53]

50. Hollenweger, *Geist und Materie*, p. 314: 'Der Geist ist nicht nur in der Kirche am Werk, sondern auch in der Welt.'

51. On speaking in tongues outside Christianity, Hollenweger makes reference to D. Christie-Murray, *Voices from the Gods* (1978), C.G. Williams, *Tongues of the Spirit* (1981), W.J. Samarin, *Tongues of Men and Angels* (1970) and W.E. Mills (ed.), *Speaking in Tongues* (1986).

52. Hollenweger, *Geist und Materie*, pp. 325-35 (329): 'Für mich ist daher die Trinitätslehre ein Denkmal archetypischer Zusammenhänge, ein archaisches Dokument, das uns fortwährend an unsere Bedingtheit erinnert, ein Grenzstein an der Grenze kaum beantwortbarer Fragen, die wir—eben weil wir sie nicht beantworten können—als unbeantwortete offen halten müssen.'

53. Hollenweger, *Geist und Materie*, p. 329. In the same year that *Geist und Materie* was published, 1988, Hollenweger presented a paper entitled 'Kosmische Gottheit und Persönlicher Gott: Gespräch mit der Anthroposophie' ('Cosmic Deity and Personal God: A Conversation with Anthroposophy') to a conference at the Evangelische Akademie Bad Boll (*Protokolldienst* 33.88, pp. 13-22). Here, under the heading, 'God as Person', he explains to the audience how the debate with Marcion set the context for the making of the Apostles' Creed. At that time 'persona' was the name given to the masks worn by actors in a play, which has caused confusion since by being understood as 'person'. He then discusses the Old Testament understanding of the *ruach Yahweh*, and the charismata in the New Testament, affirming here again the natural, not supernatural nature of the gifts, p. 18: 'All these phenomena [organization, teaching, healing, speaking with tongues etc.] are not specifically Christian. They

The Dignity of the Spirit

In giving attention to God's role as the *ruach Yahweh*, the Creator Spirit, Hollenweger ascribed a dignity to the Holy Spirit not often found in Western conceptual formulations. This dignity essentially rested on the Spirit's freedom as evidenced in the Bible: the Spirit could not be controlled, only responded to; the Spirit could not be circumscribed by definition, only described in a variety of ways as experienced by different groups of people.[54] Making this point in a 1995 lecture, 'How Did the First Christians Experience the Holy Spirit?' Hollenweger drew attention to three Spirit-traditions in the New Testament. Here, as well as in the Old Testament, there is an understanding of the Spirit as the giver of life, given to all people: Matthew's story of the pagan astronomers who brought their gifts to Jesus is of particular interest (luckily, says Hollenweger, Matthew did not have to submit his Gospel to a doctrine commission for examination—he got away with it). Another interesting narrative is the conversion of Cornelius, or as Hollenweger prefers to refer to it, the conversion of Peter; Cornelius and his household receive the gift of speaking in

belong to the realm of the Creator Spirit... But they become Christian in the moment when they are placed in the service of the Kingdom of God.' ('Alle diese Phänomene sind nicht spezifisch christlich. Sie gehören zum Bereich des Schöpfergeistes... Sie werden aber christlich in dem Moment, wo sie in den Dienst des Reiches Gottes gestellt werden.') Protestant theology has neglected, he said, what the Bible and Third World churches know—that God is the soul of the cosmos in the *ruach Yahweh*, and that is why people are leaving the churches in Europe and travelling to places like Asia in search of spirituality (p. 19). For an introduction to anthroposophy see Robert A. McDermott, 'Rudolph Steiner and Anthroposophy', in A. Faivre and J. Needleman (eds.), *Modern Esoteric Spirituality* (London: SCM Press, 1992), pp. 288-310.

54. Hollenweger, 'Wie erlebten die ersten Christen den Heiligen Geist?', in *idem*, *Wie erlebten die ersten Christen den Heiligen Geist? und Predigt über Joh.20.29b*, pp. 1-14 (14). 'Erstens müssen wir zur Kenntnis nehmen, dass die Bibel keine durchgehende Definition des Geistes gibt. Sie ist nicht interessiert an einer logisch-kohärenten und systematischen Erarbeitung der Theologie. Sie beschreibt, wie der Geist von verschiedenen Gruppen von Menschen erfahren wurde.' 'If we even in the natural sciences do not know what is, but only how it is encountered', Hollenweger continued, 'it is not surprising that we cannot say what the Spirit is, but only how he encounters different people.' ('Wenn wir schon in der Naturwissenschaft nicht wissen, was ist, sondern nur, wie es uns begegnet..., ist es nicht verwundlich, dass wir nicht sagen können, was der Geist ist, sondern nur, wie er verschiedenen Menschen begegnet.')

tongues before Peter has finished preaching and before they are baptized. Even Jesus himself, the Son of God, learnt something about the gospel from the heathen woman who wanted him to heal her daughter.[55] Secondly, there is the Pauline understanding of the Spirit that brings Christians together as a body, which is limited to Christians. The third tradition is found in Luke, described as a crisis experience of those who have already become Christians. These three Spirit-traditions also continue to be found in contemporary denominations: the first in Eastern Orthodoxy and old Liberals (e.g. Albert Schweitzer or Paul Tillich); the second in the Reformation churches, derived from Paul and swallowed up in Christology; and the third in the Lukan-Catholic tradition with the two stages of salvation derived from Paul and Luke and whose followers expect a special experience of the Spirit. All three streams are important to get a whole picture of the Spirit, suggested Hollenweger, but not so that one group wants to convince the others that they are right and the others are wrong. 'Theology is a process, not a definitive result—we still have to learn that.'[56]

An important part of this ongoing theological process for Hollenweger is awareness that pneumatology should not be reduced to Christology and the recognition of the Spirit outside the churches and outside the influence of the Christian gospel. For him the awareness and recognition arose

---

55. Hollenweger, 'Wie erlebten', pp. 2-3.

56. Hollenweger, 'Wie erlebten', Summary, pp. 13-14. 'Wir haben gesehen, es gibt in der Bibel mindestens drei Geisttraditionen: 1. Der Geist als Lebensspender, allen Menschen gegeben, 2. Der Geist, der die Christen zu einem Leib zusammenführt, der auf die Christen beschränkt ist (Paulus), und 3. Der Geist als Krisiserfahrung derjenigen, die schon Christen geworden sind (Lukas). Diese drei Geisttraditionen finden sich auch in unseren heutigen Konfessionen wieder: Die erste Tradition wird vertreten durch die östliche Orthodoxie und die alten Liberalen (zum beispiel Albert Schweitzer oder Paul Tillich). Die zweite Tradition findet sich in den reformatorischen Kirchen, allerdings ohne die dramatische Erfahrungsdimension des Paulus. In der reformatorischen Tradition werden die nichtpaulinischen Traditionen in der Bibel konsequent von Paulus her ausgelegt. Man nennt das "was Christum treibet". Das heisst, der Geist wird von der Christologie verschluckt. Er hat keine eigene Würde und ist im Grunde in den reformatorischen Kirchen arbeitslos. Drittens, gibt es auch heute die lukanisch-katholische Tradition mit dem zweistufigen Heilsweg, die Paulus von Lukas her auslegt und von ihren Anhängern erwartet, dass sie eine besondere Geisterfahrung machen... Um aber ein Gesamtbild des Geistes zu bekommen, sind wohl alle drei Ströme nötig, aber nicht so, dass die eine Gruppierung die andere davon überzeugen will, dass sie recht und die anderen unrecht haben... Dass daher Theologie ein Prozess und nicht ein definitorisches Ergebnis ist—das müssen wir noch lernen.'

primarily from Pentecostal and intercultural (mission) studies. This is articulated in *Pentecostalism: Origins* in the following way. Having argued in
other chapters that an important element of Pentecostal spirituality, and in
its growth as a movement, comes from the black slave religion and the
pre-Christian African past from which it derived; that many elements of
pre-Christian African religions have been selectively integrated and
transformed in African Pentecostal churches; that elements of Korean
Shamanism re-emerge in Korean Pentecostalism; that elements of American Indian culture re-emerge in Latin American Pentecostalism; and that
elements of Western middle-class culture become dominant in Western
Pentecostalism, then, he suggests, these elements could belong to the
realm of the *Creator Spiritus*, 'to the good but confused order of creation',
to the Holy Spirit as *ruach Yahweh*.[57] The realities of the variety of
Christian experience, practice and understanding, plus the interaction of
Christianity with pre-Christian and non-Christian cultures, present, for
Hollenweger, impelling reasons for consideration of the Spirit in a broader
field of vision.

What has happened, or is continuing to happen, in history is for Hollenweger a fruitful field to pursue. This can be seen clearly in his preference
for 'real history' rather than ideology in Pentecostalism, and his champion-
ing of William Seymour rather than Charles Parham as the key figure in
the contemporary movement.[58] It is in Seymour and the events of the

57. Hollenweger, *Pentecostalism: Origins*, p. 219. On syncretism, see above,
Chapter 4, 'Comment'.

58. See, for example, the following: 'Pfingstkirchen' (pp. 1163, 1164), where
Hollenweger deals with Parham and speaking in tongues as the initial sign under the
heading of 'Ideological-historic historiography' ('Die ideengeschichtl. Geschichtsschreibung') and Seymour and the black and Catholic influences under the heading
'Realistic historic historiography' ('Die Realgeschichtl. Geschichtsschreibung'). See
also 'From Azusa Street' where Hollenweger states (p. 4): 'The most important root of
the Pentecostal and charismatic movements is a revival in a Black church on Azusa
Street in Los Angeles under the leadership of the Black ecumenist William J. Seymour
(1870–1922).' In this article Hollenweger summarizes the historical traditions of
Pentecostalism under the headings of 'The Black oral root', 'The Catholic root', 'The
Evangelical root', 'The critical root' and 'The ecumenical root'. These are the headings
developed at length in *Pentecostalism: Origins*. In this book see ch. 3, 'The
Beginnings', where Hollenweger deals with the discussion within Pentecostalism on
the founders, challenging James R. Goff's assessment of Parham (*Fields White Unto
Harvest: Charles F. Parham and the Missionary Origins of Pentecostalism* [Arkansas:
University of Arkansas Press, 1988]). He wrote (p. 23): 'Parham's pacifism, his
doctrine on the "destruction of the wicked", his animosity to medicine, his Anglo-

revival at Azusa Street, where experiences broke down the barriers between black and white, educated and uneducated, men and women, slaves and free people, and people of different ethnic groups and denominations, rather than in Parham with his emphasis on the doctrine of baptism of the Spirit evidenced by speaking in tongues at Topeka, that he sees the strength of the movement. The Azusa street origins signal the potential contribution of Pentecostalism to the overcoming of racism. Extraordinary (not super-natural) experiences are undoubtedly significant for individuals, but they should not be raised to normative status. In Hollenweger's view, as we have noted, experiences such as speaking in tongues belong to the realm of creation; they become Christian when they are used, in Paul's words, 'for the common good of the community' (1 Cor. 12.7). Not all Pentecostals subscribe to the doctrine of the 'initial sign'. Those who don't include Seymour himself, Chilean Pentecostals, and Jonathan Paul, the founder of the German Pentecostal movement, and perhaps a decreasing proportion of members of those who do subscribe actually speak in tongues.[59] It does not help for the most powerful groups (North American classical Pente-costals) to make strong attempts to revive the doctrine of the 'initial sign', according to Hollenweger (who also notes that in the Roman Catholic Church, the less priests live a celibate life, and the more women take a leading part in liturgy, 'the more the Vatican condemns such behaviour'). 'The heavy doctrinal emphasis is almost always a sign that the experience is waning. And no doctrinal emphasis is going to change this.'[60]

Israel theories, his sympathy with the Ku Klux Klan—all this has been contradicted by Pentecostalism… there is hardly a Pentecostal movement in the world that is not built on Seymour's oral black modes of communication. Furthermore, Pentecostalism has not yet come to its maturity. It could very well be that it offers the key to overcoming racism in the world today, as some of the more enlightened Pentecostals are now discovering that Pentecost is more than Parham's narrow ideology.'

59. See Barrett, 'Statistics, Global', where he states, 'Most Pentecostal denominations teach that tongues-speaking is mandatory for all members, but in practice today only 35% of all members have practised this gift either initially or as an on-going experience' (p. 820). On Chilean and German Pentecostalism see Hollenweger, *Pentecostalism: Origins*, chs. 10 and 25. For an introduction to the subject of speaking in tongues see R.P. Spittler's entry, 'Glossolalia', in Burgess and McGee (eds.), *Dictionary of Pentecostal*. On Spirit-baptism in the charismatic movement see Henry Lederle, *Treasures Old and New: Interpretation of Spirit-Baptism in the Charismatic Renewal Movement* (Peabody, MA: Hendrickson, 1988) and Hollenweger's review in *Pneuma* 10.1 (1988), pp. 62-64.

60. W.J. Hollenweger, 'The Contribution of Critical Exegesis to Pentecostal Hermeneutics', *The Spirit & Church* 2.1 (2000), pp. 7-18 (10-11).

In a recent comprehensive article reviewing the official Roman Catholic–Pentecostal dialogue which began in 1972, Hollenweger, after pointing out their shared understanding of the active power of the Holy Spirit and their differences in deciding who should judge 'present revelation' (though he thought Pentecostals would increasingly come to adopt the Catholic belief that it should be judged by the official church institution), continued by pointing both groups to concrete historical realities. Few Christians had fought for the Jews in the 1939–45 war—only one Pentecostal, as far as he knew, Louis Dallière of France, a few Protestants, for example Dietrich Bonhoeffer and Karl Barth, and many secularists.

> So was the Holy Spirit perhaps blowing more outside Pentecostalism and Catholicism? And if so, might we also expect him (or her) today outside the church, according to the testimony of Acts 2.17 (the Holy Spirit is poured out on *all* flesh) or the prophetic understanding of the pagan king Cyrus as an anointed one, a Messiah, a Christ (Isaiah 45.1)? Are Pentecostals prepared to realize that the Holy Spirit blows also outside the Christian community?[61]

In moving from life to theology, re-engaging with the Bible to retrieve aspects of the Spirit of God submerged in much subsequent Christian thinking, recalling the disputed *filioque* clause of the Nicene–Constantinople Creed, and highlighting the international, multidisciplinary and ecumenical dimensions of discussion, Hollenweger ascribes dignity and

---

61. W.J. Hollenweger, 'Roman Catholics and Pentecostals in Dialogue', *Ecumenical Review* 51.2 (1999), pp. 147-59 (152-53). Reference to the shared Roman Catholic and Pentecostal understanding is taken from Gerald O'Collins, 'Revelation Past and Present', in René Latourelle (ed.), *Vatican II: Assessment and Perspectives, Twenty Years After (1962-1987)* (New York: Paulist Press, 1988), p. 129. On Dallière (1887–1976), see *Pentecostalism: Origins*, pp. 338-42. Had the August 2000 Vatican document *Dominus Iesus* (signed by Cardinal Joseph Ratzinger, Prefect of the Congregation for the Doctrine of the Faith, and Archbishop Tarcisio Bertone, Secretary, and confirmed and ratified by the Pope) been published when Hollenweger wrote this article for the *Ecumenical Review*, he might have asked the same question directly of the Roman Catholic Church. Recalling bishops, theologians and all the Catholic faithful to Christian doctrine, warning of the danger of 'relativistic theories' to the 'absolute truth' of the church and 'the subsistence of the one Church of Christ in the Catholic Church', it proceeds to affirm in relation to salvation, 'the action of the Spirit is not outside or parallel to the action of Christ'. Congregation for the Doctrine of the Faith ' "Dominus Iesus": Declaration on the unicity and salvitic universality of Jesus Christ and the Church' (London: Catholic Truth Society, 2000). For some comments see *The Tablet* 9, 16 and 30 September 2000.

freedom to the Holy Spirit. It may be considered, however, by various groups of Christians whose interpretations of their experiences of the Holy Spirit are relativized by this line of thinking, that there is too high a price to pay for subscribing to it. The Holy Spirit cannot be monopolized, restricted, possessed or confined—no group can claim authority over it.[62]

Comment

Hollenweger is not a renegade who thinks the unthinkable. There is, arguably, in his writing, not one area relevant to pneumatology which has not been addressed and debated by others—biblical scholars, historians, anthropologists, systematic theologians, missiologists, natural scientists, psychologists or sociologists. And yet his approach is particularly unsettling. With the bombardment of material brought together, often in original juxtapositioning, Hollenweger redraws the field of play. A panorama of interconnected issues is offered revealing the complexity of sources for reflection, issues which cannot be satisfactorily dealt with from narrow denominational, cultural or academic disciplinary perspectives. Readers are compelled to respond and rethink because questions are raised for which there are no ready-prepared answers.

If his sources were not the Bible, church history, diverse contemporary Christian experiences and interpretation, and worldwide cultural contexts, he might be considered a theological trouble-maker looking for ways to undermine the church. As they are, however, commonly held legitimate sources of academic research, Hollenweger can be viewed as a creative realist. Focusing on the 'grey areas' of Christian understanding, overlapping disciplinary fields and dogmatic controversies, he sees not threat, but opportunity.

Opportunity for what? Not for dogmatic consensus on the Holy Spirit, nor for elevating any one denominational practice or pneumatology to normative status. Nor does Hollenweger seek the opportunity to hold court on the particular interpretations of the experience of the Holy Spirit forged

62. See, for example, Richard Massey's 'Response' to Hollenweger's paper 'Rethinking Spirit Baptism', in Anderson and Hollenweger (eds.), *Pentecostals after* (pp. 173-75), where he comments on p. 175: 'My own concern is with the whole problem of reductionism within any area of Christian faith and experience. Professor Hollenweger may well have to explain more clearly, for most Pentecostals, how he avoids this charge.' Dr Massey was at the time of the Conference the Principal of Birmingham Bible Institute.

in different geographical, historical, social and political contexts. We are offered no conceptual closures. A doctoral student remarked in a seminar when presented with some of the material in this chapter, 'Hollenweger throws all the cards up in the air'.[63] I think this comment is apposite. The opportunity Hollenweger exposes is for continuing fresh consideration. The 'cards' are from the standard deck but some have rarely been brought into play in this game. Hollenweger brings diverse perspectives into dialogue with the effect, not of reducing variety to a false synthesis, but of revitalizing reflection.

Recalling the topic of healing reminds us how effective this is. African traditional healers, English spiritualists, scientific Western medicine, parapsychology, and Christian liturgies for the sick are all brought into one discussion for critical examination. Intercultural and intracultural dimensions receive equal attention along with more conventional considerations and are not treated as peculiar asides. This is only possible on the basis of an understanding of the Spirit as *ruach Yahweh*. The specifically Christian contribution to healing is located in practice: how gifts are used becomes the critical factor and for this the biblical records of Jesus' ministry are the guide. The ambiguous role of faith in healing, manipulation of the sick and vulnerable, and the self-propaganda of healers are identified by Hollenweger as requiring attention by Christians, alongside his conviction that healing is given high profile in the Gospels and healing liturgies today are necessary and helpful.[64] As an evangelist, Hollenweger engages dialogically with healing as a multifaceted issue of public concern about which the public have some experience and whose thoughts and questions are valid. He is not the first to do this. Earlier in the twentieth-century, for example, the Revd Dr Leslie Weatherhead, a British Methodist minister, broadcaster and writer with wide influence throughout the English-speaking world, was a pioneer in relating psychology, religion and healing who engaged in research, experimental practice and public debate.[65]

63. Paper entitled 'Einstein, Hollenweger and Pneumatology' given to joint seminar of Mission and Pentecostal Studies postgraduate students, University of Birmingham, 11 May 2000.

64. Reference has already been made to Hollenweger's active facilitation of such liturgies in Chapter 6. A weekend conference at Berneuchener House in February 2001 entitled 'Heilsame Berührung' explored the rite of anointing with oil through a play. Hollenweger worked with artistic facilitators, including Estella Korthaus, and participants to perform the play incorporating an anointing rite in Sunday morning worship (2001 Programme, Berneuchener Haus).

65. See Price, *Faithful Uncertainty*, ch. 7, 'Healing: the Exploration of Uncharted

Of course, many of the particular areas Hollenweger brings into discussion on pneumatology are in themselves controversial. The relation between the natural sciences and theology is one of them. Hollenweger is not (and would not claim to be) an original thinker on this subject; what he does is to use the work of scientists and theologians where he sees possible relevance to the increasing body of research in the areas of Pentecostalism, intercultural studies and mission. Thus Einstein's observations on matter and energy are taken up in relation to healing and parapsychological phenomena because of their importance in reality, particularly, but not exclusively, in contemporary non-Western contexts and in the Bible. For Hollenweger, Ted Peters's objections to Wolfhart Pannenberg's opinion that 'the Spirit *is* a force field' would carry little weight. Peters asks, 'How long will field theory stay afloat? If someday, it should sink, will Pannenberg's theology of Spirit sink with it?'[66] Theology, Hollenweger believes, is always in process. If it goes, it goes—whether it has been constructive in passing is more to the point.

Which brings us directly to the historic creeds. Hollenweger has made his position very clear. Christians—all Christians, worldwide, whether or

Territory'. Weatherhead 1893–1976; his magnum opus *Psychology, Religion and Healing* (London: Hodder & Stoughton, 1951), was the outcome of years of pastoral care and psychotherapeutic counselling experience, private research into parapsychological phenomena related to Spiritualism, and doctoral research. Weatherhead, like Hollenweger, addressed all three publics of society, the church and the academy at various times, publishing with national newspapers and magazines, as well as the religious press and publishers, lecturing to non-church-going groups as well as preaching. On the doctrine of the Holy Spirit, in his last major work written in retirement Weatherhead wrote: 'In regard to the Holy Spirit I retreat into agnosticism. Few Christians, whom I know, think of the Holy Spirit as a separate person... When the Psalmist cried, "Whither shall I go from Thy spirit?" [Ps. 139.7] he had no thought of a third person. When Isaiah cried, "The Spirit of the Lord is upon me" he had no thought of a third person in the Godhead, and nor did Jesus when he quoted Isaiah [Isa. 61.1-2; Lk. 4.18]... Here, I think, a reverent agnosticism may be allowed. It cannot matter fundamentally whether one spells the word "spirit" with a small or with a capital S.' (*The Christian Agnostic* [London: Hodder & Stoughton, 1965], pp. 250-51.)

66. Ted Peters, 'Introduction' to *Wolfhart Pannenberg. Toward a Theology of Nature Essays on Science and Faith* (Louisville, KY: Westminster/John Knox Press, 1993), pp. 13-14 (14). See particularly Pannenberg's ch. 5, 'The Doctrine of the Spirit and the Task of a Theology of Nature'. Peters somewhat undercuts his own objection by already having noted Pannenberg's thesis that field-force theory pre-dates Socrates and through the Stoics became associated with the *pneuma*, the divine Spirit, without challenging it.

not they belong to the historic churches—need the Trinity, not as doctrine to be passively assented to but as focus for active reflection on God's relation to the world. This may be a middle road that pleases few, though the few may be increasing in number. Roger Haight, SJ, a systematic theologian, at the end of his 1999 christological study, turns attention to the historical genesis and development of Trinitarian doctrine. He comments:

> Trinitarian language cannot be taken as providing objective information about God; such a mistake in categories at this primary level creates insoluble problems. The world of religious symbolism, the world of language about God, is not one of facts and digital information; it is a world of religious experience; it is based on a narrative of a symbolic encounter with God in history.[67]

Hollenweger's pneumatological explorations support—or partially derive from—his understanding of 'mission as participation' examined in Chapter 6. According to Hollenweger, the Spirit of Life is what makes it possible for people from different cultures to become Christian. It is also what makes possible—and desirable—the participation of non-Christians in Bible study, liturgy and evangelism: participation of non-churchgoers, with their God-given charisms, in the artistic interpretation and production of his dramas is essential to a dialogical, non-colonial approach. 'Outsiders', he believes, are needed to assist Christians in their understanding of the gospel and this is also evident in the respectful consideration he gives to other faiths and non-Christian cultural contexts. God's Spirit is at work outside the churches as well as within them.

Haight sees the doctrine of the Trinity as affirming a dramatic view of a God who saves:

> God, symbolized as Father, Son and Spirit is one God who is loving creator, and who was present and active for the salvation of humankind in Jesus, and who is consistently present in the Christian community, in individuals within it, and, indeed, in all human beings.[68]

---

67. Roger Haight, SJ, *Jesus Symbol of God* (Maryknoll, NY: Orbis Books, 1999), p. 473. Haight was Professor of Historical and Systematic Theology at the Weston Jesuit School of Theology, Cambridge, Massachusetts, when the book was written. According to Gerald Renner, 'Rome targets another Jesuit', in *National Catholic Reporter* of 11 August 2000, after the book's publication Haight was made the subject of an investigation by the Vatican Congregation for the Doctrine of the Faith, headed by Cardinal Joseph Ratzinger. Haight argues that Jesus is 'normative' for salvation for Christians, though other world religions may also offers ways to God and salvation. See n. 61 above.

68. Haight, *Jesus*, p. 485.

Rethinking Christology systematically, it seems, can lead to insights similar to those Hollenweger arrived at with his 'from life to theology' approach to pneumatology.

The 'from life to theology' method encompasses a broader spectrum of source material (contemporary, historical, biographical as well as theological and biblical) from more groups (worldwide, not just Western) and embraces other disciplines in the discussion (natural sciences, social sciences). In overtly engaging with the realities of life, praxis and reflection are related in an intimate and complex way. There is not 'the Truth' about the Holy Spirit which can be discovered and subsequently applied, but a continuous experience–dialogue–reflection–action process. Hollenweger's exploration of pneumatology relates at various times to each facet of the process, underlining the importance of the subject of the Holy Spirit, which, in his view is vital, literally vital, for the sustenance and maintenance of all life—religious and otherwise.

Chapter 7

FINAL COMMENTS

Hollenweger as boundary-crosser is inevitably out of place. Moving between Christian traditions, geographical locations, oral and literary forms of theology, between historical roots and the present, between churched and unchurched, the academy, the public and church institutions, his extensive scholarly interests and practical implementation of insights gained cut through conventional approaches and narrowly defined subject areas.

Conversely, this displacement makes him very much at home in the postmodern, post-colonial, post-literary and post-Christian environment that characterizes Western society at the beginning of the third millennium. Accustomed as a Pentecostal scholar, ecumenist and intercultural theologian to studying Christianity in diverse social and historical contexts, he has responded positively rather than negatively to the real situations underlying the conceptual labels applied to our times. Unity and diversity, particularity and universalism are addressed pragmatically, not philosophically. 'This is the way things are now; how shall Christians respond?' sums up his approach. It is essentially a biblical approach according to his understanding. The Bible provides his model, with all its rich variety of material, literary genres and differing theological interpretations, tensions between tradition and innovation, and sense of ongoing involvement in a life of faith in God with the life of the world.

The particular contribution Hollenweger brings to the Western academy is the insistent reminder that the whole Christian *oikumene* worldwide is— or should be—involved in the process of analysis, critique and solution-finding. Not only has he played a key role in pointing out the importance of the Pentecostal and Pentecostal-type churches (by promoting academic research and their active involvement in the WCC), recognizing their international significance before most theologians gave the movement any attention, but also raising awareness of the many worldwide contexts and theological issues being addressed in the post-colonial period. Further, he has suggested, and acted upon the insight, that even all the Christians cannot find the answers without the help of 'the others'. The reality is that different responses are given by Christians in different situations and even by Christians in the same situation—understanding of the Lord's Supper; compliance or resistance to political structures; fighting or pacifism; monogamy or polygamy; prescribed written liturgies or oral, more fully participative forms of worship, and so on. Hollenweger stands clearly against the implicit or explicit assumption that there is one right answer for all times, decided by one group claiming normative status for its views. A dialogical process with mutual enrichment and correction is the only practical option, precarious though it may be.

The pragmatic approach is also reflected in his essential concern for this life, not the hereafter, which he regards as being in safe hands. Whether writing on Pentecostal/charismatic experiences, formal WCC reports, Bible study, particular local histories or theological treatises, Hollenweger invariably includes the aspect of social relevance; Paul's injunction that all gifts should be used 'for the common good' comes repeatedly to mind. Criteria for assessing 'right' response are often difficult to come by in general terms; on specifics like Christian healing, Hollenweger is more direct, on other issues judgment cannot be humanly made, or only, perhaps, retrospectively, as in the case of Bonhoeffer's traitorous stand against National Socialism. Life is as much 'An Adventure of Faith' now as in New Testament times.

In turn, his social concerns are reflected in his enthusiastic commitment to the church as 'the church for others' applying itself to 'the agenda of the world'. The church does not exist for itself, should not be driven by the desire to grow in numbers and should seek flexible structures to meet current needs. The participation of lay people and non-church members in liturgy and theological reflection is vital for this, and is actively promoted through his method of Bible study and drama, which engages people intellectually, physically and emotionally with contemporary and scriptural issues, and his frequent use of narrative, rather than conceptual propositions, for communicating the fruits of scholarship.

Hollenweger's very practical approach to reflection on Christian faith and life leaves little room for exploration of the 'mystic path' or seeking 'the kingdom within'. In fact, from one not given to direct adversarial controversy with other scholars, his criticism of Eugen Drewermann's psychological approach is exceptional.[1] The inner depths of the individual soul are much too dubious a source of guidance and inspiration for Hollenweger; for him the open processes of dialogue, experiment and social engagement, combined with informed study of the Bible for guidance, are preferable.

Is Hollenweger's complex research/communication/reflection/dialogue/ practical experiment methodology confusing, subversive or the most appropriate way forward in the coming decades? Readers will have to decide for themselves. For myself, his multifaceted approach to life and theology, with all its ragged edges, offers a scholarly encounter with the contemporary world which is excitingly stimulating and demanding. Hollenweger makes us as Christians, all of us—of different colour, historical and geographical context and church affiliation—face our limitations and prejudices. The Bible and life's realities are often irritating thorns in the flesh of dogmatics and institutional structures, of propositional certainty and authoritarian control. This is nowhere more clearly demonstrated than in Hollenweger's practice of dialogical, non-colonial evangelism, reinforced by his radical pneumatology, and articulated clearly in *Evangelism Today*: 'A Christian's understanding of the Good News is always in the making, fundamentally in the making.'[2]

---

1.   See, for example, Hollenweger, *Pentecostalism: Origins*, pp. 323-25. Summarizing from Drewermann's *Tiefenpsychologie und Exegese*, I (1984), pp. 14-15, in the context of a consideration of hermeneutics Hollenweger agrees with his critique that historical-critical exegesis has not produced help for most Christians, but doubts whether 'digging deep into the depths of our souls' is a viable alternative. 'The depths of our souls also contain some ugly things: it is good that this stuff comes out, but it is not necessarily the pure water of God's revelation. To distinguish between the two is only possible if we can in fact still recognize the difference between clean well-water and chlorinated water; and the taste for good water is given to us in the Bible. I am not against diving into our own depths. But we should not do it uncritically. There are sources *extra nos*, outside of us.' These sources include the Bible and the whole universal church.

2.   Hollenweger, *Evangelism Today*, p. 94.

BIBLIOGRAPHY

General

Anderson, Allan H., *Moya The Holy Spirit in an African Context* (Pretoria: University of South Africa, 1991).

Anderson, Allan H., and Hollenweger, Walter J. (eds.), *Pentecostals After a Century: Global Perspectives on a Movement in Transition* (Journal of Pentecostal Theology Supplement Series, 15; Sheffield: Sheffield Academic Press, 1999).

Ariarajah, S. Wesley, *Gospel and Culture: An Ongoing Discussion within the Ecumenical Movement* (Geneva: WCC, 1994).

Barr, James, *The Bible in the Modern World* (London: SCM Press, 2nd edn, 1990 [1973]).

Barrett, David (ed.), *World Christian Encyclopedia* (Oxford: Oxford University Press, 1982).

—'Statistics, Global', in Burgess and McGee (eds.), *Dictionary of Pentecostal and Charismatic Movements* (Grand Rapids: Zondervan, 1996 [1988]).

Bartylla, Eva, 'Der leise Laut der Liebe: Beeindruckende Premiere des Theaterprojekts "Eine unerhörte Frau" ', *Nordbayerischer Kurier* (16 June 1998), p. 11.

Beozzo, José Oscar, 'Documentation: The Future of Particular Churches', *Concilium 1999: 1, Unanswered Questions* (ed. Christoph Theobald and Dietmar Mieth; London: SCM Press, 1999), pp. 124-38.

Bismarck, Ruth-Alice, von and Ulrich Kabitz (eds.), *Love Letters From Cell 92: Dietrich Bonhoeffer and Maria von Wedemeyer 1943–1945* (trans. John Brownjohn; London: Harper Collins, 1994 [German original 1992]).

Bittlinger, Arnold (ed.), *The Church is Charismatic: The World Council of Churches and the Charismatic Renewal* (Geneva: WCC, 1981).

Bliss, Karen, 'Oldham, Joseph Houldsworth', in Lossky *et al.* (eds.), *Dictionary*, pp. 746-47.

Bloch-Hoell, Nils, *The Pentecostal Movement: Its Origins, Development and Distinctive Character* (London: Allen & Unwin, 1964 [Norwegian original 1956]).

Boff, Leonardo, 'The Contribution of Liberation Theology to a New Paradigm', in Küng and Tracy (eds.), *Paradigm Change in Theology*, pp. 408-23.

—*Church, Charism and Power* (London: SCM Press, 1985).

Bonhoeffer, Dietrich, *Letters and Papers from Prison* (ed. Eberhard Bethge; London: SCM Press, enlarged edn, 1971).

Bosch, David, Review of Hollenweger, *Glaube, Geist und Geister*, *Missionalia* 4.1 (1976), pp. 43-44.

—Review of Hollenweger, *Umgang mit Mythen*, *Missionalia* 10.3 (1982), pp. 128-29.

—*Transforming Mission* (Maryknoll, NY: Orbis Books, 1991).

Bundy, David, 'Pentecostalism as a Global Phenomenon: A Review Essay of Walter Hollenweger's *Pentecostalism: Origins and Developments Worldwide*', *Pneuma* 21.2 (1999), pp. 289-303.

Burgess, Stanley M., and Gary B. McGee (eds.), *Dictionary of Pentecostal and Charismatic Movements* (Grand Rapids: Zondervan, 1996 [1988]).

Clines, David J.A., *The Bible and the Modern World* (Biblical Seminar, 51; Sheffield: Sheffield Academic Press, 1997).

Cobb, John, 'Response to Johann Baptist Metz and Langdon Gilkey', in Küng and Tracy (eds.), *Paradigm Change in Theology*, pp. 384-89.

Coggins, R.J., and J.L. Houlden (eds.), *A Dictionary of Biblical Interpretation* (London: SCM Press, 1990).

Congregation for the Doctrine of the Faith, *"Dominus Iesus"*. *Declaration on the Unity and Salvific Universality of Jesus Christ and the Church* (London: Catholic Truth Society, 2000).

Conway, Martin, 'Helping the Ecumenical Movement to Move On: Hollenweger and the Rediscovery of the Value of Diversity', in Jongeneel *et al.* (eds.), *Pentecost, Mission and Ecumenism*, pp. 273-87.

—'Honorary Fellows 1996', in *Selly Oak Colleges News and Views* 20 (1996), p. 3.

Cooper, Howard, 'Living with the Questions: Psychotherapy and the Myth of Self-Fulfilment', in Sidney Brichto and Richard Harries (eds.), *Two Cheers for Secularism* (Northamptonshire: Pilkington Press, 1998), pp. 93-106.

Cox, Harvey, *Fire from Heaven* (London: Cassell, 1996 [1994]).

Davies, J.G. (ed.), *Looking to the Future* (Institute for the Study of Worship and Religious Architecture: Papers read at an international symposium on prospects for worship, religious architecture and socio-religious studies; Birmingham: University of Birmingham, 1976).

—*A New Dictionary of Liturgy and Worship* (London: SCM Press, 1986).

—*Research Bulletins 1974, 1977, 1978* (Institute for the Study of Worship and Religious Architecture; Birmingham: University of Birmingham).

Davis, R., *Locusts and Wild Honey: The Charismatic Renewal and the Ecumenical Movement* (Risk Book Series, 2; Geneva: WCC, 1978).

Dayton, Donald W., *Theological Roots of Pentecostalism* (Metuchen, NJ: Scarecrow Press, 1987).

Duraisingh, Christopher, 'Editorial', *International Review of Mission* 85.337 (1996), pp. 155-70.

Flesseman-van Leer, Ellen (ed.), *The Bible: Its Authority and Interpretation in the Ecumenical Movement* (Geneva: WCC, 1980).

Ford, David F. (ed.), *The Modern Theologians: An Introduction to Christian Theology in the Twentieth Century*, I, II (Oxford: Basil Blackwell, 1989).

Friedli, Richard, 'Hollenweger als Theologe', in Jongeneel *et al.* (eds.), *Pentecost, Mission and Ecumenism*, pp. 15-25; Also as 'Walter J. Hollenweger: Als Christ zusammen mit Gleichgültigen und Ungläubigen das Evangelium entdecken', in Stephen Leimgruber and Max Schock (eds.), *Gegen die Gottvergessenheit: Schweitzer Theologen im 19 und 20 Jahrhundert* (Basel: Herder, 1990), pp. 652-62.

—'Intercultural Theology', in Müller *et al.* (eds.), *Dictionary of Mission*, pp. 219-22.

Gerloff, Roswith, 'Theological Education in Black and White: The Centre for Black and White Christian Partnership (1978–1985)', in Jongeneel *et al.* (eds.), *Pentecost, Mission and Ecumenism*, pp. 41-59.

Gittins, Anthony J., *Bread for the Journey: The Mission of Transformation and the Transformation of Mission* (Maryknoll, NY: Orbis Books, 1993).

—'Missionary Myth Making', in Scherer and Bevans (eds.), *New Directions in Mission and Evangelization* 2, pp. 143-57.

Goodall, Norman (ed.), *Missions Under the Cross* (London: Edinburgh House, 1953).

Green, Garrett (ed.), *Scriptural Authority and Narrative Interpretation* (Philadelphia: Fortress Press, 1987).

Greinacher, Norbert, and Norbert Mette (eds.), *Concilium 1994: 2, Christianity and Cultures* (London: SCM Press, 1994).

Haight, Roger, SJ, *Jesus Symbol of God* (Maryknoll, NY: Orbis Books, 1999).

Hardy, Daniel W., 'God in the Ordinary: The Work of J.G. Davies (1919–1990)', *Theology* 98.792 (1996), pp. 427-40.

Hart, Trevor A. (ed.), *The Dictionary of Historical Theology* (Carlisle: Paternoster Press; Grand Rapids: Eerdmans, 2000).

Hartley, L.P., *The Go-Between* (Harmondsworth: Penguin Books, 1970).

Harvey, David, *The Condition of Postmodernity: An Enquiry into the Origins of Cultural Change* (Oxford: Basil Blackwell, 1990).

Hasted, John, *The Metal Benders* (London: Routledge & Kegan Paul, 1981).

Hauerwas, Stanley, 'The Church as God's New Language', in Green (ed.), *Scriptural Authority and Narrative Interpretation*, pp. 179-98.

Hoekendijk, J.C., 'The Call to Evangelism', *International Review of Missions* 39 (1950), pp. 167-75.

Hunsinger, George, and William C. Placher (eds.), *Theology and Narrative: Selected Essays on Hans W. Frei* (Oxford: Oxford University Press, 1995).

Imhof, Fritz, 'Besser gespielt als gepredigt', *Leben und Glauben* 75.10 (2000), pp. 32-37.

Janowski, Hans Norbert and Michael Strauss, 'Glauben lernen wie das Violinspiel: Gespräch mit Professor Walter Hollenweger', *Evangelische Kommentare* 6 (1993), pp. 343-47.

Jeanrond, Werner, 'Biblical Criticism and Theology: Towards a New Biblical Theology', in Werner G. Jeanrond and Jennifer L. Rike (eds.), *Radical Pluralism and Truth: David Tracy and the Hermeneutics of Religion* (New York: Crossroad, 1991), pp. 38-48.

Jones, Charles Edwin, *Black Holiness: A Guide to the Study of Black Participation in Wesleyan Perfectionist and Glossolalic Pentecostal Movements* (ATLA Bibliography Series No.18; Metuchen, NJ: the American Theological Library Association and Scarecrow Press, 1987).

—*A Guide to the Study of the Holiness Movement* (Metuchen, NJ: Scarecrow Press, 1974).

—*A Guide to the Study of Pentecostalism* (Metuchen, NJ: Scarecrow Press, 1987).

—'Holiness Movement', in Burgess and McGee (eds.), *Dictionary of Pentecostal and Charismatic Movements*, pp. 46-49.

Jongeneel, Jan A.B., (ed.), *Experiences of the Spirit*: Conference on Pentecostal and Charismatic Research in Europe at Utrecht University 1989 (Frankfurt am Main: Peter Lang, 1991).

Jongeneel, Jan A.B. *et al.* (eds.), *Pentecost, Mission and Ecumenism: Essays on Intercultural Theology* (Festschrift in Honour of Professor Walter J. Hollenweger; Frankfurt am Main: Peter Lang, 1992).

Jongeneel, J.A.B. and J.M. van Engelen, 'Contemporary Currents in Missiology', in Verstraelen *et al* (eds.), *Missiology: An Ecumenical Introduction* (Grand Rapids: Eerdmans, 1995), pp. 438-57.

Kinnamon, Michael, and Brian E. Cope (eds.), *The Ecumenical Movement: An Anthology of Key Texts and Voices* (Geneva: WCC; Grand Rapids: Eerdmans, 1997).

Korthaus, Estella, 'Sprechende Bilder: Wie die Bibel in Kopf und Herz dringt', *Evangelische Kommentare* 7 (1995), pp. 404-407.

Küng, Hans, 'A New Basic Model for Theology: Divergences and Convergences', in Küng and Tracy (eds.), *Paradigm Change in Theology*, pp. 439-52.

Küng, Hans, and David Tracy (eds.), *Paradigm Change in Theology: A Symposium for the Future* (Edinburgh: T. & T. Clark, 1989).

Kwok Pui-Lan, *Discovering the Bible in the Non-Biblical World* (Maryknoll, NY: Orbis Books, 1995).

Laan, Paul N. van der, 'Walter Hollenweger: A Pluriform Life', in Jongeneel *et al.* (eds.), *Pentecost, Mission and Ecumenism*, pp. 5-13.

Lamb, Matthew, 'Paradigms as Imperatives Towards Critical Collaboration', in Küng and Tracy (eds.), *Paradigm Change in Theology*, pp. 453-60.

Lartey, Emmanuel Y., and George M. Mulrain, 'Hollenweger as Professor of Mission', in Jongeneel *et al.* (eds.), *Pentecost, Mission and Ecumenism*, pp. 33-40.

Lederle, Henry, *Treasures Old and New: Interpretations of Spirit Baptism in the Charismatic Renewal Movement* (Peabody, MA: Hendrickson, 1988).

Leinberger, Bodo (ed.), *Getanztes Leben: Heilende Liturgie* (Hammersbach: Verlag Wort im Bild, 1993).

Lembke, Ingo, Review of Jongeneel *et al.* (eds.), 'Pentecost, Mission and Ecumenism, Festschrift für Professor Walter J. Hollenweger', in Verband Evangelischer (ed.), *Jahrbuch Mission 1993* (Hamburg: Missionshilfe Verlag, 1993), pp. 200-201.

Linn, Gerhard, Review of Hollenweger, 'Glaube, Geist und Geister: Professor Unrat zwischen Bangkok und Birmingham', *International Review of Mission* 65.260 (1976), pp. 461-63.

Lossky, Nicholas *et al.* (eds.), *Dictionary of the Ecumenical Movement* (Geneva: WCC, 1991).

Loughlin, Gerard, *Telling God's Story: Bible, Church and Narrative Theology* (Cambridge: Cambridge University Press, 1996).

Margull, Hans Jochen, 'Structures for Missionary Congregations', *International Review of Missions* 52.208 (1963), 433-46.

—'We Stand in our Own Way', *Ecumenical Review* 17.4 (1965), pp. 321-31.

—'Gathering at the Point of Mission', in Wieser (ed.), *Planning for Mission*, pp. 146-48.

Martin, David, *Tongues of Fire* (Oxford: Basil Blackwell, 1993 [1990]).

Martin, David, and Peter Mullen (eds.), *Strange Gifts? A Guide to Charismatic Renewal* (Oxford: Basil Blackwell, 1984).

McGavran, Donald, 'Church Growth Strategy Continued', *International Review of Missions* 57 (July 1968), pp. 335-43.

Metz, Johann Baptist, 'Theology in the New Paradigm: Political Theology', in Küng and Tracy (eds.), *Paradigm Change in Theology*, pp. 355-66.

Moltmann, Jürgen, 'The Interlaced Times of History: Some Necessary Differentiations and Limitations of History as Concept', in Küng and Tracy (eds.), *Paradigm Change in Theology*, pp. 320-39.

Müller, Christoph, Review of Hollenweger, 'Geist und Materie', *Reformiertes Forum* 38 (22 September 1988).

Müller, Karl, *et al.* (eds.), *Dictionary of Mission: Theology, History, Perspectives* (Maryknoll, NY: Orbis Books, 1997).

Nyamiti, Charles, 'African Christologies Today', in Robert J. Schreiter, *Faces of Jesus in Africa* (Maryknoll, NY: Orbis Books, 1992), pp. 3-23.

Oldham, J.H., *Christianity and the Race Problem* (London: SCM Press, 1924).

—*The World and the Gospel* (London: Church Missionary Society, 1916).

O'Mahoney, Patrick, *Swords and Ploughshares: Can Man Live and Progress with a Technology of Death?* (London: Sheed & Ward, 1986).

Peck, Chris, 'Back to the Future: Participatory Bible Study and Biblical Theology', *Theology* 98.785 (1995), pp. 350-57.

Peters, Ted (ed.), *Wolfhart Pannenberg. Toward a Theology of Nature: Essays on Science and Faith* (Louisville, KY: Westminster/John Knox Press, 1993).

Pluess, Jean-Daniel, Review of Hollenweger, 'Geist und Materie', *EPTA Bulletin* 7.2 (1988), pp. 70-72.

Poewe, Karla (ed.), *Charismatic Christianity as a Global Culture* (Columbia: University of South Carolina Press, 1994).

Pope-Levison, Priscilla, and John R. Levison, *Jesus in Global Contexts* (Louisville, KY: Westminster/John Knox Press, 1992).

Potter, Philip A., 'Mission', in Lossky *et al.* (eds.), *Dictionary*, pp. 690-96.

Price, Lynne, *Faithful Uncertainty: Leslie D. Weatherhead's Methodology of Creative Evangelism* (Frankfurt am Main: Peter Lang, 1996).

—'Scholarship and Evangelism: Oil and Water?', in Anderson and Hollenweger (eds.), *Pentecostals after a Century*, pp. 197-208.

—'Hollenweger, Walter J.', in Trevor A. Hart (ed.), *The Dictionary of Historical Theology* (Carlisle: Paternoster Press; Grand Rapids: Eerdmans, 2000), pp. 259-60.

Price, Lynne, Juan Sepúlveda and Graeme Smith (eds.), *Mission Matters* (Frankfurt am Main: Peter Lang, 1997).

Renner, Gerald, 'Rome targets another Jesuit', in *National Catholic Reporter* (11 August 2000).

Saayman, William, and Klippies Kritzinger (eds.), *Mission in Bold Humility: David Bosch's Work Considered* (Maryknoll, NY: Orbis Books, 1996).

Said, Edward W., *Culture and Imperialism* (London: Vintage, 1994).

Scherer, James A., and Stephen B. Bevans (eds.), *New Directions in Mission and Evangelism.* 1. *Basic Statements 1974–1991* (Maryknoll, NY: Orbis Books, 1992).

—*New Directions in Mission and Evangelism.* 2. *Theological Foundations* (Maryknoll, NY: Orbis Books, 1994).

Schreiter, Robert J. (ed.), *Faces of Jesus in Africa* (London: SCM Press, 1992).

Sepúlveda, Juan, 'To Overcome the Fear of Syncretism: A Latin American Perspective', in Price, Sepúlveda and Smith (eds.), *Mission Matters*, pp. 157-68.

Simpfendörfer, Werner, Review of Hollenweger, 'Umgang mit Mythen', *Ecumenical Review* 35 (1983), pp. 103-105.

Spittler, R.P., 'Glossolalia', in Burgess and McGee (eds.), *Dictionary of Pentecostal*, pp. 335-41.

Stransky, Tom, 'International Missionary Council', in Lossky *et al*, *Dictionary*, pp. 526-29.

Stroup, George, *The Promise of Narrative Theology* (London: SCM Press Ltd., 1981).

Sugirtharajah, R.S. (ed.), *Asian Faces of Jesus* (London: SCM Press, 1993).

Sullivan, SJ, Francis, A., *Charisms and Charismatic Renewal: A Biblical and Theological Study* (Dublin: Gill & MacMillan, 1982).

Sundermeier, Theo, 'Inkulturation als Entäusserung', in Jongeneel *et al.* (eds.), *Pentecost, Mission and Ecumenism*, pp. 209-14.

Theobald, Christoph, 'The "Definitive" Discourse of the Magisterium', *Concilium 1999: 1, Unanswered Questions* (eds. Christoph Theobald and Dietmar Mieth; London: SCM Press, 1999), pp. 60-69.

Thomas, Norman (ed.), *Readings in World Mission* (London: SPCK; Maryknoll, NY: Orbis Books, 1995).

Tracy, David, *The Analogical Imagination* (London: SCM Press, 1981).

Ustorf, Werner, *Christianized Africa—De-Christianized Europe? Missionary Enquiries into the Polycentric Epoch of Christian History* (Seoul, Korea: Tyrannus Press, 1992).

—'The Documents that Reappeared', in Price, Sepúlveda and Smith (eds.), *Mission Matters*, pp. 63-82.

—'The Magpies Gotta Know: Hollenweger as an Ecumenical', in Jongeneel *et al.* (eds.), *Pentecost, Mission and Ecumenism*, pp. 27-32.

—*Sailing With the Next Tide: Missions, Missiology and the Third Reich* (Frankfurt am Main: Peter Lang, 2000).

Utok, Efiong S., 'From Wheaton to Lausanne', in Scherer and Bevans (eds.), *New Directions in Mission and Evangelization*, 2, pp. 99-112.

Verstraelen, F.J., *et al.* (eds.), *Missiology: An Ecumenical Introduction* (Grand Rapids: Eerdmans, 1995).

Walls, Andrew, 'Christianity in the Non-Western World: A Study in the Serial Nature of Christian Expansion', in James P. Mackey (ed.), *Studies in World Christianity* 1.1 (1995), pp. 1-25.

—*The Missionary Movement in Christian History: Studies in the Transmission of Faith* (Maryknoll, NY: Orbis Books; Edinburgh: T. & T. Clark, 1996).

Weatherhead, Leslie, *The Christian Agnostic* (London: Hodder & Stoughton, 1965).

Weber, Hans-Ruedi, *Experiments in Bible Study* (Geneva: WCC, 1981).

Werner, Dietrich, 'Missionary Structure of the Congregation', in Lossky *et al.* (eds.), *Dictionary of the Ecumenical Movement*, pp. 699-701.

Wieser, Thomas, *Planning for Mission* (London: Epworth Press, 1966).

Wiles, Maurice, 'Scriptural Authority and Theological Construction: The Limitations of Narrative Interpretation', in Green (ed.), *Scriptural Authority and Narrative Interpretation*, pp. 42-58.

Wind, Renate, *A Spoke in the Wheel: The Life of Dietrich Bonhoeffer* (trans. John Bowden; London: SCM Press, 1991).

World Council of Churches, *The Church for Others and The Church for the World* (Geneva: WCC, 1967).

—*Drafts for Sections: Prepared for the Fourth Assembly of the World Council of Churches, Uppsala, Sweden, 1968* (Geneva: WCC, 1967).

—'WCC Evangelism Secretary heads Bible Study in Mexico', *Ecumenical Press Service* (Geneva: WCC 6 April, 1970).

—*From Mexico City to Bangkok* (Report of the Commission on World Mission and Evangelism 1963–1972; Geneva: WCC, undated).

—*Minutes and Reports of the Commission for World Mission and Evangelism of the World Council of Churches, December 31 1972 and January 9–12 1973* (Geneva: WCC, 1973).

—*Confessing the One Faith: An Ecumenical Explication of the Apostolic Faith as it is Confessed in the Nicene-Constantinopolitan Creed (381)* (Faith and Order Paper, No. 153; Geneva: WCC, rev. edn, 1992).

World Missionary Conference 1910. IX. The History and Records of the Conference together with Addresses delivered at evening meetings (Edinburgh: Oliphant, Anderson and Ferrier, 1910).

Yates, Timothy, *Christian Mission in the Twentieth Century* (Cambridge: Cambridge University Press, 1994).

Works by Walter J. Hollenweger

Books

Besuch bei Lukas (Munich: Chr. Kaiser Verlag, 1986 [1981]).

Conflict in Corinth & Memoirs of an Old Man: Two Stories that Illuminate the Way the Bible Came To Be Written (New York: Paulist Press, 1982). German: *Konflikt in Korinth/ Memoiren eines alten Mannes* (Munich: Chr. Kaiser Verlag, 5th edn, 1987 [1978]).

Das Fest der Verloren. Die Bibel erzählt, getanzt und gesungen (Munich: Chr. Kaiser Verlag, 1984 [1983]).

Erfahrungen in Ephesus. Darstellung eines Davongekommenen (Munich: Chr. Kaiser Verlag, 1985 [1979])

Erfahrungen der Leibhaftigkeit: Interkulturelle Theologie I (Munich: Chr. Kaiser Verlag, 2nd repr. edn. 1990 [1979]).

Evangelism Today: Good News or Bone of Contention? (Belfast: Christian Journals Limited, 1976). German: *Evangelisation gestern und heute* (Stuttgart: J.F. Steinkopf, 1973).

Geist und Materie: Interkulturelle Theologie 3 (Munich: Chr. Kaiser Verlag, 1988).

Glaube, Geist und Geister: Professor Unrat zwischen Bangkok und Birmingham (Frankfurt: Otto Lembeck, 1975).

Der Klapperstorch und die Theologie: Die Krise von Theologie und Kirche als Chance (Kindhausen: Metanoid Verlag, 2000).

Pentecost between Black and White: Five Case Studies on Pentecost and Politics (Belfast: Christian Journals Limited, 1974).

Pentecostalism: Origins and Developments Worldwide (Peabody, MA: Hendrickson, 1997). German: *Charismatisch-pfingstliches Christentum* (Göttingen: Vandenhoeck & Ruprecht, 1997).

The Pentecostals (Peabody MA: Hendrickson, 3rd edn, 1988 [1972]). German: *Enthusiastisches Christentum: Die Pfingstbewegung in Geschichte und Gegenwart* (Zürich: Zwingli Verlag, 1969). The full ten-volume work, *Handbuch der Pfingstbewegung*, 1965–67, is available at ATLA, Board of Microtexts, Divinity School, Yale University, New Haven, CT.

Umgang mit Mythen: Interkulturelle Theologie 2 (Munich: Chr. Kaiser Verlag, 2nd edn, 1992 [1982]).

Züritüütschi Gibätt: Gebete–Prières–Prayers (Meilen: Ch. Walter Verlag, 2000).

Edited Volumes

The Church for Others and The Church for the World (Geneva: WCC, 1967).

Kirche, Benzin und Bohnensuppe: auf den Spuren dynamischer Gemeinden (Zürich: TVZ, 1971).

Pentecostal Research in Europe: Problems, Promises and People (Frankfurt am Main: Peter Lang, 1985).

Co-editor with Allan H. Anderson, *Pentecostals After a Century: Global Perspectives on a Movement in Transition* (Journal of Pentecostal Theology Supplement Series, 15; Sheffield: Sheffield Academic Press, 1999).

Articles and Lectures

'After Twenty Years' Research on Pentecostalism', *Theology* 87.720 (1984), 403-12; *International Review of Mission* 75.297 (1986), pp. 3-12; extended version in *idem* (ed.), *Pentecostal Research in Europe*, pp. 124-53.

'Agenda: The World', *Concept* 11 (1966), pp. 19-20.

'All Creatures Great and Small: Towards a Pneumatology of Life', in David Martin and Peter Mullen (eds.), *Strange Gifts? A Guide to Charismatic Renewal* (Oxford: Basil Blackwell, 1984), pp. 41-53.

'Als die Ökumene noch jung war und die Studenten die Welt gewinnen wollten...: Versuch über Hans Jochen Margull, der 1995 70 Jahre alt geworden wäre', in *Jahrbuch Mission 27 1995* (Hamburg: Missionshilfe Verlag, 1995), pp. 175-86.

'Aus christlicher Verantwortung lügen: Eine Würdigung von Dietrich Bonhoeffers nachgelassener "Ethik" ', *Der Kleine Bund* (9 September 1995), p. 5.

'Aus dem weltweiten Echo auf Emil Brunners Theologie', *Reformatio* 12.8 (1963), pp. 441-48.

'Black Competence', *Christian Action Journal* (Autumn 1982), p. 17.

'The Chair of Mission at the University of Birmingham', *The Selly Oak Journal* 4 (1986), pp. 13-17.

'The Challenge of Reconciliation', *Journal of the European Pentecostal Theological Association* vol. 19 (1999), pp. 5-16.

'Charismatic and Pentecostal Movements: A Challenge to the Churches', in Dow Kirkpatrick (ed.), *The Holy Spirit* (Nashville, TN: World Methodist Council Tidings, 1974), pp. 209-33.

The Christian and the Church of the Future, *Audenshaw Papers* 39 (1973).

'Christus extra et intra muros ecclesiae', in Thomas Wieser (ed.), *Planning for Mission* (London: Epworth Press, 1966), pp. 56-61.

'A Church for Others', *Study Encounter* 3.2 (1967), pp. 84-99.

'The Church for Others: Discussion in the DDR', *Study Encounter* 5.1 (1969), pp. 26-36.

'The Church for Others—Ten Years After', in Davies (ed.) *Research Bulletin 1977*, pp. 82-96.

'Church Growth or Political Prophecy: The Question of Priorities', review of Eberhard Bethge's *Dietrich Bonhoeffer: Theologe, Christ, Zeitgenosse* (Munich: Chr. Kaiser Verlag, 1967), *International Review of Missions* 57 (July 1968), pp. 377-80.

'The Common Search—Experiment and Tradition', *Pax Romana* 4 (1966), pp. 19-21.

'Community and Worship', in Davies (ed.), *A New Dictionary of Liturgy and Worship*, pp. 183-84.

'The Contribution of Critical Exegesis to Pentecostal Hermeneutics', *The Spirit & Church* 2.1 (2000), pp. 7-18.

'Creator Spiritus: The Challenge of Pentecostal Experience to Pentecostal Theology', *Theology* 81.679 (1978), pp. 32-40.

'Criteria for Reforming the Church', in Johannes B. Metz (ed.), *Concilium* 6.7. *Fundamental Theology in the Church* (London: Burns & Oates, 1971), pp. 116-24.

'The Critical Tradition of Pentecostalism', *Journal of Pentecostal Theology* 1 (1992), pp. 7-17.

'Dietrich Bonhoeffer and William J. Seymour: A Comparison between Two Ecumenists', *Norsk Tidsskrift for Misjon* 39.3-4 (1985) (Festschrift for Nils Bloch-Hoell), pp. 192-201.

'The Discipline of Thought and Action in Mission', *International Review of Mission* 80.317 (1991), pp. 91-104.

'Does Efficiency Imply the Destruction of Human Values? A Theological Action-Research-Report of Co-Decision in Industry', in Davies (ed.), *Research Bulletin 1974*, pp. 114-18.

'The Ecumenical Significance of Oral Christianity', *Ecumenical Review* 41.2 (1989), pp. 259-65.

'Efficiency and Human Values: A Theological Action-Research-Report on Co-Decision in Industry', *Expository Times* 86 (May 1975), pp. 228-32.

'Das einzige wirklich interressante Thema ist "Gott"', *Der Evangelische Erzieher* 46.3 (1994), pp. 219-28.

'The Embrace of Africa with the West', *Reform* (March 1981), p. 7.

'Evangelism: A Non-Colonial Model', *Journal of Pentecostal Theology* 7 (1995), pp. 107-28.

'Experimental Forms of Worship', in Davies (ed.), *A New Dictionary of Liturgy and Worship*, pp. 231-36.

'La Fonction prophétique de l'Eglise dans la société', *Hokma* 72 (1999), pp. 109-23.

'From Azusa Street to the Toronto Phenomenon: Historical Roots of the Pentecostal Movement', *Concilium 1996.3 Pentecostal Movements as an Ecumenical Challenge* edited by Jürgen Moltmann and Karl-Joseph Kuschel, pp. 3-14.

'Funktionen der ekstatischen Frömmigkeit der Pfingstbewegung', in T. Spoerri (ed.), *Beiträge zur Ekstase. Biblioteca Psychiatrica et Neurologica* 134 (Basel: Karger, 1968), pp. 53-72.

The Future of Mission and the Mission of the Future (Selly Oak Colleges Occasional Paper, 2; Birmingham: Selly Oak Colleges, 1989).

'Guest Editorial', [church growth] *International Review of Missions* 57 (July 1968), pp. 271-77.

'Hans Hoekendijk: Ein ökumenischer Souffleur', *Leben und Glauben* 52.15 (1977), p. 10.

'Healing through Prayer: Superstition or Forgotten Christian Tradition?', *Theology* 92.747 (1989), pp. 166-74.

'Heilungsbewegungen', in Hans Gasper, Joachim Müller and Friederike Valentin (eds.), *Lexikon der Sekten, Sondergruppen und Weltanschauungen* (Freiburg: Herder, 1990), pp. 449-53.

'Im Gottesdienst Zärtlichkeit und Lebonskraft feiern', *Wendekreis* (June 1998), pp. 18-19.

'Interaction between Black and White in Theological Education', *Theology* 90.737 (1987), pp. 341-50.

'Intercultural Theology', in Davies (ed.), *Research Bulletin 1978*, pp. 90-104.

'Intercultural Theology', *Theology Today* 43.1 (1986), pp. 28-35.

'Johannes Christian Hoekendijk: Pluriformität der Kirche', *Reformatio* 16.10 (1967), pp. 663-77.

'Karl Marx (1818–1883) and his Confession of Faith', *Expository Times* 84.5 (1973), pp. 132-37.

'Kosmische Gottheit und Persönlicher Gott: Gespräch mit der Anthroposophie', *Protokolldienst* 33.88, pp. 13-22.

'Kultur und Evangelium: Das Thema der interkulturellen Theologie', in Verband Evangelischer (ed.), *Evangelische Mission Jahrbuch* 17, *1985* (Hamburg: Missionshilfe Verlag, 1985), pp. 52-60.

'Marxist and Kimbanguist Mission—A Comparison' (Inaugural Lecture, 23 November 1972; Birmingham: University of Birmingham, 1973).

'Marxist Ethics', *Expository Times*, 85.10 (1974), pp. 292-98.

'Monocultural Imperialism vs Intercultural Theology', *International Review of Mission* 73: 292 (1984), pp. 521-26.

'Minjung-Theologie in der Schweiz?', in Samuel Jakob and Hans Strub (eds.), *Kirche Leiten im Übergang-Konturen Werden Sichtbar* (Festschrift für Ernst Meili; Zürich: TVZ, 1993), pp. 284-90.

'Mr. Chips Goes Back to Philadelphia', in *Minutes and Reports of the Commission on World Mission and Evangelism of the World Council of Churches, Bangkok Assembly, 1973* (Geneva: WCC, 1973), pp. 15-17.

'Mr. Chips Goes to Bangkok', *Frontier* 16.2 (1973), pp. 93-100.

'Mr. Chips in Switzerland', in Davies (ed.), *Looking to the Future*, pp. 13-33.

'Mr. Chips Looks for the Holy Spirit in Pentecostal Theology', *Journal of Theology for Southern Africa* 12 (1975), pp. 39-50 also in *Theological Renewal* 4 (1976), pp. 12-20.

'Mr. Chips Reviews Bangkok', *International Review of Mission* 63.249 (1974), pp. 132-36.

'Music in the Service of Reconciliation', *Theology* 92.748 (1989), pp. 276-86.

'My Fair Lady—ein theologisches Gleichnis', *Kunst und Kirche* 4 (1976), pp. 161-64.

'The Other Exegesis', *Horizons in Biblical Theology* 3 (1981), pp. 155-79.

'The Pentecostal Elites and the Pentecostal Poor: A Missed Dialogue?', in Poewe (ed.), *Charismatic Christianity as a Global Culture*, pp. 201-14.

'Pentecostalism and Academic Theology: From Confrontation to Co-operation', *EPTA Bulletin* (Journal of the European Pentecostal Theological Association) 11.1-2 (1992), pp. 42-49.

'Pentecostalism, Growth and Ecumenism', *Priests and People* 12.4 (1998), pp. 153-56.

'The Pentecostal Movement and the World Council of Churches', *Ecumenical Review* 18.3 (1966), pp. 310-20.

'Pfingstkirchen', in Ekkehard Starke, Birgit Bender-Junker and Notger Slenczka (eds.), *Evangelisches Kirchenlexikon: Internationale Theologische Enzyklopädie vol. 3* (Göttingen: Vandenhoeck & Ruprecht, 1992), pp. 1162-1170.

'A Plea for a Theologically Responsible Syncretism', *Missionalia* 25.1 (1997), pp. 5-18.

'Pluralismus als Gabe und Aufgabe: Die Zukunft des Christentums in multireligiöser Gesellschaft', in Johannes Lähnemann (ed.), *Das Wiedererwachen der Religionen als pädagogische Herausforderung* (Hamburg: E.B. Verlag Rissen, 1992), pp. 65-76.

'Pneumatologie des Lebens', *Evangelische Kommentare* 16.8 (1983), pp. 446-48.

'Priorities in Pentecostal Research: Historiography, Missiology, Hermeneutics and Pneumatology', in Jongeneel (ed.), *Experiences of the Spirit*, pp. 7-22.

'Prophecy', in Müller *et al.* (eds.), *Dictionary of Mission*, pp. 368-72.

'Religion in a Silenced Culture' (=Foreword), in Roger B. Edrington, *Everyday Men: Living in a Climate of Unbelief* (Frankfurt am Main: Peter Lang, 1987).

'A Reminder from Church History', in Thomas Wieser (ed.), *Planning for Mission* (London: Epworth Press, 1966), p. 153.

'Ripe for Taking Risks?', *Pneuma* 18.1 (1996), pp. 107-12.

'Roman Catholics and Pentecostals in Dialogue', *Ecumenical Review* 51.2 (1999), pp. 147-59.

'Roots and Fruits of the Charismatic Renewal in the Third World', in Martin and Mullen (eds.), *Strange Gifts?*, pp. 172-91.

'Saints in Birmingham', in A. Bittlinger (ed.), *The Church is Charismatic* (Geneva: WCC, 1981), pp. 87-99 also in Hollenweger, *Pentecostalism: Origins*, pp. 6-15.

'Syncretism and Capitalism', *Asian Journal of Pentecostal Studies* 2.1 (1999), pp. 1-16.

'The Theological Challenge of Indigenous Churches', in A.F. Walls and Wilbert Schenk (eds.), *Exploring New Religious Movements: Essays in Honour of Harold Turner* (Elkhart, IN: Mission Focus Publications, 1990), pp. 163-67.

'Theologie Tanzen: Warum wir eine "narrative Exegese" brauchen', *Evangelische Kommentare* 7 (1995), pp. 403-404.

'Theologiestudium anders', *Der Ueberblick* 9.1 (1973), pp. 51-52.

'Theology and the Future of the Church', in Peter Byrne and Leslie Houlden (eds.), *Companion Encyclopedia of Theology* (London: Routledge, 1995), pp. 1017-1035.

'Toleranz im Islam und im Christentum', *Die Politische Meinung* 310 (1995), pp. 90-95.

'Towards a Charismatic Theology', Preface in Simon Tugwell *et al.* (eds.), *New Heaven? New Earth? An Encounter with Pentecostalism* (London: Darton Longman & Todd, 1976), pp. 9-13.

'Towards an Intercultural History of Christianity', *International Review of Mission* 76.304 (1987), pp. 526-56.

'Towards a Pentecostal Missiology', in T. Dayanandan Francis and Israel Selvanayagam (eds.), *Many Christian Voices in Christian Mission: Essays in Honour of J.E. Lesslie Newbigin* (Madras: The Christian Literature Society, 1994), pp. 59-79.

'Two Extraordinary Pentecostal Ecumenists: The Letters of Donald Gee and David du Plessis', *Ecumenical Review* 52.3 (2000), pp. 391-402.

'Verheissung und Verhängnis der Pfingstbewegung', *Evangelische Theologie* 53.3 (1993), pp. 265-88.

'A Vision of the Church of the Future', *Laity* 20 (November 1965), pp. 5-11 and *Reformatio* 15.2 (1966), pp. 90-98.

'Was Bonhoeffer in Harlem lernte: Eine frei gestaltete Reminiszenz zu Bonhoeffer's Umgang mit den Schwarzen Amerikas', *Der Kleine Bund* (8 April 1995), *Kultur-Beilage*, p. 6.

'Was ist das Wort Gottes?', *Schulfach Religion* 6.1-2 (1987), pp. 25-36.

'Was ist von Zwingli's Reformation geblieben?', *Leben und Glauben*, 59.44 (2 November 1984), pp. 6-7.

'The "What" and the "How": Content and Communication of the One Message. A Consideration of the Basis of Faith, as Formulated by the World Council of Churches. Part 1', *Expository Times* 86 (August 1975), pp. 324-28; Part 2, *Expository Times* 86 (September 1975), pp. 356-59.

'What Happens to Scripture in Church and School?', *Journal of Beliefs and Values* 4.2 (1983), pp. 14-19.

Wie erlebten die ersten Christen den heiligen Geist? und Predigt über Joh. 20.29b (Sexau: Evangelische Kirchengemeinde, 1995), pp. 1-22.

'Wurzeln der Theologie Emil Brunners: Aus Brunners theologischer Entwicklung von ca.1913 bis 1918', *Reformatio* 12.10 (1963), pp. 579-87.

'Zwingli's Devotion to Mary', *One in Christ* 16.1-2 (1980), pp. 59-68.

'Zwinglis Einfluss in England', in Heiko A. Oberman *et al.* (eds.), *Reformiertes Erbe* (Festschrift für Gottfried W. Locher zu seinem 80. Geburtstag; Zürich: TVZ, 1992), pp. 171-86.

'Zwingli Writes the Gospel into his World's Agenda', *The Mennonite Quarterly Review* 43.1 (January 1969), pp. 70-94.

Zwingli zwischen Krieg und Frieden, erzählt von seiner Frau (Kaiser Traktate, 76; Munich: Chr. Kaiser Verlag, 1983–84; repr. Kindhausen: Metanoia Verlag, 1992).

Dramas

All published by Metanoia Verlag, CH-8963 Kindhausen, Switzerland. Copies of English versions of the manuscripts indicated * can also be obtained from the publisher.

Fontana: Die Frau am Brunnen und der siebte Mann & Herr, bleibe bei uns, denn es will Abend werden: Salbungsliturgie zu Lukas 7, 36-50

Gomer—das Gesicht des Unsichtbaren

Gomer—the Face of the Invisible
Hiob im Kreuzfeuer der Religionen (music Hans-Jürgen Hufeisen)
*Job in the Crossfire of Religions
Im Schatten seines Frieden (music Hans-Jürgen Hufeisen)
Jona, ein Kind unserer Zeit (music Fritz Baltruweit)
*Jonah, a Child of Our Time
Kamele und Kapitalisten
Kommet her zu mir alle, die ihr mühlselig und beladen seid & *Die zehn Aussätzigen*
Requiem für Bonhoeffer. Den Toten aller Völker
*Bonhoeffer Requiem. To the Dead of All Nations
Das Wagnis des Glaubens (music Hans-Jürgen Hufeisen)
*The Adventure of Faith
Co-author with Estella F. Korthaus
Hommage an Maria von Wedemeyer—Bonhoeffers Braut
Neuer Himmel—neue Erde

Bible Studies

Besuch Bei Lukas (Munich: Chr. Kaiser Verlag, 1986 [1981]).
Das Fest der Verloren (Munich: Chr. Kaiser Verlag, 1984 [1983]).
Erfahrungen in Ephesus (Munich: Chr. Kaiser Verlag, 1985 [1979]).

Book Reviews

Juan Luis Segundo, SJ, 'A Theology for Artisans of a New Humanity', in John Drury (trans.), *Ecumenical Review* 27.3 (5 vols.; New York: Maryknoll, 1974 [1975]), pp. 291-93.

Gianfranco Coffele, 'Johannes Christiaan Hoekendijk: Da una teologia della missione ad una teologia missionaria', *International Review of Mission* 66.262 (Rome: Universita Gregoriana Editrice, 1976 [1977]), pp. 192-93.

Henry Lederle, 'Treasures Old and New: Interpretation of Spirit-Baptism in the Charismatic Renewal Movement', *Pneuma* 10.1 (Peabody, MA: Hendrickson, 1988), pp. 62-64.

Stanley M. Burgess and Gary B. McGee (eds.), 'Dictionary of Pentecostal and Charismatic Movements', *International Bulletin of Missionary Research* 13.4 (Zondervan Publishing House: Grand Rapids, 1988 [1989]), pp. 181-82.

M.W. Dempster, Byron D. Klaus and Douglas Peterson (eds.), 'The Globalisation of Pentecostalism', *Theology* 103.813 (Regum, 1999 [2000]), p. 231.

Kilian McDonnell, 'Presence, Power, Praise: Documents on the Charismatic Renewal', *Worship* 55.3 (3 vols.; Collegeville, MN: Liturgical Press, 1980 [1981]), pp. 267-68.

David B. Barrett, 'World Christian Encyclopedia: A Comparative Survey of Churches and Religions in the Modern World AD 1900-2000', *Times Literary Supplement* 5.11.1982 (Oxford: Oxford University Press, 1982), p. 1224.

INDEX

INDEX OF REFERENCES

BIBLE

INDEX OF AUTHORS

JOURNAL OF PENTECOSTAL THEOLOGY

Supplement Series

13 THE DEVIL, DISEASE AND DELIVERANCE:
ORIGINS OF ILLNESS IN NEW TESTAMENT THOUGHT
John Christopher Thomas
pa £15.95/$21.95
ISBN 1 85075 869 7

14 THE SPIRIT, PATHOS AND LIBERATION:
TOWARD AN HISPANIC PENTECOSTAL THEOLOGY
Samuel Solivan
pa £10.95/$13.95
ISBN 1 85075 942 1

15 PENTECOSTALS AFTER A CENTURY:
GLOBAL PERSPECTIVES ON A MOVEMENT IN TRANSITION
Allan H. Anderson and Walter J. Hollenweger
pa £15.95/$21.95
ISBN 1 84127 006 7

16 THE PROPHETHOOD OF ALL BELIEVERS: A STUDY IN LUKE'S
CHARISMATIC THEOLOGY
Roger Stronstad
pa £10.95/$13.95
ISBN 1 84127 005 9

17 RITES IN THE SPIRIT: A RITUAL APPROACH TO
PENTECOSTAL/CHARISMATIC SPIRITUALITY
Daniel E. Albrecht
pa £15.95/$21.95
ISBN 1 84127 017 2

18 RESTORING PRESENCE: THE SPIRIT IN MATTHEW'S GOSPEL
Blaine Charette
pa £10.95/$13.95
ISBN 1 84127 059 8

19 COMMUNITY FORMING POWER: THE SOCIO-ETHICAL ROLE OF THE
SPIRIT IN LUKE–ACTS
Matthias Wenk
pa £15.95/$21.95
ISBN 1 84127 125 X